The
Pearl
District

City of Portland (OR) Archives, Thirteenth Avenue Urban Design Plan, 7200-02 file 13. 1990

The Pearl District

PLACEMAKING FROM THE GROUND UP

BRUCE JOHNSON

PEARL LIGHT PUBLISHING
PORTLAND, OREGON

Pearl Light Publishing
Portland, Oregon

Printed in the United States.

Direct inquiries to: bjd2U@comcast.net

ISBN 978-0-578-28046-2 (paperback book)

This book is dedicated to Greg Baldwin.
The Pearl District is part and parcel of his legacy.

OTHER BOOKS BY THE AUTHOR

Beyond the Dream Bandon Dunes, 2014
Reflections of an Adolescence, 2018

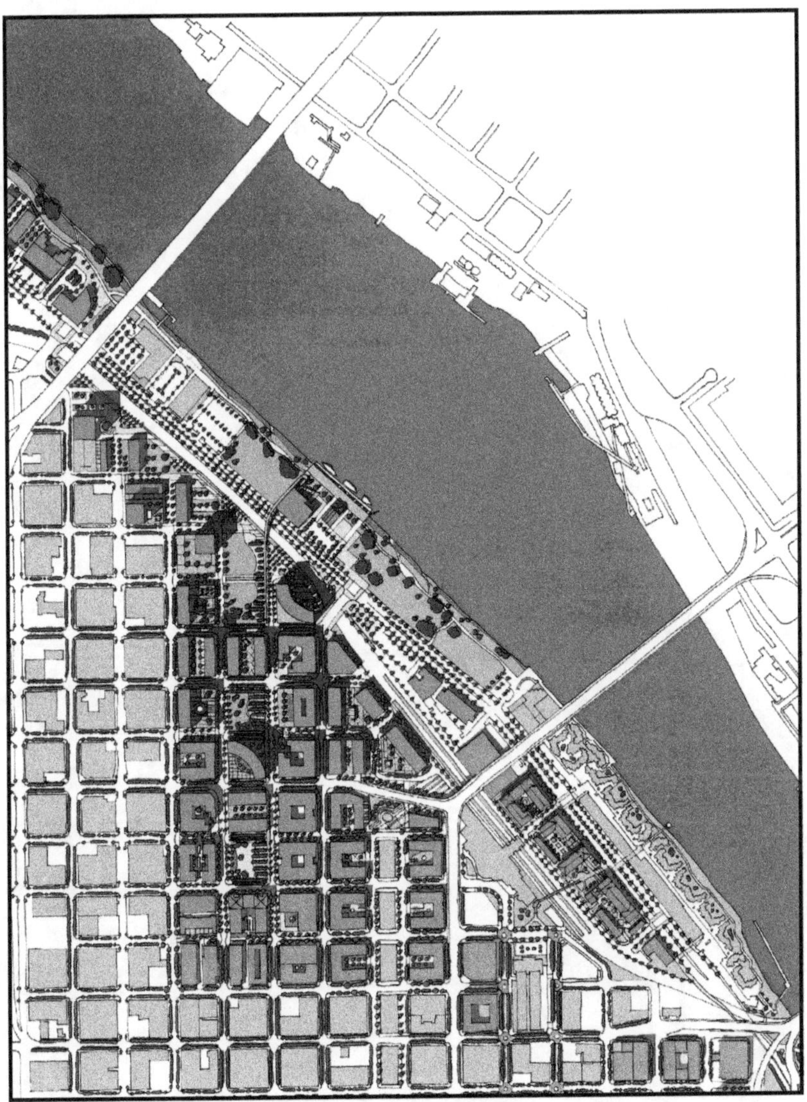

City of Portland (OR) Archives, River District: A Development Plan for Portland's North Downtown, A2005–004. 1994

CONTENTS

PART 5: THE CULTURED PEARL
An Enriched Community 1979-2020   269

PART 6: THE POSTPONED PEARL
Under The Covid Pandemic 2020-2022   319

ILLUSTRATIONS

INTRODUCTION

Back in the 1880s, before anyone conceived of the Pearl District, an ethnically diverse neighborhood existed north of Portland's downtown business district. The advent of rail service, the construction of Union Station in 1896, and the addition of the Hoyt Street switching yards eventually led to the displacement of the working and middle-class residents who lived in this inner-city community. Multistory warehouses used for the storage of goods transported by rail soon replaced the cottages inhabited by the local citizenry. For most of the early twentieth century, the area displayed the hustle and bustle of an established industrial-manufacturing district central to the economic vitality of the city.

By the 1960s and into the '70s, this industrial-manufacturing district began to slide into a period of transition. Many of the previous businesses had relocated to other inner-city industrial neighborhoods or to industrial parks in the outer suburbs. Over time, a sizeable collection of vacant or underused old warehouses displayed For Sale signs. By the early 1980s, change was afoot when a few local businesspeople bought a few of these old warehouses along NW 13th Avenue. Those vacant and underused structures were ripe for redevelopment. And here is where the storyline of this book begins.

When I set out to write this book, I did so as one of those 1980s property owners on NW 13th Avenue. So, in part, this is an insider's story, but it is also informed by many interviews I conducted with individuals who played key roles in the formation and evolution of the Pearl District.

◇ ◇ ◇

The historical development of the Pearl District spanned five decades. To discuss this vast time, this book has been organized into six distinctive parts. Part one—*Deep Roots*—discusses the foundation, as formed by local and state politics. Parts two through four—*The Northwest Triangle*, *The River District*, and *The Pearl District*—convey the emerging and substantive evolution of the district from 1979 to 2020. Part five—*The Cultured Pearl*—highlights the district's transformation in terms of its enriched, cultural branding as an arts district composed of galleries, street art, a national art college, and a new historic theater for the performing arts.

Part six, *The Postponed Pearl*, introduces the impact the Covid-19 public health crisis has had on the Pearl District, and the fact that there are several significant projects already approved and in the redevelopment pipeline by the city council. When implemented, these projects will alter the built urban form, scale, and visual character of Pearl District in the coming years.

A NARRATIVE TIMELINE

The following timeline provides the reader with a general illustration of the sequence of the narrative's major events.

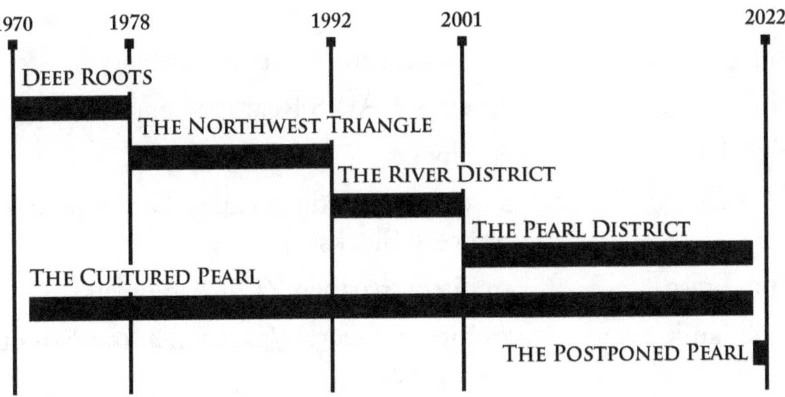

At the beginning of each of the book's parts, a list of important historical dates and events introduce the reader to the topics that follow.

LIST OF CHARACTERS

Al Solheim	developer, AWS Real Estate, partner
Bill Naito	developer
Bill Papas	artist, developer
Bill Scott	Mayor Neil Goldschmidt's chief of staff
Bill Will	artist
Bing Shelton	architect, community activist
Bob Ames	developer, AWS Real Estate, partner
Bob Ball	developer
Bob Gerding	developer, Gerding Edlen Development, Brewery Blocks
Bob Frasca	architect, partner, ZGF Architects
Bob Janik	architect, investor/partner, Hoyt Street Lofts, Inc.
Bob Koch	owner, Robert Koch Gallery
Bob Naito	developer, Old Town
Brad Cloepfil	architect, founder, Allied Works Architecture
Brad Dempy	architect, BORA Architects
Brad Rogers	artist
Brian McCarter	landscape architect/urban designer, ZGF Architects
Bruce Allen	project manager, Portland Development Commission
Bruce Forster	photographer
Bruce Johnson	author, developer, managing partner, Hoyt Street Lofts, Inc.
Bruce Nordstrom	chairman, Nordstrom
Bud Clark	Portland mayor

Carol Smith-Larson	resident, president of the Pearl District Neighborhood Association
Charles Froelick	owner, Froelick Gallery
Charles Kelley	architect, urban designer, ZGF Architects
Charles Redmon	architect, point person, R/UDAT Study
Cheryl Barton	landscape architect, Office of Cheryl Barton, San Francisco
Chris Coleman	director, Portland Center Stage Theater
Clay Fowler	developer, partner, Hoyt Street Properties
Colin Rowan	financial services advisor
Curt Gottfried	owner, Giant Steps coffee shop
Dennis Wilde	architect, Gerding Edlen Development, sustainability specialist
Don Magnusen	executive vice president, US Bancorp,
Don Stastny	architect, urban designer
Don Vallaster	developer, architect
Earl Blumenauer	Portland city commissioner, US congressman
Elizabeth Leach	owner, Elizabeth Leach Gallery
Ethan Seltzer	professor, Portland State University
Gary Reddick	architect, urban designer
George Crandall	architect, urban designer
Geoffrey Pagen	artist
Gordon Davis	architect, Pearl District resident
Greg Baldwin	architect, ZGF Architects
Herbert Dreiseitl	landscape architect, artist, Atelier Dreiseitl
Hiroshi Iwaya	photographer, investor/partner, Hoyt Street Lofts, Inc.
Homer Williams	developer, partner, Hoyt Street Properties
James Pettinari	architect, R/UDAT
Jane Beebe	owner, PDX Contemporary Gallery
Jeffrey Thomas	partner, Jamison/Thomas Gallery

Jim Kalvelage	architect, owner, Opsis Architecture
Jim Winkler	developer, DeSoto Project
Joe Angel	developer
Joe Weston	developer, partner Hoyt Street Properties
John Carroll	developer, John Carroll Investments
John Jay	advertising executive, Global Creative
John Meadows	architect, BOORA
John Russell	developer
John Tess	owner, historic preservation, Heritage Consulting Group
John Thompson	architect, ZGF Architects
Julie Vigeland	fundraiser, Portland Center Stage Theater
Ken Unkeles	developer, artist working spaces
Liz Mapelli	artist, developer
Marilyn Anderson	principal broker, sales manager, Hoyt Realty Group
Mark Edlen	developer, Gerding Edlen Development, Brewery Blocks
Mark Siebert	contractor, investor/partner. Hoyt Street Lofts, Inc.
Margaret Strachan	Portland city commissioner
Martha Bergman	Portland's executive director, American Institute of Architects
Marty Houston	architect
Marty Sevier	project manager, Glacier Park
Mary Josephson	director, Jamison/Thomas Gallery, artist
Mike Powell	founder/owner, Powell's Books
Namita Wiggers	director, Museum of Contemporary Craft
Neil Goldschmidt	Portland mayor
Neilson Abeel	resident, president of the Pearl District Neighborhood Association

Paddy Tillett	architect, urban designer, ZGF Architects
Pat Prendergast	developer, Urban Homes and Prendergast & Associates
Peter Walker	landscape architect, founder, Peter Walker Partners
Phil Beyl	architect, president, GBD Architects, Brewery Blocks
Phil Sylvester	teacher, artist, Oregon School of Design (OSD)
Ralph Kunselman	investor/partner, Hoyt Street Lofts, Inc.
Rich Ford	developer, real estate broker
Richard Brown	architect
Rick Gustaffson	executive director and COO, Portland Streetcar, Inc.
Rod O'Hiser	senior city planner, City of Portland
Roger Breezley	past chairman and CEO, US Bancorp
Roger Shiels	architect, Shiels, Obletz, Johnson, cofounder
Ron Buel	advisor to Mayor Neil Goldschmidt
Russell Keune	historic preservationist, R/UDAT Study
Sam Rodriguez	project manager, Mill Creek Residential
Spencer Beebe	environmentalist, founder, Ecotrust
Steve Cridland	photographer
Steve Schell	attorney, First Oregon LCDC
Susan Hodges	art gallery owner
Tad Savinar	artist, urban designer
Terry Brandt	developer, City Lofts building
Tessa Papas	artist, developer
Tiffany Sweitzer	developer, president, Hoyt Street Properties
Tom Manley	president, Pacific Northwest College of Art
Vera Katz	Portland mayor

Vic Rhodes	director, engineer, Portland Bureau of Transportation
Vickie Diede	project manager, Portland Bureau of Transportation
Victoria Frey	owner, Quartersaw Gallery
William Jamison	partner, artist, Jamison/Thomas Gallery
Zari Zantner	director, Portland Bureau of Parks and Recreation

PLACEMAKING AND THE PORTLAND WAY

BUILDING WITH A CLEAR SENSE of purpose is fundamental to good city planning. This approach can result in, among practical benefits, a strong sense of place. Examples from the ancient world include the Acropolis in Athens, the Roman Forum, Notre Dame in Paris, and Piazza San Marco in Venice. Centuries later, we have the White House in DC, Central Park in New York City, Disney parks in California and Florida, and other distinguished, or at least famous and popular, historical places and iconic buildings. More recently, the tenet of providing a sense of place has been codified as a core urban design principle termed *placemaking*.

Like other metropolitan cities, Portland, Oregon, undertook renewal of its downtown core in the 1960s. Unfortunately, this renewal effort displaced an existing residential neighborhood. Many Portlanders considered this a mistake. They took note.

In the next decade, the election of Neil Goldschmidt as mayor led to changes in local sensibilities and values regarding city planning and historic preservation. Creative leadership by city bureau leaders, officials, and initiatives by local developers then resulted in dramatic changes to local planning and urban design decision-making processes. Underlying these processes, city and community leaders embraced a useful modus operandi appropriately known as the *Portland Way.*

NEIGHBORHOOD PLACEMAKING

In the 1970s, Oregon was nationally recognized as a wellspring for progressive land-use planning. Two decades later, Portland witnessed the early transformation of an inner-city industrial-manufacturing area into a mixed-use residential neighborhood. The emergence of this community, known as the River District and later as the Pearl District, became an exceptional example of good urban design and placemaking. Shortly thereafter, the district became the envy of many cities looking to revive their downtown centers.

This transition occurred when local developers began targeting, purchasing, and converting existing warehouses in the 1980s. Artists and other businesses filled these repurposed warehouses with new energy. City officials embraced this neighborhood as ground zero after a report—*The Last Place in the Downtown Plan*—was published in 1983.

The plan—the product of a Regional/Urban Design Assistance Team (R/UDAT) initiated by the Portland Chapter of the American Institute of Architects considered five possible development alternatives for improving an outdated inner-city industrial-manufacturing area. Team members presented city officials with a series of recommendations on how to either make the area "work better" versus a public intervention to create a richer mix of land uses with a greater economic return to the city in the future. The report spotlighted development opportunities, notably future riverfront development along the Willamette River, creation of a warehouse preservation district, consideration of a multi-block business park, and the extension of the City's Transit Mall to Union Station accompanied by development of a transportation center at this railway terminal.

During the 1980s, no one foresaw the extent and density of redevelopment that would blossom in this old industrial-manufacturing district. Later visitors from metropolitan cities across the United States and as far away as Japan and China traveled to and witnessed what was happening and more warehouses were repurposed into condominium lofts. And new mid-rise buildings began to rise out of what had once been a storage yard for railway boxcars. These visitors marveled at what they saw. They came to Portland to find the recipe for the wonderful urban renewal that had occurred in the district. They were looking for lessons, the planning model, and the secret sauce if one existed. As they asked questions and sought answers, a few may have discovered a facet of Portland's DNA—something referred to as the Portland Way.

THE PORTLAND WAY

Portland experienced sociological and cultural changes in the 1970s that contributed to Portlanders' choices about making plans for their city. These choices were uncharacteristic compared to similar decisions made in other major American cities. In the decades that followed, Portland found a different path to revitalize its downtown area and surrounding inner-city neighborhoods.

The national Knight Foundation wanted to understand how past urban living transformations had happened in Portland and why they had not in other places. Portlanders had made choices that created a kind of urbanism not seen in many other American cities.

To do so, Carol Coletta, the foundation vice president in 2014, convened two panels composed of Portland community leaders. Ten individuals, including several architects, a city planner, a governmental affairs person, and a couple of ex-politicians, served as panelists. The participants took on the task of digging beneath past events. During their discussions, everyone agreed upon one central fact, as expressed by one of the participants Don Stastny. He had been a prominent figure in the formulation of Portland's 1988 Central City Plan—and he had remarked that the misconception was "that there was some grand plan, and there never was."

The panelists discussed a wide range of topics, but they all agreed that peoples' attitudes had shifted and evolved. Every panel member was well aware of how Senate Bill 100 had upended state and local land-use planning processes. Once this regulatory mandate was in place, statewide planning became more comprehensive in scope. Rick Gustafson, another panelist, reminded everyone that lots of local professionals had twenty years of professional experience gained from the 1970s to the 90s before working on the River District Vision. Many of them had arrived in Portland as young people in the 70s. They had learned to be flexible in their problem-solving methods. Most had embraced a comprehensive planning approach. And most of them hadn't lost all their idealism while also being more pragmatic and tolerant in their thinking. Tolerance was appreciated because sometimes, an over-commitment to an established comprehensive planning concept can restrict an alternative approach. Rick remembered how the planning for a future streetcar line was done under the radar and in complete opposition to the regional transportation planning effort. It had to be "a hollow end…You had to hold it until you had your plan together, or it wouldn't have been done."

Another topic discussed was that having a vision and ideas was fundamental to the process. Beginning with an intriguing vision invited lots of ideas. There was also the recognition that as one looked at various solutions, it was apparent that there was no one solution to solve many of the problems associated with urban renewal. Behind this mode of thinking was the realization that the answers were tied up with the chemistry of the people making value-weighted planning decisions about improving and respecting their community core values.

Bill Scott, another panelist, had been Neil Goldschmidt's chief of staff when he was mayor of Portland in the 1970s. He reminded the other panelists that the mayor had focused on the voters when he ran for office. Neil had wanted votes and had sought out the opinions and advice of the people who lived in the city. Instead of proposing a bunch of new projects, he had offered a more open government in contrast to the way previously elected officials and community leaders had run things.

Another panelist, Ethan Seltzer, a professor at Portland State University, made several key points that established context for why Portland was different from other major cities. Portland was not part of the established East Coast or Midwestern heartland. Ethan pointed out that "we are at the edge; we're not stuck with the inertia of the centers of commerce and society, culture, and politics that characterize places to the east of us that are often looked to not for the cutting edge, but for the view in the rearview mirror."

Besides location, the scale of Portland relative to other metropolitan centers was an essential factor. Ethan pointed out that Oregon was a place of small things, but Portland was the most populated city in Oregon. He emphasized that Portlanders and visitors can experience a day trip to the wilderness, an outing to Mount Hood, or a day hike in Portland's Forest Park—a 5,200-acre urban park. That's a profoundly different experience than is available anywhere else in the United States. Ethan said, "The landscape keeps us honest. It's not so much all about the city as it's all about creating a life in the Pacific Northwest. This is not a great place to get rich, but a great place to live well."

PART ONE

DEEP ROOTS

THE FOUNDATION YEARS

1970–1978

Deep Roots Timeline

The Foundation Years

1972	The Portland City Council approves a plan for downtown Portland
1973	Neil Goldschmidt is elected Portland mayor.
1973	The Oregon State Legislature passes Senate Bill 100
1975	Skidmore, Owings & Merrill submit an urban design study— an update to the 1972 Downtown Plan—to the city

1

THE NEW POLITICS

THE PEARL DISTRICT HAS ITS genesis in Oregon's past local and statewide politics. In the late 1960s, Portland underwent a local political transformation. The entrenched power brokers and established politicians had had their day. Neil Goldschmidt had been student body president at the University of Oregon in the early 1960s. After he graduated with a bachelor's degree in political science, he went to Washington, DC. There, Neil interned for a senator and participated in Mississippi's 1964 Freedom Summer civil rights campaign. He then obtained a law degree from UC Berkeley Law School, a hotbed of political activity in the revolutionary 1960s. The mayor-to-be was grounded in the politics of the day.

THE GOLDSCHMIDT ADMINISTRATION

Newly minted as a lawyer, Neil moved to Portland in 1967 because he was interested in urban issues. He took a job as a legal aid attorney. He felt being in a big city was the best place to apply his abilities and realize his youthful ambitions. Two years later, Neil asked Ron Buel, the St. Louis bureau chief of the *Wall Street Journal*, to run his campaign for city commissioner. In 1970, Neil was elected to the Portland City Council, winning over sixteen other candidates in a runoff election. Neil was at the cutting edge of political change.

As a city commissioner, he asked Mayor Terry Schrunk to appoint him to a significant bureau, like planning. Instead, the mayor put Neil in charge of animal control. Citizens were concerned about unleashed dogs running wild in the city and scaring people. If the intent was to sideline Neil, this was a total miscalculation. Ron and Neil saw this as an opportunity to build a political base.

Neil went to endless neighborhood meetings and coffees. He was attentive to the voters' concerns. And in so doing, he built a grassroots voter base of support. Ron's insight was to use this time to introduce Neil to the city and build an infrastructure for a campaign. Instead of running a city bureau, Neil was, in actuality, running for mayor. Portland was on the verge of learning about the value of citizen participation in local politics, specifically how citizen concerns about alternative transportation modes and housing policies could change the city's urban form.

The Goldschmidt mayoral era brought a breath of fresh ambiance to City Hall. In his early twenties in 1973, Neil became the youngest mayor of any American city. Once in office, as Neil began organizing his political agenda, he realized he had a big problem. Among large American cities, Portland was, and as of this writing continues to be the only city with a commission form of government. Power—legislature, administrative, and quasi-judicial—was divided then among a mayor, four commissioners, and an auditor. To maximize his control over the levers of power Neil realized he had to change the organizational structure of the operational departments. He created the Office of Planning and Development and the Portland Development Commission (PDC). Each one was a power center, and Neil used them holistically to direct and reshape the city's future and urban form.

The mayor wanted new talent—people with creative ideas and youthful energy. Several individuals—Bill Scott, Don Mazziotti, Steve Dotter, Denny Wilde, Leo Williams, and Ernie

Bonner—came from the East Coast or the Midwest. Ernie became the new director of the Bureau of Planning and then convinced Doug Wright, with whom he had worked in Cleveland, to join him in Portland. Doug became the first chief of the Comprehensive Planning Section. Later Doug redirected his talents to transportation issues, and together with another hire, Ernie Munch, they redesigned the city's transportation system.

It's difficult to say precisely when Neil formed an ambitious vision to make Portland a thriving town, but that was what happened.

There was a strong surge of planning in Portland in the 1970s. The Oregon Department of Transportation funded a design and environmental impact study in 1971 for a proposed major transportation project—the Mt. Hood Freeway—to link neighborhoods in Southeast Portland from 122nd Avenue to downtown. After the submittal and review of an environmental impact study for the freeway, the mayor and city council rejected the idea of a freeway in July 1974. The freeway was never built. Two years later, the mayor convinced the federal government to transfer $600 million of allocated funds for the proposed freeway to another local project—the Banfield Freeway improvement project. At first, city planners viewed the Banfield Freeway corridor as a possible bus transit way. As the study progressed, the affected community asked that light rail be considered an alternative mode of public transit. By 1979, the Banfield Freeway became a designated a light rail transit corridor. Funding for the project followed a year later.

The downtown core now witnessed the construction of two important public improvement projects. TriMet—Portland's metropolitan transit company—studied, funded, and began operating a bus-oriented downtown transit mall in 1977. The public Pioneer Courthouse Square, a design competition product won by a local architectural design team, opened seven years later as the city's "open-air living room." Downtown Portland had become a more attractive place to shop, dine, enjoy a movie or cultural event, or hang out.

Alan Webber, one of the new City Hall hires, came to Portland in 1970 to visit relatives and stayed. He became the mayor's speech-writer and worked on a range of policy issues. Alan appreciated the local sensibilities, different from what he'd perceived elsewhere, and separated from the rest of the country. Oregon had defined attributes. Years later, Alan told me he used to say to his friends on the East Coast "that the difference between the East and West Coasts was, respectively, the same as the difference between American and Swiss cheese. American cheese had no holes, while the Swiss variety had holes. You could slip into these holes and fill them in your own way." He was speaking about opportunities because Oregon was much less structured and less judgmental back then.

2

THE DOWNTOWN PLAN

THE DOWNTOWN MEIER & FRANK Department Store was a popular place to shop in the early 1950s. To attract customers and offer convenience to those who drove into the city, Julius Meier and Aaron Frank tore down the luxury Portland Hotel in 1951 and built a two-story parking structure. By 1969, the partners had decided to erect a taller garage because the downtown core had expanded and retailing activity had grown. They wanted an eight-hundred-car parking garage on the old hotel site, and they weren't going to follow any official plan.

The proposal was perceived as a laissez-faire development. Portlanders reacted with immediate outrage and outcry. The city planning commission met and denied a conditional use permit request by Meier & Frank. The expressed public disapproval and bureaucratic denial subsequently gave birth to the realization that the downtown needed a plan. The question was: What kind of plan?

THE CITY, THE DOWNTOWN, AND A NEW PLAN

Robert Moses—known as a master builder—had proposed a Portland Improvement Plan in 1943. From the mid-1940s to the late 1960s, the city's form reflected elements of Moses' plan.

Initially referred to as a "masterpiece" by *Collier's* magazine, the plan envisioned a future city based on a massive highway system enabling free fluid access to a "24-block civic center" as a major downtown destination. Fortunately, the lack of adequate financing hindered the full implementation of the plan. By the mid-1960s, the Interstate 405/I-5 freeways had been built around downtown Portland and a portion of the Willamette River. Eventually a freeway loop completely encircled the downtown core, the river, and the east bank of the river when the Fremont Bridge opened in 1973.

Portland had evolved from an early seaport and timber town that had shipped wood products worldwide to an industrious, mercantile city with several corporate headquarters based in downtown Portland by the 1960s and early 1970s. The city was recognized as "progressive" in governmental affairs while most of the citizenry embraced a conservative lifestyle. The pace of life was slow and steady. New arrivals thought the town's atmosphere was sleepy. I remember someone telling me back in the '70s how amazed they were because city drivers sometimes made a left-hand turn from the right-hand lane.

No one used the word *networking* back then, but membership in the Multnomah Athletic Club, or MAC, was highly desirable for business and social reasons. Plus, the club offered access to excellent athletic facilities. Restaurants in downtown were scarce. However, the Ringside on West Burnside was a popular choice for a prime steak dinner and fried onion rings. Most of the downtown offices were closed by five o'clock. Some office workers stayed a while afterward to enjoy a beer or two and then drove or took a bus home. Sometimes people came back for a movie night or special cultural event at the Civic Auditorium. Usually, they entertained friends at home. Downtown tended to be dead at night except for the guys and gals cruising Broadway in their cars and trucks. Local artists and young people could always find more exotic, underground entertainment at local dance clubs or halls near downtown or elsewhere.

Young people seeking an alternative lifestyle had found paradise in rural Oregon through cooperative living arrangements. Local events like the Rose Festival brought out large groups. However, generally, the public realm held no daily attraction for a leisurely city lifestyle. Eventually, Pioneer Square addressed this type of need, offering a European-style public plaza with city-managed, programmed events.

A new youthful community activist movement had grown and was now actively engaged in city planning affairs. Downtown property owners became more vocal about their loss of retail, commercial, and residential markets to the surrounding, expanding suburban areas in Multnomah and Washington Counties. The business community wanted additional parking spaces to compete with Lloyd Center, a shopping mall located in Portland's inner eastside. There was also a concern about increasing levels of vehicular congestion. At the time, many downtown blocks were used exclusively for surface parking. To developers, city planners, and architects, those blocks were future building sites.

Adding to these issues was the fact that Portland had dirty air. Federal air quality standards were violated one out of every three days. Planners eagerly sought solutions to this collection of problems. Restricting more uncontrolled vehicular access was viewed as a nonstarter. Ongoing discussions led to the notion of improving local public transit service. The idea to build the downtown bus transit mall was seen as part of the solution to reduce traffic congestion and improve air quality downtown.

Initially, local businesspeople wanted and asked the city leaders for a parking plan for downtown. CH2M-Hill, a local engineering firm, realized an array of complex issues now faced the city. The firm rose to the challenge and suggested preparing a comprehensive downtown plan. To assist in the planning process, the business community contributed $110,000. CH2M staffers Dick Ivy and Richard Brainard led the effort, working side by side with city planners. Greg Baldwin, a local architect, remembered the mayor had advised the planning team to "develop a specific plan and strategy that did not require any condemnation of property." The mayor wanted the city to implement the plan by leveraging public dollars with private investment.

The final downtown plan was not that conceptually original. It was a collection of proposed projects from the past that everyone could endorse and support in many ways. Instead, it was innovative in terms of the process. There was a significant concern among local citizens that City Hall and the business community would have too much input and control of the planning process. This apprehension was put to rest when a Citizens Advisory Committee (CAC) involving local citizens and activists was formed as an integral part of the planning process. The notion of creating CACs proved beneficial because it laid the groundwork for continued citizen participation in preparing, updating, and revising future downtown and neighborhood plans. As the city embarked on this enterprise, Greg said: "The specific objective was to create an urban community sufficiently attractive as a place to encourage citizens and activities in the immediate region to concentrate their energies and resources in the downtown. The goal was simply to make downtown Portland the best *place* to be."

POLITICAL LEADERSHIP

The 1972 Downtown Plan recommended more investment in retail. The mayor held a meeting with staff and advisors, including Bing Shelton, a local architect and activist, to strategize on how to accomplish this objective. They concluded that another major retailer was needed in the Central Business District.

The assembled group knew that Lloyd Center on the eastside, especially Nordstrom department store, competed and drew customers away from the Central Business District. What was needed was a downtown Nordstrom. The group decided on an action plan. The mayor and a few advisors would go up to Seattle and convince Bruce Nordstrom to build and open a new department store downtown. Having that store in the city core would be a catalyst to spur more retail activity there.

Mayor Neil Goldschmidt's leadership style was both old-fashioned and legendary. Sometimes a leader has to take the bull by the horns to make things happen. In Seattle, Bing remembered, that Bruce had listened politely as Neil expounded on this idea. Bruce responded by saying he needed some time to consider. A couple of weeks later, Neil received a letter from Bruce. The letter stated that Nordstrom was building stores in malls and didn't have any interest in building a new Portland store.

Neil never took no as an answer. He immediately directed his staff to draw up a concept plan that illustrated a new Nordstrom store on a site directly across from a proposed city square. Two years later, the mayor, his planning director, Ernie Bonner, and others flew to Seattle and showed Bruce the plan. As the mayor explained the advantages of the concept plan, one of his advisors added, "You couldn't ask for a better site."

Bruce responded by saying again that he had to think about it. Later, he replied, agreeing to build a new store if several conditions could be met: First, the site had to be guaranteed. Second, the department store had to be within easy walking distance from a parking structure—the Morrison Parking Garage was built to meet this requirement. Third, the city had to find a developer and contractor capable of constructing the building to Bruce's standards and specifications. And fourth, Bruce needed financial assistance. If the city could meet these conditions, the city and Nordstrom had a deal.

The mayor put the project into motion. However, a hiccup developed. Bruce's position was that he needed the right price for the land, the site for his new store. He also required an acceptable interest rate for a construction loan. These conditions didn't quite align because interest rates were high back then. The financing issue needed to be solved, and First Interstate was the store's bank of choice.

Neil sorely wanted that department store downtown, so he inserted himself into the financial process. Pondering the situation, the mayor called his friend Bob Ames, the local president of First Interstate Bank. Shortly after that, Bob ended up in the mayor's office. The mayor informed him he needed a favorable interest rate for this deal. Bob responded by saying, "You're talking about something I can't do. We don't cut rates for what would be an unprofitable level. We make donations, but we don't play with rates."

Bob went back to his office. Ten minutes later, the phone rang. It was the mayor. "Look," he said to Bob, "do you mind if I go over your head?"

Bob didn't object since he knew anybody Neil saw at the bank would turn him down. "Do whatever you want—you're the mayor." Bob hung up the phone and walked down the corridor to the chairman's office, and he told him about his exchange with the mayor.

The chairman responded by telling Bob he'd straighten the mayor out. "I can handle this guy. This will be fun." Twenty minutes later, Bob was back in his office when the mayor walked by. The mayor waved and gave Bob a big smile. The mayor proceeded down the corridor and entered the chairman's office. Bob was now thinking this was going to be a very short meeting. Ten minutes went by. Then it was twenty minutes, and finally, after an hour, the mayor walked back down the corridor, and as he passed Bob's office, he smiled again and waved. After the mayor had gotten on the elevator, Bob rushed down the hall to find out what happened. "The SOB talked me into it," said the chairman.

AN URBAN DESIGN PLAN

As welcomed as the 1972 Downtown Plan was, it had a serious shortcoming. It lacked specific design details and recommendations for plan implementation. More work was needed. Fortunately, the approved plan included a preliminary design program that called for a second-phase study effort to identify design concepts and implementation guidelines. After three years of discussion, the city hired an interdisciplinary team that included a local architecture firm Skidmore, Owings & Merrill (SOM), a San Francisco-based planning firm, a traffic-engineering consultant, and other consultants. The team began analyzing the downtown traffic patterns and parking demand, identifying redevelopment opportunities, assessing the feasibility of creating historic districts, and exploring linear park open space development along the Willamette River. Harbor Drive—a major arterial road that had been a physical barrier between the downtown core and the Willamette River—was closed and removed in 1974. Consequently, an extensive swath of undeveloped land between downtown and the river seawall was viewed as a prime land for use as a multiple purpose waterfront park and special community events.

Howard McKee, an architect and urban designer with SOM, led the urban design component of the study. The urban design plan consisted of a layered series of improvements for a downtown retail/office core, Old Town, Union Station, and the surrounding area around the railway station including portions of the Northwest Triangle District. The plan specifically recommended replacing existing surface parking uses with new buildings that needed to step down in height in city blocks immediately west of the waterfront open space. To reduce traffic congestion, a row of multi-level parking garages was planned to intercept vehicular bridge traffic entering the downtown from the eastside of the river. Key to the preservation of historic buildings was the designation of two historic districts. The study also explored development opportunities at and around Union Station and the North Park Blocks.

In 1975, the city published *The Urban Design Plan and Program Waterfront Renewal Area* as a newspaper-style broadsheet report. The broadsheet set forth an urban design framework plan for downtown and contained specific illustrative concept plans, design guidelines, and detailed recommendations for each sub-district. The report also outlined a rezoning strategy and recommendations about tax increment financing and tax incentives for housing development and historic preservation.

It rains a lot in Portland. From October to May, it was common to see lots of wet weather gear downtown. Therefore, the idea of requiring rain protection over sidewalks seemed like a good idea back in the mid-70s. And if you needed property owners to provide awnings, why couldn't the city permit tables and chairs on portions of the public sidewalk? The city took this notion to heart, given the duration of seasonal rains the town experienced. The outcome, over time, was pronounced rain protection along downtown streets. The present-day prevalence of street cafes and the increased street life in the city's public realm resulted from these early changes to the city's physical environment. Back in the 1970s, the local architects and planners talked about improving the sense of place in the downtown. They weren't using the term *placemaking*, but that was what they were envisioning.

THE AFTERMATH OF THE PLAN

Whatever happened to that proposed parking garage next to the Meier & Frank department store? The downtown plan recommended the city build a plaza at that location. This wasn't a new idea. When Lloyd Keefe was the city-planning director in the early 1960s, his staff had considered building this public square. A young, local architect, Bob Frasca, and a part-time city employee, Greg Baldwin, had prepared conceptual designs for a future public square.

By 1975, the mayor had convinced the potential garage project owners to sell the property to the city. Five years later, a competition was held for the square's design. A design team led by local architect Willard Martin and the firm of Walker Macy won the Pioneer Square competition. Pioneer Square—Portland's downtown outdoor "living room"—opened on April 6, 1984. Portland continues to enjoy it. This central city plaza, under active programming management, hosts many unique and seasonal events throughout the year and demonstrates how distinctive placemaking promotes urban vitality and livability.

In acknowledging the downtown plan's value, the Rudy Bruner Award Selection Committee in 1989 recognized the 1972 Downtown Plan as a pivotal event. The plan featured a mix of inclusive and creative design elements, a high degree of physical adaptability to new conditions, the redefinition of public transit needs, the provision of structured parking garages downtown, and conceptual plans that targeted public open space and waterfront improvements. The downtown plan incorporated many, if not most, of the ideas and projects already accepted by the downtown business community. It was admittedly a short-term plan; it would require several revisions in the following decades.

The Goldschmidt mayoral era was a harbinger for profound change in local citizens' ability to participate in the community and neighborhood planning process. It may not have seemed like a big deal at the time, but those coffee get-togethers Neil attended in people's homes were game-changers. They bought people together to discuss political, social, and environmental issues. No local politician had ever used this simple, effective way to build a political base.

People who attended these coffees were able to have a personal dialogue with a politician. They could tell him what was needed to make the city better and more livable. The commissioner used these public views and opinions in formulating policy changes that eventually changed the way city planning process for the better. These neighborhood sessions ultimately led his administration to formally institute a citywide public participation policy for neighborhood planning affairs.

◇ ◇ ◇

The same year the Portland City Council adopted the 1972 Downtown Plan, state senators in Salem, Oregon, heatedly debated the passage of Senate Bill 100. After its enactment, this controversial legislation radically changed attitudes, pro and con, about how land-use planning should and would proceed in the future.

3

SENATE BILL 100

A RADICAL CHANGE TO OREGON'S land-use planning system took place in the 1970s. Hector Macpherson, Jr., a Linn County dairy farmer, was convinced that continued suburbanization of the Willamette Valley was a threat to the state's productive agricultural industry. Hector and others addressed this threat by proposing new statewide policies and regulations that changed the way metropolitan, municipal, and county jurisdictions went about planning their respective communities. New legislation, Senate Bill 100, was enacted to protect and enhance the state's agricultural investment, forestry resources, and coastal lands.

This new comprehensive land planning process became more democratic due to mandated citizen participation statewide. The result created a highly progressive regulatory environment that required all municipalities and countries to prepare comprehensive plans. And these had to comply with a broad set of established goals and administrative rules. Out-of-state onlookers marveled at how Oregon became so progressive in the spheres of land-use and city planning.

Furthermore, local politicians, business and community leaders, and neighborhood activists all voiced concern about urban renewal, air pollution, transportation, public transit planning, and the livability of neighborhoods. All of the new statewide land-use regulations, coupled with a newfound passion for local historic building preservation, brought about urban renewal quite different from the previous effort in Portland's South Auditorium Area. In effect, all these efforts changed the social and environmental consciousness of Oregonians.

PROTECTING FARMS AND FORESTS

The changes state politicians enacted through Senate Bill 100 rippled through Oregon's land-use planning and decision-making processes with a targeted objective of limiting suburban sprawl in outlying Portland metropolitan areas. These new land-use regulations restricted the conversion of farm and forestlands into residential subdivisions.

In the 1960s, there was concern about emerging residential development along the I-5 freeway corridor from Portland to Eugene. This had resulted in the loss of both agricultural and forestlands. Continuing urbanization was already evident between these two cities, where two-thirds of the state's population lived. The surrounding farmland was some of the most productive in Oregon. Environmentalists and others who remembered how California's orange tree farms in Orange County and associated agricultural industries had been devastated to make way for Los Angeles's bedroom communities began to wave a red flag.

While the vision behind Senate Bill 100 had many supporters and advocates in the legislature, Hector has been recognized as the principal originator of the legislation. Writing about Governor Tom McCall—he played a critical support role in the controversy surrounding Senate Bill 100—Laura Jane Gifford has shared an anecdote about suburbia's expansion into farmland in her 2014 article "Planning for a Productive Paradise: Tom McCall and the Conservationist Tale of Oregon Land-Use Policy." As the story goes, one day Hector drove past his neighbor's farm in the late 1960s and noticed a Caterpillar tractor turning over the soil.

What ya planning to grow here?" he shouted out the window. 'Houses," replied the tractor driver. Farmers and environmental activists threw their support behind this far-reaching legislation.

An alliance of statewide interests supported by various businesspeople, including state officials, attorneys, planners, and farmers, led the charge for change. In response, the governor created the Willamette Valley Environmental Protection and Development Planning Council. An enlightened staff took time and watched Ian McHarg's movie *Multiply and Subdue the Earth*. Inspired by that approach to planning with nature, the council hired noted landscape architect Lawrence Halprin to undertake Project Foresight in 1972.

The passage of earlier legislation led to the creation of the Oregon Land Conservation and Development Commission. Steve Schell, a Portland attorney, had been appointed to the commission. As vice-chair of the commission, he was intimately involved in discussions that led to draft versions of Senate Bill 100. Steve believes Halprin's study "provided the kind of intellectual framework for what we were talking about. Halprin had designs for what would happen if there was future sprawl in the valley, and what would happen if there was containment." The project became an investigation of alternative scenarios about how the Willamette Valley would be impacted by growth pressures. It included the idea of developing the valley hillsides to preserve the valley floor for agriculture. This planning study encouraged lawmakers to pass statewide land-use planning regulations that preserved and protected the Willamette Valley and associated agricultural uses along the interstate corridor from the encroachment of endless waves of residential subdivisions.

AN URBAN GROWTH BOUNDARY

The passage of SB 100 had been preceded by adoption of Senate Bill 10. Sy Adler made the point in his book *Oregon Plans, the Making of an Unquiet Land-Use Revolution*, that the former bill "required every city and county government to adopt comprehensive land-use plans and to zone its jurisdiction 'border-to-border' by the end of 1971."

Afterward, Senate Bill 100 established nineteen statewide planning goals and guidelines that dealt with land-use planning affairs, transportation, housing, open spaces, energy conservation, and urbanization that applied to counties and all incorporated municipalities. One of the goals—Goal 14: Urbanization—dealt with the expansion of residential land development at the outer edges of the Portland greater metropolitan area. The idea of building residential uses vertically instead of horizontally was one of the main ideas in the original vision for the River District and subsequent development that evolved into the Pearl District. Public officials and developers were able to envision and implement policies that increased residential densities in the central city. Senate Bill 100 also mandated public participation in the ongoing process of goal and guideline development as well as requiring the appointment of a statewide Citizens Advisory Committee (CAC) to oversee the process. In Portland, this reaffirmed the grassroots role citizens needed to play in local politics and the new city planning process initiated by the Goldschmidt mayoral administration.

Goal 14 fundamentally recognized that population and job growth would require more land for urban development. Therefore, compliance with Goal 14 required cities, counties, and regional governments "to identify and separate urban and urbanizable land from rural land." All these jurisdictions were required to inventory, analyze, and delineate a boundary between urban and rural lands while allowing an adequate supply of urbanizable land based on a twenty-year population forecast. This boundary was termed an urban growth boundary (UGB) and included delineated urbanizable land. The underlying goal was to reduce urban sprawl.

The basic idea behind Goal 14 and the UGB was to protect farm and forestlands, but it also had the effect of constraining suburban expansion, thereby preserving rural land for agricultural use. The underlying goal was to reduce urban sprawl while accommodating the need for twenty years of population growth in an "orderly and efficient" manner.

In 1978, voters approved Ballot Measure 6 statewide, and the existing Metropolitan Service District was renamed Metro. Metro became an elected regional planning authority responsible for planning and policy-making dedicated to preserving and enhancing the quality of life and environment in and around Portland. Metro was given the task of establishing the UGB for the Portland metropolitan area.

The process to establish a UGB was prescribed by an Oregon administration rule that stated the boundary "shall be determined by evaluating alternative boundary locations consistent with ORA 197.298." The rule also considered several factors, including accommodation of identified land needs, provision of public facilities and services, comprehensive environment analyses, and compatibility with farm and forest use immediately outside the UGB.

In reality, the determination of the UGB was a subjective exercise. To determine the initial boundary, several legislative leaders flew over the metro area in a Forest Service spotter plane—the kind with a glass nose. They looked for indications on the ground where there were transitions from rural to urban uses. Sometimes it was difficult to determine where the line should be, and in the end, the boundary generally came to be located where sewer service stopped. The rationale was to limit development to locations where public infrastructure allowed hookups but not in areas where new utility services were not available.

The UGB directly affected the evolution of the Pearl District. It pointedly underscored the fact that building infill was feasible even if land costs in the urban core were higher than at the suburban fringe since utility trunk lines didn't have to be extended to service newly proposed subdivisions. And, of course, the idea of urban living was becoming more popular in response to changing societal trends. This further validated the notion that building housing units in and near the downtown core was a good idea. The city also got behind the idea because new development in the district would mean increased long-term dividends in tax revenues.

It's also important to realize that the UGB is a long-term planning tool. It's not a market-oriented device. The expectation has always been that the UGB is speaking not to the next year or the next eighteen months, the classic short-term business cycle. Instead, it is a planning tool that reaches out twenty years or further.

Embedded in Goal 14 was the realization there was always going to be additional land available for development. Goal 14 allowed for future adjustment of the boundary if the amount of land designated for urban development within the boundary area diminished significantly. Yet it wouldn't operate in a standard supply and demand manner.

Goal 14 also had another meaningful impact on the local development marketplace. Developers tend to be risk-averse people. They take risks, but these are calculated and based on experience. Developers are not in the business of throwing caution to the wind. They focus on the bottom line—can they make a profit or not. What developers looked for back then—and now—were reasons to believe that the investments they wanted to make were good bets or at least better than the average bet. What the UGB said to the developer was this: It's going to be very difficult to double the amount of urban land inside the boundary or exceedingly hard to push the boundary farther up to accommodate potential market demand for new residential use. Many began to think, maybe it's better to build in the inner city and go up as opposed to look for land on the fringe of the metropolitan area. However, where could you find multiple blocks of developable land in the inner city? Alternatively, you could buy a building and tear it down.

In many ways, the impact associated with having a UGB was psychological. It gave the development community a strong feeling that the public sector and its policies would not run away with the market. Will the market be there? Nobody knew or knows for sure even now. But the UGB gave developers the reassurance to believe that their decision to build new housing was not foolish. Furthermore, this gave them the assurance that the public sector would not undermine their assumptions about why this was a good bet.

Everyone, notably the bureaucrats and politicians, knew the cost of expanding utility infrastructure into new rural areas would be expensive. This contrasted with the 1970s when across the nation, cities were expanding urban areas using federal dollars for transportation, water, and sewer systems. By the 1990s, after the Reagan era, federal funds had dried up. The federal block grants that had enabled local jurisdictions to invest on behalf of local developers were gone too. The "rug" that had supported those efforts was gone, gone, gone.

Fundamentally, the UGB gave developers a sense of certainty about the local policy that made them think that investing in the Northwest Triangle District and the emerging River District was defensible. Private investment was the name of the game. The city was still sitting on the sidelines, watching and waiting to see how this new trend termed *loft living* would play out in the marketplace. The early developers in the Northwest Triangle—these new pathfinders—had to form private investment partnerships to buy old buildings they wanted to convert to new uses or tear down to build new buildings.

By the early 1990s, the real estate game in the Northwest Triangle was on the cusp of a big change. The opportunity arrived when a sizable tract of surplus rail yards was sold to a local Portland development company. Previously, developers had been renovating and repurposing a collection of old warehouses from another era. The rail yards were developable and allowed for new building construction. Loft living had become a trendy choice for people seeking an urban lifestyle. So, residential condominiums began to sprout and rise vertically as the new owners traded a backyard for a balcony.

The residential densities associated with mid-rise structures increased in stark contrast to the more traditional detached family dwellings and garden apartments found in Portland's inner eastside and the suburban, low-density, horizontal, single-family dwellings that dotted the West Hills and Tualatin Valley. Once construction began, no one seemed to know what the saturation point was for new housing units. Without the passage of Oregon Senate Bill 100 and Land Use Goal 14, it's debatable whether the Pearl District would exist in its present urban form.

PART TWO

THE NORTHWEST TRIANGLE

AN EMERGING NEIGHBORHOOD

1978-1992

THE NORTHWEST TRIANGLE TIMELINE

An Emerging Neighborhood

1978	Artist Tad Savinar rents a workspace in the Chown Pella building
1980	Al Solheim establishes the real estate firm AWS and rehabilitates an old warehouse into Downtown Self-Storage.
1980	Oregon School of Design (OSD) opens
1982-1987	The Northwest Artists Workshop operates out of a space on NW 12th Avenue
1983	An AIA-sponsored Regional Urban Design Assistance Team publishes the report *The Last Place in the Downtown Plan*
1984	Victoria Frey and Luis Lopez open PDXS
1984	Hoyt Street Lofts, LLC purchases the Gadsby building and proposes to build condo lofts
1985	The City approves the *Northwest Triangle Report*
1986-1987	The NW 13th Avenue Historic District is approved by the National Park Service and the City of Portland
1987	Blue Sky Gallery relocates to the district
1988	The City approves the Central City Plan
1989	Curt Gottfried opens Giant Steps, a coffee shop on NW Glisan Street
1989	Joe Angel begins the Everett Station Lofts and Honeyman Hardware Lofts projects
1989-2005	Pulliam Deffenbaugh Gallery operates on NW 12th Avenue
1990	Glacier Park sells the Hoyt Street rail yards to Prendergast & Associates
1990	The City approves the Thirteenth Avenue Urban Design Plan
1992	The roadway surface for NW 13th Avenue is upgraded to paved concrete

4

ADAPTIVE REUSE

AL SOLHEIM FOUND NW 13TH Avenue in the 1980s. Walking the street he saw a collection of older, multistory warehouses, many which were vacant or partially occupied. Al was also quite aware that NW 13th Avenue was different from all the surrounding streets. There were no public sidewalks along the building faces. Instead, elevated loading docks projected out into the street. And there were no street trees. There were also vestiges of steel rails, evidence of past railroad spur lines to the loading docks. These facts sparked his imagination.

Al quickly realized these structures were excellent candidates for adaptive reuse. Moreover, they were aesthetically pleasing. This grouping of old buildings along NW 13th Avenue—a collection of early-to-mid-twentieth-century structures—defined and gave this local street a special historical character all its own. In his eyes, these buildings and the streetscape were worth preserving for future generations.

However, although these old warehouses appeared structurally sound, the City required developers to make structural upgrades. Building owners now had to meet the new seismic earthquake code requirements.

VERTICAL STORAGE

Al—a tall, lanky, energetic, personable guy with a tendency to listen before speaking his mind—had decided to get into the real estate business by opening the company AWS Real Estate. Earlier, he had become friends with John Gray, a successful local businessman. John was a developer who became Al's mentor and business partner.

Before Al met John, he had worked with Homer Williams, another local developer. Homer had been building rows of one-story self-storage facilities. Al's job had been to scout out potential sites of at least two and a half acres. As Al pondered self-storage development using only one-story buildings, he had a thought: *Why not store and stack things vertically?* That was the original purpose for which most of these old warehouses had been built. Al ran this idea past Homer. Homer passed on it.

Later, when John asked Al if he had any good ideas, Al told John about his idea of repurposing a vacant, multistory warehouse for storage. John liked the idea. They formed a partnership and bought a four-story industrial warehouse, the Woolgrowers building at NW 13th Avenue and Johnson Street, for about $300,000.

Once renovated, the building opened as Downtown Self-Storage. It was the first recycled building project in the district. Afterward, Al continued to walk up and down NW 13th Avenue thinking about the next real estate deal. There were a lot of buildings he could buy. One has to remember what incredible real estate opportunities were at hand—mostly invisible to other realtors until later. And Al liked the prices. I've heard him say it was like "walking into a candy store."

The upper floors of the Woolgrowers building become a remote storage closet for many people who later sold their detached single-family homes and moved into apartments or condominiums, as the district became a fashionable place to live. The ground floor, however, would serve another purpose for almost the next decade.

OREGON SCHOOL OF DESIGN

Many Portland-based architects in the late 1970s felt that new architectural graduates lacked the necessary skills to work in established architectural firms. Firms wanted graduates to be familiar with traditional drawing and technical skills. Dismayed, three Portland architects—Don Stastny, Chuck Gordon, and Clark Llewellyn—decided to start a new program in Portland in 1980. Until then, the University of Oregon had had the only architectural school in the state. The new school was called the Oregon School of Design (OSD).

The founders needed funding, and they were rewarded with $40,000 seed money from two local architectural firms—Skidmore, Owings & Merrill (SOM) and Zimmer, Gunsul, Frasca Partnership (ZGF). What the school needed next was cheap space. Clark chased down Al, who had purchased the Woolgrowers building that same year. Fortunately for the school, the ground floor was still unrented. Al agreed to rent the school space in the western half of the building along NW 14th Avenue. The agreed-upon rental rate turned out to be too much for the school, and Al eventually forgave much of the rent.

OSD needed a curriculum. A local architect, Phil Sylvester, had gone to Reed College for his undergraduate studies. Afterward, he attended Princeton University and graduated with a degree in architecture and returned to Portland to work at a local architectural firm. He soon realized that corporate architecture wasn't what he expected. So, he took a leave of absence to work on a personal design project. Around the same time, he was asked to teach architectural history at OSD. He now had a way to pay his rent.

At first, the school was undisciplined and without apparent context. Phil characterized it as "a ragtag band of professionals in a rough space." Phil eventually took on more responsibilities and became the director of academic affairs. He also hired several local architects to teach, and he designed the academic curriculum. Phil convinced several East Coast schoolmates and some exceptional architects from Europe and South America to become OSD instructors.

The school began having Friday lectures and discussions open to the public. Occasionally, the school hosted a design charrette—a specialized kind of workshop—to educate the public and community leaders on local building design issues. When the eastside convention center was proposed, the school challenged the initial design. They suggested alternatives. By engaging in the public arena of debate over the facility design, the school took an active role in civic planning affairs.

When the school closed in 1989, Phil walked out the door, setup a studio two blocks away, and started teaching drawing classes.

MIXED-USE BUILDING CONVERSIONS

John Gray had been on the First Interstate Bank board when Bob Ames was the bank's president in Portland. Bob had been John's personal banker. When John decided to retire, he advised Bob to partner up with Al. The new partnership worked because Al and Bob displayed different yet complementary roles. Al was the visionary, and Bob was the conservative, analytical half of the partnership.

Their first acquisition was the Maddox building in 1982. Originally a moving-and-storage company and later a furniture store, the Maddox was a four-story brick warehouse at the corner of NW 13th Avenue and Hoyt Street. When asked why they bought the buildings they bought, including the Maddox, Al said, "They (the previous owners) didn't screw them up."

They initially converted the warehouse to studio spaces for artists. Later, many of the studios were reconverted for commercial office use. To make the building attractive to renters, an atrium was created in the middle of the building to bring more light into the interior. They upgraded the elevator and put in a new mechanical system and a seismic upgrade. They ended up leasing space ranging from twenty to fifty cents a square foot.

Photographer Steve Cridland was one of the first tenants in the revamped Maddox building. In 1987, his friend Geoffrey Pagen had told Steve there was cheap space available in the Maddox. For $350 a month, you could rent a studio space. Fifteen years later, when Steve left, he was paying $2,300 a month.

Steve remembers the Northwest Triangle in the late 1980s and '90s as being desolate. In particular, he couldn't get a good martini anywhere. But a person could walk over to what is now called the Low Brow on Hoyt Street for a beer. Or you could go to Bogart's Joint for a hamburger and a beer.

A lot of district artists worked under the radar. They were young people, some with new and growing families, scrambling to get to the top economically. For many of them, this was the first time they were making money. Steve told me the most money he ever made was in the 90s in what became the Pearl.

Geoffrey had rented a studio space in the Maddox building starting around 1984 or 85. He'd heard about the Maddox from a photographer named Doug Petty, who worked as an assistant for photographer Bruce Forster. The Stash Tea Company had rented the basement and the first floor in the Maddox. They were storing bales of tea from all over the world, and they would repackage it. So, at times, the freight elevator and the entire building smelled like peppermint or black tea.

Geoffrey felt Al was someone who was genuinely interested in artists, how they worked and what they made. He felt Al was curious about the creative act. Bill Will had mentioned something very similar when he told me people are attracted to artists because they're curious about why artists dance or play music or paint. Generally, artists don't make a lot of money for their efforts. Most need a day job until their art sells, and even afterward.

◇ ◇ ◇

Al—aware of the popularity of loft workspaces and loft living across the nation—decided to take a few research trips. He visited New York City, Boston, Los Angeles, and Vancouver, BC, to see what others had done. Based on this research, Al decided to continue buying and renovating more of these older warehouses. However, one of his advisors wanted an economist to validate the demand and feasibility for this type of development.

Al's response was, "Great, you pick the economist, but before they start, have them talk to me." Al told them to go to specific places like the ones he had visited earlier.

They came back and reported: "That should work." It was 1988, and their reports confirmed in both Al's and John's minds that repurposing a warehouse for rental apartment use was timely. They purchased another warehouse and converted the interior floors into apartments and office spaces. This project became the Irving Street Lofts building.

I met and got to know Al when I was involved in the district as a building owner and manager. Then and years later, I'd bump into Al when he was walking around the Pearl District checking on activities at buildings he managed. I'd stop and say hello, and we'd talk about what was happening in the district. I knew he liked these old warehouses and that he wanted to see them preserved to serve other purposes in a new era. But I couldn't quite figure out what fundamental itch he was trying to satisfy.

Then someone told me he was a birder, and that helped me understand. I had known Al was an outdoorsman. He's still a hiker, a skier, and according to one of his buddies, he craves nature. He will travel across continents to experience mountains, deserts, lakes, and woods. One day back before the Pearl was a thought in anyone's head, as we were again sharing recollections about the district, I asked him if he was indeed a birder.

Al didn't respond by telling me the last species he saw, so I figured birding wasn't a hardcore activity for him. But he did say he'd done some birding. I like to think he exhibits the personal attributes we associate with birders. Birders have to spend lots of time looking. One needs patience, and one also needs to listen for the birdcalls or songs to identify each bird and its location.

These two traits—the ability to be patient and to listen—are reflected in Al's character and how he goes about his business. No one in Portland had thought about vertical storage before he transformed the Woolgrowers building into a cash cow. Later, he bought another building located farther south on the same street and repeated this business model. Three decades later, these two warehouses function like ATMs, automatically paying out monthly cash dividends to Al and his partners.

Al's patience pays off when it comes to acquiring buildings. He can wait years for just the right opportunity to make a real estate deal. Plus, he does it quietly. Sometimes Al courts people; other times, he merely waits them out.

There's another interesting aspect of his business acumen. Sometimes you can find him in his office. At other times he's outside walking around the Pearl. He likes to operate "on the street," and there's a magnetic aura about him. People are attracted to him, and he brings people together.

So, like a birder, he moves around, "glassing" for new properties—identifying buildings to repurpose. While engaged in his real estate affairs, he doesn't seem to have a grand plan or agenda. I believe both pursuits reflect a passion that fuels and gives purpose to his life. My conversations with Al had left me with the impression that when he first got into renovating old warehouses, he hadn't thought the whole thing out ahead of time.

There was another old warehouse—the old Union Pacific building—located along NW 13th Avenue. Al and Bob liked the location and the look of it so they built it. The project turned into design collaboration between Al and his architects. When Holst Architecture saw an opportunity to create a special interior circulation corridor during the renovation work, Al and Bob differed on whether this was a good idea. Bob initially thought the idea of making the hallway an artistic statement meant losing too much rentable space.

The principal architects, Jeff Stuhr and John Holmes proposed designing the hallway as a kind of internal *allée*—a French term for an alley in a formal garden or park. The architects envisioned the hallway as a special movement corridor. They knew they could direct natural light into the building's interior through the building's large roof light monitors. The hallway design incorporated a long, sweeping series of sculptured, curved wall formations that flowed throughout the first floor and second floors. Holst also incorporated a large atrium in the building similar to the one in the Maddox building. Together with clerestory windows, the atrium allowed natural light to pour into this commercial office/retail building, illuminating the interior. These artistic wall elements united the overall building circulation and lobby space into a visually dynamic environment.

Al liked and supported the concept even though it added additional expense to the interior renovations, and the converted building turned out to be a great success. The partnership went through three five-year tenants, and the partnership never spent a nickel attracting new tenants. Everyone loved the artistic treatment of the hallway, and it demonstrated Al's visionary attention to architectural ideas and details.

◇ ◇ ◇

Al and Bob continued to acquire properties along NW 13th Avenue as the 1980s turned into the 1990s. One of their key acquisitions during this time was the Maytag building at the corner of NW 12th Avenue and Hoyt Street. This two-story corner building was a "must acquisition" because its owner also owned the paved parking lot next door to the Maddox building. Al and Bob had observed that on-street parking was becoming problematic. Al became tenacious about buying the Maytag because he wanted to ensure a convenient parking supply.

The circumstances surrounding the purchase of the Maytag building offer a telling example of how Al works. Al had told Bob he wanted to "tie up this building." Back in the 80s, a developer couldn't get a 75 percent loan on a building in this part of town, so the partners put together a local investment group that included Warren Rosenfield, Bob Walsh, and Roger Paul. They split up the entry money among the investors so no one was hurt financially—what each individual could afford to do, he did.

Compared with the cost of acquiring a similar multistory building decades later, these initial purchases were bought for next to nothing. However, at the time, it did take real money, and the buildings were acquired incrementally. After the Maytag real estate deal closed, Al and Bob established their business offices on the second floor.

A pivotal event was about to happen in the Northwest Triangle. An idea had arisen in the mind of a Portland architectural activist. This individual wanted to demonstrate how local architects could make a meaningful contribution to their community.

SPOTLIGHTING
THE DISTRICT

THE LAST PLACE IN THE Downtown Plan was the brainchild of Bill Church, a talented Portland architect and architectural activist. In this role, his contribution was like the guy who waves the starter's flag at the Indy 500. Maybe he just unfurled the flag, but others then picked it up and ran with it. His commitment to community service was nothing short of outstanding when it came to thinking about redevelopment in the Northwest Triangle.

Bill had been a partner with Roger Shiels, another architect, for ten years. In 1972, the partnership ended, and Bill continued as a sole practitioner. One of Bill's special interests was solar architecture and sustainability issues. He had a real desire to advance the profession and believed the architectural community should be engaged in public service and civic projects.

Besides designing buildings, Bill was interested in city planning and historic preservation. He was keenly aware that a century had passed since the City's first planning effort of any magnitude. To Bill, the Northwest Triangle presented an opportunity for the architectural community to contribute and make a difference in the evolution of the city. Bill was saying, let's focus on the historical character of the district and preserve its architectural heritage. He, as well as others, didn't want to witness another tragic misstep like the one that had led to the irreplaceable loss of cast-iron facades along downtown's Front Avenue.

LOCAL ARCHITECTS ACT

Bill was elected as chair of the board of directors of Portland chapter of the American Institute of Architects (AIA) in 1982. Back then the natural resources economy in Oregon had collapsed, and work was scarce for architects. After thinking about how this was affecting local architects, Bill decided one of the best courses of action for local architects was to identify critical areas for development. If they couldn't design and build, instead they could insert themselves into worthwhile public planning projects. As a leader in the architectural community, Bill believed it was time for the local AIA chapter to assert itself into the public planning arena.

Martha Bergman was the chapter's executive director. She told me how Bill came into the office one day, sat down in a swivel chair, started rolling around the office, and musing about getting the national AIA involved in a Portland project. The AIA had the capability to organize volunteer assistance teams to put out fires—to deal with problems people were having in a particular location. His thinking then jumped to the notion that you could get the experts to come before there was a fire—in other words, come when there was an opportunity.

To Bill, what was needed was an important project that would have public visibility. The downtown was in good shape. The past decade had seen the implementation of the 1972 Downtown Plan that included the city square, the transit bus mall, and the city's public parking garage system called SmartPark. The new Nordstrom department store and other retail establishments had flourished, bringing more shoppers back to the downtown core. Now people had begun to look at other areas of blight.

The local AIA chapter began having meetings and discussions where the idea of transformational power became a central topic.

The chapter decided that they were looking for a project that would allow architects to be seen as agents of change. At one point, they had twenty or so ideas that were later winnowed down to five for assessment by the chapter's board of directors.

Initially, Bill liked the development potential around the Memorial Coliseum. Bill Wilson suggested looking at how to develop more affordable housing. Gary Reddick wondered about the warehouse district adjacent to his office in Old Town. The latter idea intrigued Bill Church. He noted that land-use changes were already underway in the Northwest Triangle. Bill also remembered this industrial-manufacturing area had not been included when the 1972 Downtown Plan was prepared a decade earlier.

The board met and whittled the choices down to three: an affordable housing project in East Multnomah County, the area around the Memorial Coliseum, and the Northwest Triangle. A committee met to discuss and select the project to study. The Triangle was judged to have the highest probability of success.

Bill looked across the table at Dave Pugh, an AIA fellow. Dave was the managing partner at Skidmore, Owings & Merrill. Bill knew Dave had always been a dependable financial patron for community service projects. Looking directly at Dave, Bill asked him if the Northwest Triangle was in the Downtown Plan. Dave didn't think so, and the committee agreed. Bill then asked Dave which project would make his job easier. Dave laughed because he knew he'd just been tapped to raise the money to fund the project. He also agreed the Northwest Triangle project was the best idea.

THE R/UDAT STUDY

Bill, with committee approval, formally requested the aid of a Regional/Urban Design Assistance Team (R/UDAT). Before the national AIA would commit to sending a team, they sent architect Charles Redmon to Portland in March 1983. Charles's task was to assess the request and need for a proposed urban design study. Fitted out in borrowed rain gear, he toured the warehouse district with city officials and local architects. One of Charles's first observations was: "The thing that sets this area (the warehouse district) apart from other efforts is it isn't a case of bailing out a totally decrepit neighborhood, but of catching it before that happens."

Charles walked the fifty or so blocks of the study area that locals referred to as Portland's back office—a service area with printers, publishers, graphic designers, label makers, marketing firms, supply houses, and businesses like Premier Press. He said, "There's vitality and strong businesses established here." The fact that many of the buildings were still occupied by operational businesses increased the probability of success. He noted that congestion was a problem caused by freight and delivery trucks idling and parking in the streets. He also saw that many warehouses had vacant upper floors. The neighborhood had the untapped capacity for new development.

In conversations with local business owners, Charles learned that land values were relatively low, considering the area's proximity to the downtown core. He also believed the historical role of the district should be maintained, and that its architectural character was as important as the economic potential. A collection of well-maintained late-nineteenth and early-twentieth-century warehouses and other industrial buildings sprinkled throughout the area gave the Northwest Triangle historical architectural interest and value.

Charles summed up his observations by saying, "It's an area where there is a stock of pretty interesting older buildings that could be converted to other uses." He asked if developers were already buying up the best of these buildings. The central question in Charles's mind was: *How are we going to influence the repurposing?*

He knew a change was inevitable. However, timely planning could influence the outcome, so Charles recommended that the national AIA approve the project. He suggested that the national office select a team leader and other team members.

In late April 1983, an eight-person team led by Charles Zucker assembled in Portland. Charles was deputy director of the Design Arts Program of the National Endowment for the Arts. A practicing architect with expertise in participatory planning, he directed the team as they concentrated on developing conceptual plans and recommendations for urban design and economic development.

Robert Sommer, an environmental psychologist, was on the team. He was concerned about the effects of converting old warehouses into new uses. "How can the emerging neighborhood economically impact the region?" asked Dale Henson, an economist. William Flesissing, an architect and urban designer, wondered what it would take to redevelop and then integrate the rather ratty "back office" land uses with the existing Central Business District.

James Pettinari was an architect and an associate professor at the University of Oregon's School of Architecture. For many years, his professional architectural practice had focused on waterfront industrial renovation. When the study was announced, the university asked him to observe the process. After James had attended a few organizational meetings, Bill invited him to join the team. James accepted. He, along with his university students, worked with the R/UDAT members and participated in several charrette sessions. James wanted them to have the opportunity to work with national experts to gain a ground-level understanding of community design.

After arriving in Portland, the team met with civic leaders, local architects, and urban planners. The Oregon School of Design opened its doors to the project. Workstations were set up and spaces designated to facilitate discussions, charrette sessions, and workshops on how best to redevelop this industrial-manufacturing area while also preserving its architectural character.

Architect Justin Dune from the Portland Bureau of Buildings functioned as a resource person on city zoning and building code issues. He had provided a copy of the city's historic building survey to Russell Keune. Russell, who had worked as senior vice president of the National Trust for Historic Preservation, was the team's historic preservation expert. He had worked all over the United States studying how historical districts can function to preserve architectural buildings and local and regional history. Russell was aware of one of the recurring problems in designating historic preservation districts: how does one determine where to draw the boundary lines?

Russell looked at this "last place" through the lens of how historical districts were formed, the zoning issues, and preservation strategies for historic structures. Working with Portland historian Lewis McArthur, Russell concluded that the study area didn't have a lot of landmark building candidates. However, the Northwest Triangle did have integrity as an urban industrial district. This part of the city was still functionally active. Many of the original warehouses were still occupied by businesses. More than three decades later, he remembered the area as being very horizontal in character because there was a uniform scale of building heights throughout the district. Most of the buildings were four stories or fewer at the time of the study.

The study's recommendations were organized around five distinctive subareas and a recreation/open-space concept. Earlier in 1975, several undeveloped blocks around Union Station had been viewed as a potential site for a multimodal transportation center. Just north of Burnside, the study noted that Old Town/Chinatown could be rehabilitated as an expanded office and retail area. Farther west of the North Park Blocks, this area was viewed as a candidate for incremental improvement as a mixed-use preservation district. A narrow strip of land along the Willamette River was envisioned as a linear zone for riverfront development. NW 13th Avenue had been identified as unique due to the presence of a rail spur line and elevated loading docks.

It took only a couple of days for the team to survey the study area and formulate their opinions on a development strategy for the Northwest Triangle. Then the team turned their conclusions and action plans over to volunteer editors and graphic designers, who spent hours laying out and pasting up report pages. Within twenty-four hours, the print production team assembled and produced a final bound report for Bill's presentation to the Portland City Council. While a few property owners objected to some of the study recommendations, city commissioners wholeheartedly embraced the study report's conclusions and proposals.

The published report recommended an implementation strategy under the headline "How to Make It Happen." This was a preliminary work plan that outlined a series of actions for both the public and private sectors. For a study that had taken less than a week to complete, city officials—the mayor, commissioners, staff from the Portland Development Commission and the Bureau of Planning—and community leaders had paid incredibly close attention to this effort. The study sparked continued urban planning work by city staff that culminated two years later in the form of an urban design plan for NW 13th Avenue.

The Northwest Triangle neighborhood had been in decline for several years. The architectural community's intervention was an effort to stop and reverse this trend. Many believed the R/UDAT resulted in a shift of consciousness within City Hall, the city's bureaus, and the public community at large. The final report changed the way architects, developers, city commissioners, and others thought about the area. The publicity generated during the study gave people hope and encouragement to redo this part of town.

Included in the final report was a simple plan diagram. Over the years, it would appear over and over again in numerous published consultant and city documents. The conceptual intent expressed in that diagram contributed to the later emergence of vision for what would be known as the River District. The R/UDAT study was a pivotal event because it happened precisely at the right time and in the right place. It would take another decade for ongoing planning and private sector development to start the ball rolling.

◇ ◇ ◇

The R/UDAT study's spotlight on the district became a welcoming alert for the local real estate and developer community. Now more and more For Sale signs began to appear on many of these old warehouses. A few insightful Portlanders had seen what Al had done. Now they were more than willing to risk their financial assets, buy a building, and take on debt. Their commitment propelled redevelopment forward.

The early developers used adaptive reuse as their business model. However, this model had a built-in limitation. Typically, these old structures never exceeded four or five stories in height. This meant there was a set, low amount of leasable space achievable in this type of redevelopment model as compared to new mid-to-high rise construction.

Nationally, there was another factor that would be pivotal to redevelopment of the district. Railroad companies were saddled with a huge potential liability. They had land holdings contaminated with toxic materials. Burlington Northern was realizing it would be prudent to dispose of the surplus rail yards they owned next to Portland's railway terminal, Union Station.

As adaptive use efforts continued, the milieu and inexpensive rental rates for raw space attracted a new group of renters. In a symbiotic relationship with the developers, this gritty, industrial, blue-collar neighborhood on the doorstep of downtown had unintentionally laid out a welcome mat for artists.

6

THE PIONEERS ARRIVE

IT'S AN OLD STORY, REPEATED across the nation: cities creating loft spaces for artists. Studios and urban residential living had occurred in New York City's SoHo neighborhood, also in the Los Angeles Arts District, and even in Lincoln, Nebraska's Haymarket district. All these places had a healthy dose of the arts among a potpourri of other land uses that always included residential use. Now this story came to Portland.

Tad Savinar was the first artist to rent space in the Northwest Triangle District. In 1978, he leased raw, open space in the Chown Pella building. Tad had to invest sweat equity to create his studio on the fourth floor. He walled off a section of clear-span warehouse installed the drywall material himself to get privacy and security. He ended up with a five-thousand-square-foot dream studio. Tad stayed at Chown Pella for six or seven years until John Gray sold the building to John Carroll, an early developer in the Northwest Triangle District.

These old industrial buildings were perfect places to make paintings, ceramics, glass art, or sculptures, hold drawing classes, or open an art gallery. The loading docks were littered with dumpsters and fifty-gallon metal barrels containing scrap metal, cast-off objects, and industrial debris. The docks were a treasure trove for "found objects," and artists turned these raw materials into art.

NORTHWEST ARTISTS WORKSHOP

Northwest Artists Workshop initially leased space in Portland's Old Town on NW 5th Avenue. The Portland Center for the Visual Arts (PCVA) had also rented space there. In 1982, the workshop relocated and rented space at 522 NW 12th Avenue in the Northwest Triangle. Local artists had created the Northwest Artists Workshop as a place to exhibit their art. The workshop probably operated on a shoestring budget of $10,000 or less annually in the '80s.

To pay the rent and host events, the workshop held fundraisers. One of the best was a tropical-themed event held in 1985. It was lovingly referred to as the Beach Party. Someone suggested putting sand on the gallery floor. Someone else ordered the sand. There was a slight mistake, quantity-wise. A truck arrived, and eleven cubic yards were off-loaded in the street.

A crew of volunteers with shovels and wheelbarrows was summoned, and they moved the sand into the building. The heat was turned up for several days to warm up the sand and give the place a tropical feel. Fake palm trees were added, and people showed up in Hawaiian shirts and bathing suits. Some guests brought their beach blankets as they had four to six inches of sand to recline on. Bill Will remembered about 100 to 150 people showed up—the place was packed. Everyone had a great time, and no one got sunburned.

Many artists, locally and nationally, considered the center to be one of the country's most progressive, best alternative spaces for art, a space with a strong emanating energy. By the late '80s, the workshop was gone—a victim of lost funding from the National Endowment for the Arts in 1987. PCVA also lost their funding, which reduced their revenue from $105,000 to $10,000 in one year.

Bill Will, a sculptor, was another early pioneer. He has an interesting view and memories about those early years. He thinks the artists were the developers. In saying that, he meant the artists had just as much right to claim they had discovered the district, as did the property developers who profited from renovating the old warehouses. Bill has pointed out that because the artists didn't work on the same schedule as the manufacturing workers in the district, the artists brought life to the district, legitimizing it as a place to work and live.

At first, lots of people didn't want to come to the workshop offices because the district was dark and desolate at night. The moneyed people who chose not to come to artist studios in the Pearl in the early days now choose to live there in condominiums.

THE LOCAL ART SCENE IN THE DISTRICT

The 1970s and '80s saw the embryonic development Portland's art world. Both the PCVA—they had had a good run from 1972 to 1987—and the Fountain Gallery owned by Arlene Schnitzer were important contributors to the art scene. This energy was magnified by the arrival of art galleries that found homes in the Northwest Triangle. Blackfish, Quartersaw, and Blue Sky were three of the first galleries to set up shop. The galleries added another layer to the social and commercial ambiance of the neighborhood. Together, the artists and galleries formed an emerging, rudimentary arts scene in the western half of the district. Blackfish was a cooperative gallery that opened at 420 NW 9th Avenue in 1979. It was still in operation in 2022.

In the early 1980s, Victoria Frey was an architecture student at the Oregon School of Design. By 1984, while still in her twenties, she opened PDXS, an alternative space supporting an eclectic array of ideas, at 528 NW 12th Avenue with Luis Lopez, an artist and fellow architecture student. At first, she rented. Later, Victoria and her husband, Peter Leitner, bought the building. She changed the name of the gallery to the Quartersaw Gallery in 1987 when Luis left the business.

Besides running the gallery, Victoria lived in the gallery. That meant living with a bit of noise. Directly in front of the gallery was a rail-switching station for an active railroad spur line. Three times a night, seven days a week, trains that served the brewery on NW 12th Avenue rumbled by the gallery. Because of the switching station, the train had to go past the gallery, then back up past the gallery, and go by again. This was most irritating for people trying to sleep.

Victoria remembered there was much discussion about a name for the district. Many thought the Pearl, which had been suggested early on, was too metaphorical or too clean or characterless. It really didn't describe the scrappy, rough edges associated with the district's physical environment. Among the other names considered were NoBo (North of Burnside) and the Triangle.

While studying architecture at OSD, Victoria didn't have any notion that the district would gentrify and include full-block redevelopment. She also didn't consider the Northwest Triangle a real arts district back then. To her, the area was just a source of underutilized spaces that drew artists to this industrialized warehouse neighborhood.

Al Solheim, aware of the importance art would play in the mix as new commercial activity was attracted to the neighborhood, recruited Victoria to be on the Northwest Triangle Business Association. She had a following, and artists felt her voice could represent them at association meetings.

Blue Sky Galley has been the exhibition space for the Oregon Center for the Photographic Arts since 1975. The center was founded by a group of five young photographers and has endeavored for almost five decades to exhibit photographs by emerging and established artists. Besides presenting gallery exhibitions, the center has focused on art education by hosting artist talks and programs and publishing books to "further the careers and artistic development of the artists shown." In doing so, they built "a concrete, permanent record of their work through print and digital publications," according to Chris Rauschenberg, one of the founders.

The gallery was first located at 2315 NW Lovejoy Street. Ann Hughes, Bob DiFranco, and Christopher Rauschenberg rented a backroom and later the whole storefront for sixty dollars a month. Craig Hickman joined to make it a foursome and suggested they hang pictures and have a photo gallery. Ann thought that was a good idea because if a visiting photographer came to town, they'd come into the gallery, and they'd all expand their networks. Chris saw this as a "visual honey trap." Terry Toedtemeier later joined the group, and the gallery operated out of the Lovejoy location until 1977.

As they considered a new space, someone told them that the Northwest Artists Workshop had available space on the second floor of a building in Old Town to rent. PCVA also occupied a space there. So, Blue Sky decided it would be a good place for their gallery.

A decade later, Blue Sky moved out when they lost their lease. This was a problem because Blue Sky didn't have any money in the bank. Looking for space in the Northwest Triangle, Chris saw a For Rent sign on the Maddox building. He contacted Rich Ford, the listed realty agent. Rich showed them a ground-floor space and quoted them a price around twenty-five cents a square foot. Chris figured they could afford that. To finalize the deal, Rich measured and calculated the actual square footage. Unfortunately, he found the area was 25 percent larger than estimated.

Now Blue Sky had a big problem. They couldn't afford that rent. Chris asked if Rich could rent it for the initial price as quoted. Rich told them that owner Al Solheim couldn't charge less than twenty-five cents a square foot. Chris and his partners liked the location. They wanted the space, but their budget was tight. Rich offered to accommodate them, reconfiguring the ground floor spaces, thereby reducing the area to match the original estimated square footage.

At the time, the Nine Gallery wanted to form a co-op gallery. The rental arrangement for the space they had been considering didn't work out. After discussions with Chris, Nine Gallery ended up sharing space with Blue Sky. They've been sharing space ever since, and it's worked out for both galleries. As Chris remembered, people who came to see a show at Nine Gallery afterward checked out the art at Blue Sky. It worked the other way too.

FIRST THURSDAY

When did First Thursday start in Portland? The subject came up when I asked Chris if he had known William Jamison. Chris told me with a laugh that William had stolen the idea for First Thursday, which first started in Seattle in 1986. Separately, Bob Koch told me he and William had worked together to set up the event locally.

Before First Thursday, Blue Sky might have had an opening attended by only twenty-five people. After First Thursday started, they'd have six hundred people. Art patrons now knew there were scheduled art openings monthly. Now they could make plans to attend. And now Blue Sky began publishing books using monies previously budgeted for posters, which had been needed for irregularly scheduled shows. Books had lasting value way beyond that of advertising—whose value and impact at any level had been questionable.

Chris told me that he believes attending an art opening is a cultural act, part of an in-group experience. There is an attachment—an emotional and intellectual one. Chris thought of the relationship between patron and artist as being akin to that of the Blazer fans and the city's beloved basketball team and players.

To Bob, the idea in the 80s of having First Thursday seemed viable given the number of galleries that were in Portland's downtown area. Many Portlanders interested in art were in their thirties and forties and had kids. It was difficult to imagine this group devoting six or more nights a month to go out to see art if openings were on a variety of dates. In fact, they hadn't been doing just that. Therefore, the gallery owners felt they would have a better shot at staying in touch with their client base by having a common opening date. Art lovers could do a quick survey, see what was happening in the local art scene, and then they could return at their leisure to look at specific art they were interested in buying.

First Thursday created an event for people to talk about—it created a buzz in the local art world. It was a convenient way for people to stop by after work and see what's on exhibit for the upcoming month. It helped sponsor and spur an attitude among artists and gallery owners that art fairs might be another way to attract clients. People together would build energy that might translate into sales.

NEIGHBORHOOD COMMUNITY CENTERS

The industrial, service, and office workers, together with those new arrivals—artists and people enjoying a loft lifestyle—of course needed to eat and drink every day. Rusty's and Giant Steps on Glisan Avenue filled that need. Rusty's served food. If you just wanted a cup of coffee, you probably ended up next door at Giant Steps. If you wanted to smoke, then you traipsed back to Rusty's because Curt Gottfried, who owned Giant Steps, didn't allow smoking.

Curt had long wanted to be in the coffee business. So, in 1989, he opened Giant Steps. Together with Rusty's his café served a function in the neighborhood beyond providing sustenance. They were central gathering places—in effect, a blended community center for the neighborhood where all could gather and share information about the day and their work.

Before Giant Steps, the Pulliam Nugent Gallery had occupied that space. When they moved out, opening room for the coffee shop, Ted Nugent sold his interest in the gallery. Rod Pulliam stayed—he liked the neighborhood—and later partnered with

Mary Ann Deffenbaugh. The Pulliam Deffenbaugh Gallery rented the storefront next to the Quartersaw Gallery and remained there until 2005 when the gallery moved to NW Flanders Street, next door to Jane Beebe's PDX Contemporary Art gallery. Four years later, the Pulliam Deffenbaugh Gallery closed.

Today, Rusty's and Giant Steps are only vague memories of those times, as was a third commercial establishment. Bima was a bar and restaurant that opened when and where it was needed the most. In 1995, this bar became the anointed after-work, nighttime establishment. Steve Cridland finally had a place to have a decent martini. Customers raved about the interior architecture.

It was a remarkable space on Hoyt Street between NW 13th and 14th Avenues. The building had giant light monitors that flooded the interior with northern light. John Forsgren—a friend of Richard Brown, the architect of record—had been the interior designer. John's biggest challenge and reward had been to make minimal alterations to the space. He let the room do all the talking.

The interior space was voluminous and raw in appearance with bare concrete walls. Richard and John had used simple contemporary forms and intense colors for the design. This restaurant was "the most dramatic dining space in Portland" and "one of the most romantic locales in the city," according to an article written up in the *Willamette Week*. Bima closed its doors in 2000. Several restaurants graced the same premises, but they didn't last long. As of 2022, Brix Tavern was still in the space.

Before the mid-1980s, only a handful of artists rented loft-like workspaces in the Northwest Triangle for their creative endeavors. The idea of loft living had yet to take root.

7

THE GADSBY BUILDING

A HEADLINE IN THE SUNDAY Oregonian on August 26, 1984, stated: "Group has Lofty Plans for an Old Warehouse." The story announced that a local investment group wanted to build and market loft-style condominiums in Portland. The article went on to report what the group's representative (me) said: "Some people look at an old warehouse and see an old warehouse. Others look at the same building and see something they could call home." It was an ambitious idea. It was the first time anyone had proposed loft-style condos in the Northwest Triangle.

I was not a developer by profession, but I decided I wanted to live in a loft—a New York City—style open-plan arrangement with few walls. I'd observed early loft development in Minneapolis in the late 1960s and in Melbourne, Australia, where I lived and worked for the second half of the 1970s. Early in the 80s, after returning to Portland, I had followed with interest the results of the R/UDAT study. Subsequently, I got interested about buying a warehouse in the Northwest Triangle. I was familiar with the district. In the early 1970s, I had worked for Skidmore, Owings & Merrill (SOM) and had been responsible for the preparation of the early urban design concepts at and around Union Station and the North Park Blocks.

My intentions to purchase a warehouse intensified when I attended a party for a young architect I knew from SOM. Linda Christopher had organized a surprise birthday party for her husband, Grigsby. The party was held at Hung Far Low, a popular restaurant in Portland's Old Town. At the restaurant, I met Thomas Augustine, an artist and someone who was thinking about opening a gallery somewhere in Portland.

As the evening progressed, we ended up discussing loft living and the lack of such in Portland. Reflecting on this conversation decades later, I realized this unplanned conversation with a stranger had probably finalized my decision to buy an old warehouse.

Shortly thereafter, I found a building that was for sale. A dentist owned the four-story brick warehouse known as the Gadsby building at 1306 NW Hoyt Street. I contacted the listing agent, Rich Ford. We met and did a walkthrough. I liked what I saw, even though the gray exterior paint was peeling away from the red brick underneath. I figured a good pressure wash and fresh paint would fix that condition. Not the case. The exterior walls had been constructed of "soft" brick. Pressure washing the brick exterior would have further hastened the erosion of the brick walls.

To purchase the warehouse and convert it for live/work use, I put together a partnership of local individuals—an architect, a contractor, a plumber, and a photographer. Robert Janik, the architect, was a friend; R. Mark Siebert was a building contractor; and Ralph Kunselman, a plumber, was a friend of Mark's. Mark eventually located his construction company in the building. The photographer was Hiroshi Iwaya. He wanted a loft to use as a photographic studio. Each had a skill set that became useful in the building conversion process, and their expertise helped to lower the partnership's upfront expenses.

I had been aware of an emerging urban lifestyle trend nationally. Moreover, the presence of several artists' studios scattered throughout Old Town and the Northwest Triangle was evidence of local demand for loft workspaces. To me this venture didn't seem risky. It seemed like a good investment opportunity. Then again, I wanted to experience loft living personally.

The partnership bought the Gadsby building on a private sales contract for $450,000. Once the sale closed, the partnership hired Lois Portnoy. She was a local land-use attorney who was familiar with condominium conversions. We now needed a company name. We decided to incorporate as Gadsby Lofts, Inc., reflecting the history of the building. Shortly after the new enterprise became public, I received a phone call from Lois. She informed me that the Gadsby family was objecting to the use of the family name for commercial business purposes. Lois said that unless the partnership changed the name of the corporation, the family planned to sue. On the spot, I told Lois to change the name of the company. When the partners finally rented out space, they did it under the banner Hoyt Street Lofts, Inc.

HOYT STREET LOFTS

Once the new owners took possession of the building, they terminated the lease of the only tenant in the building, Kramer Manufacturing. Kramer manufactured mattresses, and when they left, they left a mess.

The partners cleaned up the mess and quickly switched to design mode. Bob and I put our heads together, and Bob drew up a conceptual set of architectural plans. The initial plans called for twelve condominium units arrayed throughout the three upper floors. The first floor was divided up into several spaces of various sizes and reserved for retail or commercial tenants. The plans called for a rooftop garden with several wood decks, potted landscaping and two overhead trellis structures, as well as the preservation of an existing old water tank. While Bob finalized the architectural plans and a set of specifications, I put together a lender prospectus. Then he began making appointments with local banks and lenders to obtain construction financing for the building improvements.

The plan was to advertise and presell units. The product offered consisted of a basic shell unit with minimum improvements: a wet area including a utility bathroom and strip kitchen, electrical power and service panel, and a mechanical package including water, waste, and natural gas service. A portion of the basement was designated for parking, and there were assigned individual storage spaces for each condominium owner's use.

To get publicity, the partners organized an open house. Hiroshi knew several local musicians, and he was able to get Mel Waldron, a jazz pianist, and David Friesen, a bassist, to provide entertainment during the event. The festivities were well attended and generated a lot of local interest.

Over the next few days, my phone rang constantly. Everyone who called wanted to know when spaces would be available for purchase. Most callers wanted a tour of the building. These inquiries confirmed my thought about there being plenty of pent-up demand for loft living or working studio spaces.

However, the partnership's efforts to secure financing ended in disaster. No local banks were interested in a mixed-use live/work type project. The bankers hadn't been presented with this kind of proposal before. Plus, it was problematic mixing residential and retail uses in a vertical, layered, sandwich arrangement. Interest rates were also a significant factor. They were at 14 percent or more. I even talked to private brokers, who wanted 16 percent to finance a deal. The project didn't pencil out.

I had a brief ray of hope when I talked with Louis Scherzer at Benjamin Franklin Savings and Loan. Louis had provided the financing for a number of brick row houses on NW Irving Street. This was project conceived by architect Bing Shelton in the early 1970s. Louis smiled and told me that Hoyt Street Lofts project was a great idea. But then, Louis's smile faded, and he said, "Unfortunately, I can't help you as I'm retiring in a couple of months."

My balloon burst. It was a gut punch. The partnership's hopes had just turned to ashes. What to do now?

Earlier, Kenny—an employee at Carton Service building next door—had asked me a question: "What're you going to do over there?" The question now was: What were we going to do now that the partnership's plan to convert the warehouse to condominiums had fallen through? What the partners needed now was plan B—or plan C, or D. Bob and I quickly reviewed their floor plans for condominiums. In short order, they realized that with a few adjustments, they could modify the architectural drawings and subdivide the floors into a variety of spaces—some small and others larger. Then they'd simply rent to artists and others. Artists like raw, unfinished space they can fix up to meet their individual needs. I called a meeting of the directors. Bob and I presented plan B. Everyone agreed it was the best way to move forward. Mark put a crew to work framing out the interior walls. I ordered drywall. The Hoyt Street Loft directors, because I insisted, hung the drywall. Because finishing a drywall installation is messy, the partners hired someone else to do that.

After the work was completed, I ordered more advertising and hung a For Rent banner from the top of the building's parapet wall. The phone calls continued, and I started renting out spaces, and not just to artists.

The partners didn't know it at the time, but Hoyt Street Lofts had just created a milieu that, in due course, became a micro-social community. Besides finding a home for their enterprises, our tenants eventually formed a social setting that allowed them to expand their professional and personal relationships. Many of these tenants were individuals in emerging and midcareer development. They included two photographers; a group of graphic artists who produced, among other products, posters for the Grateful Dead; a few artists; and a martial arts teacher.

Thomas Augustine opened an art gallery on the ground floor on the corner of NW 13th Avenue and Hoyt Street. The party conversation I'd had with Thomas had come full circle. He joined Victoria Frey as one of the pioneer gallery owners in the district.

His business generated a lot of attention for the Hoyt Street Lofts building—he was a desirable tenant.

Thomas also contributed something else to the district. He solidified the Pearl moniker. As more and more old warehouses were repurposed for new uses, each contributed additional energy to the ongoing renaissance and renovation of an expanded downtown core. Thomas compared these old warehouses to oysters. He felt the creative energy going on inside the warehouses was metaphorically like the energy that formed the pearls inside oyster shells. However, there are a couple of alternative stories about the naming of the Pearl.

In 1987, Terry Hammond—the editor and publisher of the *Portland Rose Arts Magazine*—had referred to the Northwest Triangle as the Pearl in an article that promoted the area in its infancy. Margie Boule wrote a version of a story that was posted on *OregonLive* by the *Oregonian*. This digital version reflected a story about a woman named Pearl Marie Ambara from New Orleans who had encouraged Thomas to move to Portland in 1983.

Allegedly, Thomas had also told people a freelance writer with *Sunset Magazine* had once asked him what the area was called. Thomas had said the district was named the Northwest Industrial Triangle, but he didn't think that very romantic. Thomas had amended the district's name referred to it as the *Pearl District*.

That story about a woman whose name was Pearl—I never heard that story back in the 1980s. Margie's account has a romantic ring about it. But was it true? Most of the people I interviewed during my research for this book, who worked or lived in the Northwest Triangle, told me they had never heard that story.

The renovation of both the Maddox and the Hoyt Street Lofts buildings had an explosive, rippling effect in the district. It was a straightforward model other developers could emulate. And several other developers did just that. Many artists rented workspaces in the warehouse conversions that followed the development efforts of Al Solheim, Bob Ames, and the Hoyt Street Lofts partners. And three financially successful artists renting from Hoyt Street Lofts decided they wanted to own their own studio spaces.

8

FROM ARTISTS TO DEVELOPERS

LIZ MAPELLI HAD RENTED SPACE in the basement of the Gadsby building. A site-specific glass artist, she made her artwork by fusing colored glass components onto glass panels. She had a large space that contained two large electric kilns. Liz also needed a lot of space for layout tables and lots more space to store glass panel for future work.

She was the only tenant in the basement. There wasn't a lot of foot traffic down there except for Liz and visitors to her studio. Most of the basement was unused space because Liz had rented the far end of the basement and had had a wall built at her own expense to seal off the space. She had an extremely low rate—about eight or ten cents a square foot. That left a lot of the basement free and vacant of any use, which turned out to allow for extra, non-paying tenants.

Security to the building could be lax if the exterior doors were left unlocked at night. Occasionally, Liz went to her studio late at night or early in the morning to check her kilns. Sometimes at night, she found six or eight guys sleeping on the basement concrete floor by a fire. Arriving early, Liz might encounter a group of vagrants cooking breakfast before they left their urban campsite. She never had a problem from these less fortunate denizens of the night. They just wanted shelter during the rainy fall and cold, damp winter months.

PARK STREET VENTURE

Feeling flush with cash from the sales of her artwork, Liz started walking around the neighborhood looking for a candidate building. At 321 NW Park Street, she found a narrow building that had promise. Next, she needed a partner.

A friend of hers was dating architect Don Vallaster. Liz met Don, and they became partners. Investing in a building as an owner was an art business decision for Liz. Moving glass panels in and out of a basement studio had been a hassle. Now she could have a workspace on the ground floor in the rear of a building that fronted onto the park blocks. Don drew up some plans, they arranged financing with Key Bank, and they bought the structure. The building footprint was small, so they decided to expand the project by purchasing the abutting building, owned by Joe Angel.

Not wanting to invest more of their own money, Liz and Don sought additional investors. They found and added two new partners, but things didn't work out. Their new partners couldn't qualify for the additional financial requirements. The deal became complicated and undoable as they attempted to work out a final agreement with Joe. Liz and Don ended up selling the Park Street building and moving on to other projects.

PAPASES' AMERICA

While living and working in Europe in the 1970s, Tessa and Bill Papas had bought a sixty-foot sailboat. The purchase of that boat came with an obligation from the previous owner. They had to honor two charters that had already been booked. Tessa remembered thinking, "This is a piece of cake."

The first charter turned into a disaster—"sheer hell," in Tessa's words. After recovering, Bill and Tessa found the next charter trip "utterly delightful." Two couples from Portland had booked that last charter. While the boat was docked on the island of Spetses, Greece, Tom Goodwin, one of the Portlanders, entertained Tessa with colorful, romantic stories about the Pacific Northwest. Intrigued, Tessa and Bill began having thoughts about visiting Portland. The sailboat purchase had set off a chain of events that resulted in the Tessa and Bill's decision to move to Portland in the early 1980s.

Bill was an artist—a political cartoonist and caricaturist, book author and illustrator—who had worked for *The Guardian*, *The Sunday Times*, and *Punch* in Europe. In 1984, Bill had two art shows scheduled in America. One was in Chicago, the other in Scottsdale, Arizona. A ten-day break had been scheduled between the two shows. On a lark, he and Tessa flew to Portland to visit the two couples that had chartered their boat ten years previous.

Tessa and Bill arrived on a brilliant, sunny day. The weather was freezing. But Bill decided on the spot—this was where they should stay! Mary Wall Baker—she'd been one of their charter sailors—had an apartment in her West Hill home, and Tessa and Bill rented it. A month later, they flew to Europe, sorted and packed up, sold the boat, and flew back to America, settling permanently in Portland.

PAPASES' ART STUDIO

Their experiences visiting friends in New York City had kindled the notion of working in a loft-style space. In 1985, needing a workspace, they rented 3,500 square feet on the fourth floor of the Gadsby building. The studio was a perfect workshop to produce an art book and etching project about America.

Much of the south brick wall was lined with workstations, and there were numerous worktables scattered about the studio. Bill and Tessa hired several people to assist them in producing Bill's etchings and art books. In many ways, the studio was organized as a craft-style assembly line with different individuals performing specialized tasks. Within two years, Tessa and Bill had published a limited-edition art book titled *Papas' America* and filled with Bill's wonderful watercolor images. The art project included a suite of fifty limited edition etchings.

This studio was as much their home as their apartment was. In the studio, there was more happening than the production of art. People gravitated to the workspace, and it became the building's social center. Typically around five o'clock in the afternoon, as the workday drew to a close, building tenants and visitors began trickling in. In the fall and winter months, they clustered around a three-foot-high kerosene heater that gave off waves of warmth to compensate for the lack of any building heating facilities. At all times, a tall, blue coffeepot and a squat, round teapot sat on top of a wire cage that encircled the heater. A cup of coffee or tea was always ready for guests and employees. Libations in hand, regulars and guests gathered around that central space heater like an earlier generation had huddled around a pot-bellied stove at a general store. These social gatherings helped instill a sense of community to those in attendance.

Developers showed up. Al Solheim came over occasionally, accompanied by Bob Ames and John Gray, and others, including John Carroll, Terry Brandt, and Rich Ford, all of who eventually purchased, converted, and renovated buildings in the district. Tessa, always a delightful host, welcomed one and all into this social setting.

The place had a unique ambiance—the wine and conversation flowed freely, imbued with energetic thoughts and ideas that mirrored the creative spirit that fueled the repurposed building projects happening outside the building. These individuals were excited, something new was happening, and people were having fun. Arlene Schnitzer, Portland's grande dame of the local art scene, a passionate patron of the arts, and her husband, Harold, were among the visitors, as was developer Homer Williams.

Homer—intrigued by the realization that people were actually living and working in these old warehouses—later conjured up a broader redevelopment vision for another piece of the puzzle that became the Pearl District. Visiting the studio space let people experience a loft workspace and loft living. Tessa and Bill's studio became a kind of urban incubator that showcased this new urban lifestyle.

THE PAPASES AS DEVELOPERS

After *Papas" America* was published, the Tessa and Bill decided they also wanted to own their own place of business, following Liz Mapelli's lead. In 1987, Tessa and Bill bought a two-story building on NW 8th Avenue between Glisan and Flanders Streets. The building was located almost directly across the North Park Blocks from the building Liz and Don had purchased. There Tessa and Bill established the Chetwynd Stapylton Gallery, named for Tessa's grandmother Dorothy Chetwynd Stapylton. When the City decided to make NW 8th Avenue a one-way street, Tessa and Bill became irritated since potential visitors and customers to the gallery were put off by this one-way traffic flow change.

Soon local politics and local circumstances propelled Tessa and Bill further into the development game. Baloney Joe's, an emergency homeless shelter, had purchased the building at the corner of NW 8th Avenue and Flanders. Baloney Joe's wanted to move its soup kitchen from the east side of the Willamette River to the west side of the river. City Hall had decided a soup kitchen by the North Park Blocks was a bad idea. Mayor Bud Clark thought the move would upset an agreement reached earlier that stated no more social services for the indigent population were to be planned in or around Portland's Old Town area. The deal was a response to complaints by the North Downtown business community over perceived conflicts and hardships related to homeless people.

The Burnside Community Council had bought the building for $382,000. However, under pressure from the City, they agreed to sell it. Tessa and Bill purchased the building with the intent to convert the structure to condominiums. Tessa and Bill, needing an architect, hired Don Vallaster to prepare a design for the adaptive reuse of the three-story structure. Don's design incorporated several playful new residences on the roof of the existing building. The architect placed and rotated the footprints of the new units at an angle to the geometry of the original building footprint. This created a sharp visual contrast between architectural styles—contemporary modern juxtaposed against the older historic warehouse style—and attests to the district's mixed architectural character.

Later, Tessa and Bill bought the old Harlow Hotel that was located immediately north of their gallery building. This was the historic Harlow Block, previously known as the Hayhurst building, which had been built in 1882–83. It was one of the oldest surviving commercial structures in the Pearl District, although it had a checkered history. Tessa and Bill's architect quickly determined a conversion of the building was not viable, and Tessa and Bill sold the building. Vacant for many years, this dilapidated brick structure had seemed to defy past attempts at renovation. Eventually, the building that housed the Tessa and Bill's art gallery was also sold, and their art gallery was moved downtown to 615 SW Broadway.

The Hayhurst building had passed through many owners over the past decades. Don had previously provided architectural services in the 1970s to one of the building's then owners. His client had ended up backing out of the deal. The building had a fundamental flaw. Unfortunately, the structure had been constructed on a gravel and mortar base instead of a proper structural foundation. This proved to be a hurdle none of the many previous owners could overcome when considering a renovation of the structure.

Don explained that the footings for the walls were built on a wall-like structure composed of rock. It was little more than a dry-stacked wall because the builders had used only a bit of mortar in the mix. There was no way the building could comply with the city's seismic codes. A seismic upgrade had proved to be prohibitively expensive. For years, the structure suffered from neglect, becoming a target for graffiti taggers. However, after the passage of four decades, a new owner appeared with a plan to restore the Hayhurst's historic exterior and renovate the structure for future use as a boutique hotel.

THE HARLOW HOTEL

In mid-2000, the new owner, Ganesh K. Sonpatki, hired Portland architect Stan Chesshir to draw up architectural renovation plans that included a voluntary seismic upgrade. The plans proposed installing a system of interior steel-reinforced concrete walls selectively up to the second floor. A new elevator core was also retrofitted from the basement to the top floor and tied to the outer walls, functioning like a flagpole to strengthen the entire structure. An extensive excavation was undertaken to remove and replace the inadequate perimeter wall footings. In the process, the head clearance in the basement was increased, and a new concrete floor was installed, resulting in useable space.

A proposal to add two new windows on the west-building facade to enhance the owner's plans for a ground-floor restaurant was applied for and approved by the City. The new windows allowed more natural light into the interior and views of the North Park Blocks. In early 2020, new windows had been installed, all graffiti on exterior walls had been removed from the building, and there was fresh paint on newly installed trim work along Glisan Street.

The Harlow Hotel—a building on the National Register of Historic Places—took its place among the growing collection of boutique hotels in the Pearl. All were destined to become destinations for adventurous, youthful guests looking for a base camp from which to experience Portland's urban sights, sounds, and nightlife. However, the arrival of Covid-19 interrupted these hopeful plans. In 2021, the exterior ground floor windows had been covered with plywood due to public protest and vandalism that occurred downtown and in other parts of the city in response to social unrest around racism and police actions.

◇ ◇ ◇

As more and more old buildings in the Northwest Triangle were converted to new uses, there was a growing awareness that many of the buildings, especially a grouping of structures along NW 13th Avenue reflected a collected historical importance. This served to underscore the earlier R/UDAT study's recommendation to designate and preserve a significant portion of the mixed-use warehouse district for historical reasons.

9

HISTORIC PRESERVATION

ONE OF THE PRIORITY STATEMENTS in the R/UDAT study report was a recommendation for the formation of a "Preservation District in the warehouse area." This statement was not lost on City officials and staff. They had been active study participants and had assisted in the publication of *The Last Place in the Downtown Plan.*

BACKGROUND STUDIES

After city officials had digested the final report, they immediately began a background study that included a land-use inventory that included identification of historic building resources while also examining development potential. This effort resulted in the publication of the *Northwest Triangle Study Background Document* in 1984. After that, planning bureau staff continued their work in association with the Northwest Triangle Business Association, the Bureau of Transportation, and the Northwest Industrial Neighborhood Association. This cooperative effort produced a report that recommended designation of the Northwest Triangle as a special district and suggested capital infrastructure and open space improvements as well as amendments to the zoning code. This work culminated in the adoption of the *Northwest Triangle Report* in 1985 by the Portland City Council. The final report set forth development policies and implementation measures for the newly formed Northwest Triangle Special District. Initially, decision-makers envisioned a continuance of the warehouse/wholesale land uses and character associated with the existing building stock. Aware that the area was in transition, district property owners were now on high alert, waiting to see what came next.

FORMING A HISTORIC DISTRICT

The wait was short. Al Solheim had a conversation with historic preservation consultant John Tess at the Heritage Consulting Group in Portland about what might happen in the Northwest Triangle. Both then took a trip to Seattle, where John was working on several loft projects. Al wanted to see for himself what type of loft development was occurring there.

After they returned, Al asked John if it was possible to get a historic approval for just a single building in the district. John's response was "Let's do them all!" He thought he could get a historic designation for a select group of buildings in the neighborhood. However, the critical question was: "what area would constitute a viable district?

After mulling this over, Al and John decided that the buildings that fronted onto NW 13th Avenue represented a microcosm of an earlier historical era that reflected use of the rail spur line that ran down the center of the roadway. They then contacted all the property owners between Davis and Johnson Streets to see if they would support a nomination for a historic district.

Some owners participated; others didn't. It was a pay-to-play deal, and twenty-odd owners signed up. Those property owners who supported the nomination primarily did so because they were aware of the economic benefits associated with being in a historic district. Buildings within a historic district received some tax relief—their local property tax assessments could be frozen for fifteen years, and the owners also became eligible for a state tax credit. These advantages were an attractive incentive to property owners in the 1980s. Some of these building owners also wanted to preserve these old structures for aesthetic and historical reasons.

The general public's attitude and reaction to the proposal was not promising at first. People remarked: "These warehouse buildings, what are you doing? These aren't historic structures." People at that time thought that historic buildings had to be Victorian homes or a building like the old US Bank building in downtown Portland. There was a perceived notion was that a building had to reflect a classical architecture style like an Italianate building or a bunch of buildings that had cast-iron facades.

When Russell Keune, the R/UDAT historic preservationist, surveyed the Northwest Triangle, he felt that the area didn't have a lot of historical building candidates. John, as he compiled his historical research, quickly realized that, politically, it would be impossible to make a historic district larger than a selective area that focused on NW 13th Avenue. There simply weren't enough warehouses that qualified as class I historical buildings throughout the entire Northwest Triangle District. Only a compact preservation district was doable.

Bill Hawkins, a member of the Historic Landmarks Commission, was adamantly opposed to the nomination. He favored classical buildings that denoted a particular architectural period. John believed historic preservation was not just about buildings. It was also about preserving a sense of place. He was forceful when he said, "Take the architecture away, historic preservation is about saving history as well as architecture." Therefore, a crucial part of the rationale for the NW 13th Avenue Historic District nomination was the fact that it was essential to save a collection of buildings because of their place in the historical development of the city.

John's strategy emphasized the role the street had played in the district's evolution. He argued: "You could make a story for NW 13th Avenue because the street had a railroad track in it."

Plus, many of the buildings had loading docks that were indicative of past land use. NW 13th Avenue was special, unlike the surrounding streets.

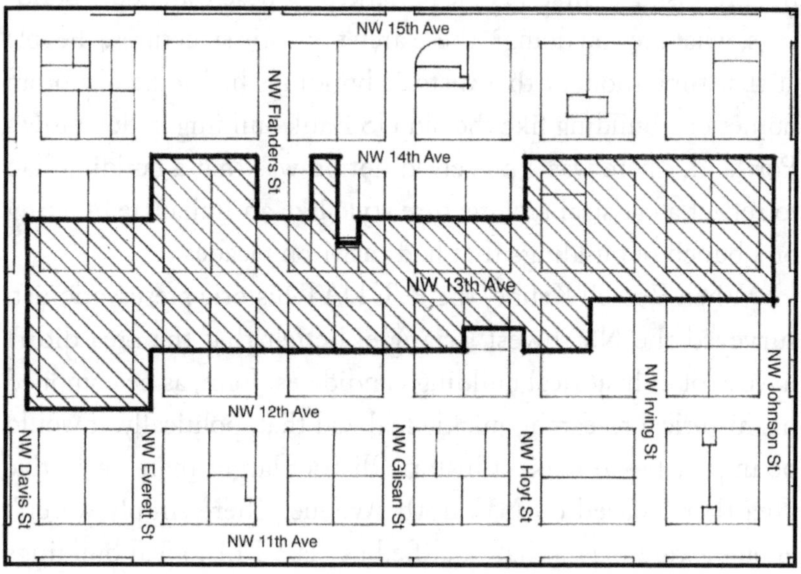

NW 13th Avenue Historic District Boundary Plan

The final boundary for the historic district turned out to be somewhat irregular; it jogged around several buildings, beginning at Johnson Street and ending at Davis Street. All of these buildings contributed to the visual land use character associated with a historical period when the storage and transport of goods and materials were dependent upon rail transport.

APPROVAL AND GUIDELINES

Getting a nomination approved required going through several review authorities: the Portland Development Commission (PDC), Portland's Historic Landmarks Commission, the Portland City Council, the State Historic Preservation Office, and the National Park Service of the United States Department of the Interior. There was some public objection to the nomination, and the Historic Landmarks Commission initially fought the nomination.

The Portland City Council proceeded to schedule a series of meetings and an application review. In advance of a meeting, Al and John went to see Commissioner Mildred Schwab. She knew Al, but it took her a moment to recognize John. John had squired her around during a scavenger clue hunt at a charity event for the Portland Junior Symphony just a week before. John reminded her of that event, and at the end of their conversation, the commissioner told Al and John she didn't have any problems with this proposal.

In 1986, the city council considered and approved the proposed nomination, declaring it an emergency to expedite the process. Heritage Consulting Group then prepared the necessary documentation that was approved by the National Park Service in 1987.

After that, an advisory committee was formed to develop design guidelines for the district. The committee prepared recommended guidelines in 1990, which were later incorporated into the public review process for the River District. The Historic Landmarks Commission approved and adopted design guidelines for the historic district in 1995. Implicit in the document was the recognition that preservation of a physical streetscape was of supreme importance in the creation of the district. The introduction to the list of design guidelines states that "the essential character of the District lies in this architectural coherence and uniformity [of the buildings], and in the street itself. Northwest 13th Avenue is the spine of the District. The District remains as the primary expression of the City's historical development as a center of commerce and distribution." A year later, the Portland City Council approved and adopted the NW 13th Avenue Historic District Design Guidelines as an integral component of the River District of the Central City Plan.

The nomination cost each property owner $80,000. It was a bargain. These owners received a fifteen-year property tax freeze on their buildings. However, now they had to meet with the City and meet whatever building code requirements applied to their properties. Many would need to negotiate the level of improvements the City required of them.

IMPROVING NW 13TH AVENUE

Everyone who spent any time on NW 13th Avenue in the '80s and '90s realized the street was in terrible shape. Heavy box-truck traffic had rutted the roadway, creating potholes. When it rained, the road filled with rainwater, acerbated by the fact there was no engineered surface drainage in place. The result was a random jumble of mud puddles sprinkled over several blocks of graveled roadways.

Past years had witnessed a decline in the use of the rail spur line, and the rails were in bad shape. Occasionally a boxcar jumped the tracks and sat in the middle of the block like an abandoned vehicle until the railroad sent out the necessary equipment to hoist it back on the rails. But a more significant issue loomed: how long were the tracks needed? Only one business—Northwestern Ice & Cold Storage—used the rails, and they were used once a month and usually at night.

Where commercial box trucks had been sometimes the sole vehicles parked along this graved streetscape, now automobiles parked there every day and sometimes overnight. A few commercial box trucks were visible, using the street in recognition that there was still some warehousing and industrial land use. But change had arrived.

Once City officials approved the historic district, it was evident to everyone that the roadway surface needed to be upgraded, and the right-of-way needed special city code treatment. For one thing, city street standards required sidewalks and street trees in rights-of-way. Compliance didn't seem appropriate in this situation. The City decided the elevated loading docks were suitable substitutes for sidewalks. And no street trees had ever been planted. It didn't seem appropriate to require them in the future, given the special nature of this street.

One of the popular ideas considered for NW 13th Avenue was the integration of a vintage trolley line connecting the district with the downtown core. City planning staff assisted by a technical advisory committee began a follow-on planning effort—a cooperative effort by the Northwest Triangle Business Association, the Bureau of Planning, and the Bureau of Transportation.

The city hired Roger Shiels, an architectural management consultant, to prepare an engineering cost analysis of what it would take to improve the existing gravel street. He also oversaw the establishment of a limited improvement district (LID) for the historic district to fund future improvements. Each property owner in the proposed landmark district was assessed and billed for a partial contribution for the upgraded improvements to the roadway. Roger had learned from personal experience that when the private sector contributed funds, then you'd have support from the bureaucrats and politicians, which is essential for these types of projects to succeed.

Roger had developed this formula over many years working in concert with Bill Naito, a local businessman who had completed several creative development projects in Portland. They always needed political and bureaucratic support, but Roger also recognized that these people were typically covering their butts, were underpaid and overworked, and were unappreciated. But if he got them in the right place on a project, they could do the job. And the timing was just right for this planning effort. Everyone supported paving this special street.

The city had decided to improve NW 13th Avenue to demonstrate certainty regarding the city's intent to support the Northwest Triangle District. The PDC paid 25 percent of the LID costs associated with the historic district and then 10 percent for the final engineering-phase costs.

As the street improvement design was nearing completion, there was the question as to whether the train tracks should remain.

Keeping them in the final design would have required installing new tracks, ties, and ballast—a full engineering design. It was not possible to simply embed new steel rails in a poured concrete slab. Laying replacement tracks would have been costly and the railroad's responsibility. And, of course, no train would ever travel on those new rails. Asking the railroad to do this was not a viable notion. Politics aside, replicating the historic rail line as a historical feature in a new paved roadway was a nonstarter.

There was also a safety concern. Roger had pointed out that bicyclists don't like to drive and ride alongside rail tracks. It's hazardous. Accidents and spills have been known to happen.

There was some opposition from a few property owners who continued to oppose the gentrification occurring in the district. However, the winds of progress prevailed. The study was concluded, and the city published the *Thirteenth Avenue Urban Design Plan* in January 1990. City planners envisioned NW 13th Avenue as an "urban alley." Sketches and development plans in the report illustrated how incorporating a trolley line, and the use of the elevated docks for outdoor dining could make the street an attractive, accessible, pedestrian-oriented environment—a idea that would resurface in 2020.

Over time, another unique visual feature associated with NW 13th Avenue was lost. For many decades, views of the First Presbyterian church steeple in the city's downtown west end had evoked an image of a Renaissance streetscape. That steeple had served as a focal object and had terminated the view looking south along NW 13th Avenue. That changed when the city installed signalized intersections at Glisan and Everett Streets at NW 13th Avenue by hanging signal lights above the middle of the intersections. Dangling and jiggling in the wind, they now reminded a viewer they were in the twenty-first century, and they disrupted a clear view of the steeple. A few years later, the construction of the Indigo Tower in the west end completely blocked the view of the steeple from any viewing position along NW 13th Avenue.

The City's adoption of an urban design plan for NW 13th Avenue was a defining moment. The City was now on record supporting redevelopment efforts in the Northwest Triangle. In 1992, Copenhagen Concrete began pouring concrete along NW 13th Avenue. Property owners in the Northwest Triangle and others perceived this as a stamp of approval. Local lending institutions and bankers now opened their purses and began funding warehouse conversions and renovations in this part of the city.

Almost two decades had passed since the city had adopted the 1972 Downtown Plan. Now people began talking about the need to upgrade and formulate a new plan. Advocates for a new plan focused on the Willamette River and the city's inner eastside commercial and residential neighborhoods. The citizenry, enamored by the successful adoption of several comprehensive inner-city neighborhood district plans wanted the new downtown planning effort to be fully transparent and driven by a high level of public participation.

10

DOWNTOWN PLAN UPDATE

CITY OFFICIALS IN THE 1980S began to say, "We're running out of gas!" Most of the projects and improvements envisioned in the 1972 Downtown Plan had been implemented. The plan had been deemed successful, but it needed updating.

Commissioner Margaret Strachan originated the idea for the Central City Plan when she served on the Portland City Council from 1981 to 1986. The council had created a committee tasked with developing a formal proposal outlining a process and first-year budget to update the previous downtown plan. Margaret, sparked by the R/UDAT study, became the committee's chairperson in 1984. Central to the vision was the need to enlarge the downtown study area to include adjoining commercial, industrial, and residential districts.

About the same time, John Russell, a local developer and community leader, hosted a lunch at Portland's University Club with business leaders and a few city staffers. He was behind several ongoing projects on the eastside. The purpose of the luncheon meeting was to actively promote expansion of the boundaries for downtown Portland. John felt the area north of Burnside and the industrial area along the east side of the Willamette River should be studied too.

A CITIZENS ADVISORY COMMITTEE

Margaret, once she had funding, went at this task with a small group of advisors—her Kitchen Cabinet. Foremost for consideration was how to continue improving the city's urban form and, most importantly, understand how it served its citizens. Central to the discussion was this question: what could be done to connect the downtown to the neighborhoods?

Don Stastny, a committee member, told me that the plan was driven by the decision to redirect the emphasis from the Central Business District to include both sides of the Willamette River and to make the river the focus instead of the downtown core. Margaret had introduced this concept to the council, and she had gotten an approval for a preplanning committee to study the proposal. Margaret put Don, an architect and urban designer, on the preplanning committee to be a neighborhood advocate. The committee's primary responsibility was to come up with an overall process that was public in its orientation. It had to have transparency, and it had to reflect citizen participation, as had happened with the 1972 Downtown Plan.

The preplanning study recommended that city bureaus were to be advisors to the advisory committee. Once the Portland City Council approved the preplanning report, a fifteen-person Citizens Advisory Committee (CAC) was established to ensure from that point forward that citizens had a voice in the planning process. Margaret then appointed Don to chair the CAC.

The CAC was also supported by a group of city planning staffers. The group, led by Rod O'Hiser, provided technical expertise. Besides the CAC, there were several subcommittees that concentrated on a variety of planning and design topics. Meetings were going on all the time. It was a cumbersome structure as the subcommittees were always coming up with ideas that clashed with what the CAC was advocating.

URBAN DESIGN INPUT

The committee wanted to add an urban design component to their efforts. So, an Urban Design Advisory Team was formed consisting of George Crandall (the team leader), Paddy Tillett, Will Martin—all of who were Portland architects—and Alan Jacobs from San Francisco. This select group oversaw the development of a general-area urban design plan, which produced detailed concept diagrams for individual districts or neighborhoods, which reflected the distinctive attributes and differences that characterized each subarea.

One of the issues the team considered was housing density. They found the allowable residential density in downtown to have been underutilized. Capacity existed to increase the number of residential units by building new row houses or urban townhouses as Skidmore, Owings & Merrill had recommended in their 1975 Urban Design Plan.

As the work progressed, George felt the urban planning had become somewhat dysfunctional because of the myriad of interests held by members of the CAC. Members had been selected geographically, and people ganged up to support things they favored and overlooked stuff they didn't like. The committee members were more interested in property values and established property rights. Preserving the status quo became a strong undercurrent during the study. This produced a lot of internal conflicts that resulted in many issues being taken off the table.

The effort produced what could best be called a contingency plan. The resulting plan totally overlooked the potential for high-density residential development in the future.

CHANGING THE PLANNING PROCESS

Things changed when Earl Blumenauer defeated Margaret in 1986 for a city commissioner position. After Earl took her place on the Portland City Council, he immediately decided the new plan, still in progress, was going to be completed by the Bureau of Planning. Michael Harrison, a senior planner at the bureau, got involved in this redirected planning effort. Michael oversaw the bureau's effort to finalize the technical portions of the plan. He focused on plan documentation enabling adoption of the new plan by the council.

The Central City Plan would introduce new changes to the design review process. Previously, development guidelines had allowed for a degree of flexibility. The new focus shifted from design guidelines to development requirements. Many in the architectural community perceived them as problematic. Many of these new development requirements were lengthy and very specific in detail. The planning bureau had changed the process from one of more performance-oriented requirements to one that was prescriptive in nature. Unfortunately, the latter approach assumed something could be presupposed or preordained—that the solution to a condition or problem had a ready-made solution. In many ways, this approach could hamper design creativity. It could frustrate architects and other professional designers thereby reducing flexibility in urban planning and design work. It was an approach that harkens back to Haussmann's approach to the redesign of Parisian boulevards in the mid to late 1800s. He had established a system of uniform development parcels and required predesigned building facades along the new boulevard corridors. Builders were told what to build.

Later in Portland as the private sector began submitting project proposals, the City would attach specific design requirements to proposed projects during the design review process. Developers and architects would soon rue these prescriptive rules.

THE CENTRAL CITY PLAN

Previously, city planners had accepted the notion that the Willamette River was the edge to the downtown area. There was now a new realization: the river could become a binding element of a larger city center. CAC participants also began discussing how a public transit loop could connect land uses on both sides of the river. Inspecting an aerial photograph of Portland, it was obvious the river was a seam between several existing mixed-use inner-city districts that included a significant number of urban housing units. The adoption of the Central City Plan in 1988 envisioned a combined area composed of the Central Eastside commercial area, Memorial Coliseum/Lloyd Center, Lower Albina, Northwest Triangle, North of Burnside, Downtown, Goose Hollow, and North Macadam as a wholly integrated city center.

The Central City Plan was published 1988 and envisioned an expanded urban center as a livable, walkable city with a focus on the river and an environment that could capture the "glitter and excitement of city living." It was viewed as a framework plan to guide development over the next twenty years.

Like many plans, there were both pros and cons to this one. The drafters of the plan had been receptive to citizen input and sensitive about recognizing the importance and value of natural resources in the urban landscape. In that regard, the Central City Plan incorporated the Willamette River Greenway Plan—a 5.3-mile pedestrian-bicycle corridor along the river—to preserve access to the riverfront for its citizens.

The plan confirmed the idea that fifty-odd acres of surplus rail yards next to Union Station was ideally suited for redevelopment because of its proximity to downtown. Older warehouses south of Lovejoy Street were identified as candidates for renovation as a public attraction, for example, a public market. Major portions of the unused rail yards were designated as a "Housing Target Area" in areas both south and north of Lovejoy. Future housing north of Lovejoy was to be required in the plan. This updated plan recommended a northward extension of the North Park Blocks with new residential use in areas adjacent to this linear open-space corridor. Feasibility studies were proposed to assess the feasibility of incorporating "water features" with new housing north of Lovejoy and along the riverfront north of the Broadway Bridge.

However, the plan did have a serious flaw. It had failed to recognize the opportunity to pursue high-density development in the urban core. Fortunately, this oversight was rectified in 1995, when the Metro Council adopted a long-range plan—the 2040 Growth Concept—for the metropolitan area. At the heart of the Central City Plan was a broad regional commitment to growth management with the idea of increasing residential densities throughout the metro area.

The Central City Plan had allocated population target figures—thirty thousand for Portland. However, the city objected to this allocation. They wanted the number to be one hundred thousand. That was fine, but the question was: where do you put the new residents?

The City replied by saying thirty thousand would be in the central city. This statement changed attitudes. Previously, it had been an abstract notion; now, they had to work out a way to achieve this goal. Before 1988, the housing goal was only five thousand units for the central city. By 1995, the goal would be thirty thousand, and then one hundred thousand units.

Furthermore, the plan recommended changes to the existing land-use zoning code in the Northwest Triangle District to allow residential development. In general, the existing Downtown Manufacturing Zone (MX) was replaced with a Commercial Employment Zone (CE) that permitted allowed residential uses together with both commercial, and industrial uses. Additionally, the Central Commercial and Services Zones (C1Z and MXZ)— both had a Downtown Development (Z) overlay designation—were replaced by the Commercial Employment Zone (CED) and the Central Commercial Zone (CXD). These new zoning designations included a new design overlay except for portions of the rail yards on either side of Lovejoy Street where the General Industrial Zone (GI) was retained. This was necessary to encourage a transition from an industrial past into a future that encouraged mixed-use development. The zoning also encouraged denser residential use with the inclusion of floor area ratio (FAR) bonus provisions in the new zoning code and new building height allowances.

The 1988 plan had focused on connectiveness as the hinge between downtown Portland and the eastside. The river was the hinge. This plan brought attention back to the Willamette River.

Loft living was about to become a developer's dream. They could build open living spaces with fewer walls that appealed to a changing, growing market demand. However, the new units would reflect compact floor plan designs as opposed to the more spacious floor plans residents in New York City had enjoyed in earlier loft development. There was money to be made, and lots of experienced and inexperienced people jumped into the game.

11

LIVE/WORK LOFT LIVING

JOE ANGEL JUMPED ON THE bandwagon to provide live/work lofts for artists in the late 1980s. He began by buying an entire city block located kitty-corner from the northwest end of the North Park Blocks. The project consisted of three buildings that included the Cotter. In 1989, Joe had nominated the Cotter for the National Register of Historic Places, and it was approved. He then executed a plan to rehabilitate and design the complex in a holistic manner he called the Honeyman Hardware Lofts. Sadly, he didn't proceed according to City requirements, and the project suffered delays.

Joe's vision was to develop the property as a mixed-use project. When completed, there were loft-style apartments, studio work-spaces, commercial-retail activity, and on-site parking for tenants. An extensive renovation process began in 1989 and involved the demolition of a three-story quarter-block structure. By 1991, all three buildings had been consolidated into a complex consisting of one hundred apartments and condominium units. Eventually, the project was sold to DiNapoli Capital Partners for $37.1 million. A $4.9 million renovation by the new owners converted some of the existing retail space into eleven live/work lofts and a new lounge for residents.

WORKING AND LIVING IN A FACTORY

Martha Bergman and Bob Gamblin needed space for a factory to make premium quality paint for artists. They found it on the third floor of the Cotter in 1987. After two years, they moved out due to uncertainty about the Joe Angel's renovation plans for the building. Fortunately, they found a larger space and the joys of loft living in the Universal Tea building at NW 12th Avenue and Hoyt.

As soon as they took possession of the building, Martha and Bob wondered if they could save money by living in the factory instead of renting a separate apartment. Their lease didn't prohibit. Still, they needed to find out if the City's zoning code allowed residential use. Martha trooped down to the Bureau of Buildings, and to her surprise, a staff person told her the City wanted to see more people living in the Northwest Triangle.

However, Martha and Bob had one more problem they had to overcome. They needed to comply with the life-safety code that required two exits in case of a fire. This presented a problem since the factory space had only one exit door.

Martha, Bob, and Bob's son Jonah demonstrated they could get out of the building using an existing window. They passed an inspection by the fire marshal and proceeded to set up housing in a walled-off section of the factory. The City was fully committed to and supportive of the idea of residences in this up-and-coming mixed-use neighborhood.

AN ARTISTS' CO-OP

After the Honeyman Hardware Lofts, Joe's next project resulted in the Everett Station Lofts. He developed a compact residential complex in Old Town and created a strong sense of community while offering rent-controlled cooperative housing. In 1989, he acquired an entire city block in Old Town for Everett Station Lofts. He wanted to create a cooperative-style residential/working studio complex for artists. When all the renovations for Everett Street Lofts were finished, there were sixty-three loft-style co-op units available for artists to rent. Sixteen of the live/work units were special. They had been designed as storefronts—right off the public sidewalk to give artists the same kind of pedestrian window-shopping exposure shopkeepers had in downtown retail stores. Unlike a traditional gallery space, these storefront studios allowed artists to curate ever-changing displays of artwork for sale.

An artists selection committee vetted artists who wanted to live in the co-op. Two of the questions were: "What would you take from living in this community, and what would you provide back to the community?" If selected, those artists had to agree to open their studios to the public during regular business hours and First Thursday events. The project was a roaring social success. Unfortunately, it was not financially sustainable.

Real estate development in the Northwest Triangle experienced a mild boom in the mid-1990s, and several developers approached Joe. They wanted to buy and convert Everett Station Lofts to condominiums for sale. Despite receiving several attractive offers, Joe turned them all down.

Still, the artists felt threatened because they might lose their homes to gentrification. Searching for a solution, the cooperative learned that a Minneapolis-based nonprofit organization called Artspace owned several arts-oriented projects across the nation. The Portland artists, following a grassroots playbook, asked Artspace if they were interested in buying the project. Joe, instead of making a significant profit by selling the buildings on the open market, agreed to sell the complex to this out-of-state company. He sold Everett Street Station in 1996 at an appraised value of $3.9 million, thereby preserving this artistic cooperative as a center of creative life in Old Town.

To make the deal happen, the PDC provided a low-interest loan for the acquisition of the property. The City wanted a broad cross-section of renters in different economic categories within the complex to revitalize this part of downtown. This was ensured by a covenant that, in effect, makes thirty of the units rent-controlled.

Because rents are controlled, there is a waiting list. Some artists stay for long periods. A handful of artists have been there for twenty years. Occasionally, space is rented to non-artists, but it's a rarity. And sometimes a family headed by an artist with children will rent a unit.

PASSIONATELY LOOKING TO LIVE IN A LOFT

Carol Smith-Larson was more than excited about the possibility of living in a loft in 1988. As construction on the Irving Street Lofts proceeded, she had petitioned Al Solheim to let her into his building to see what was happening. She then talked Al into a partial-occupancy permit before construction was completed, and Carol took up residency.

If the units had been condominiums, she'd have bought one. Unfortunately, for Carol, Al had chosen to build out the project as a rental building. Fortunately for her, in 1989, the Hotel Supply building—Richard Calhoun's Old Town Florist shop, which had once occupied the ground floor, at NW 9th Avenue and Flanders—came on the market. Al owned the building, and he sold it to Carol. Her plan was to renovate the upstairs into a loft. She hired Rick Michaelson, a building contractor, to do the renovations and to arrange project financing with a bank in Salem. Like with many of those early building conversion, there were difficulties complying with earthquake code requirements. However, Rick prevailed in his discussions with the City, ensuring that all the renovations complied with city building codes.

Carol moved out of the Irving Street Lofts and into her dream loft in February 1991. Her second-floor loft space had a tall ceiling that gave the nineteen-hundred-square-feet open floor plan a voluminous appearance. The exposed rough-edged structural beams and posts were overlaid with exposed conduit and industrial metal switch boxes. The texture of the masonry brick walls was visible through the white paint. The space had no demising walls except for an enclosed bathroom and storage area. It felt like a compact New York City loft.

Carol told me that she was "just really happy here." This was her refuge in the city. From there she could walk to not every place in the world—but exactly the places she wanted to go to. And if she didn't want to walk, she could always use the abundant public transportation running through the city's core.

She and Rick became good friends. Later, she became one of Rick's partners in an investor group that bought the Gadsby building when the Hoyt Street Lofts partnership sold the building. An early resident in the emerging neighborhood, Carol also became involved in the formation of the Pearl District Neighborhood Association (PDNA), as did Neilson Abeel.

Neilson and Tori Bryer arrived in Portland by car in the summer of 1990. Neilson had been part of a two-man real estate consulting department in New York City. In the spring of 1989, his boss retired, and Neilson was out of a job. So, he and Tori decided to take a road trip. On the Oregon coast, they decided to get married, entirely serendipitously.

They were next on to Portland because Neilson's son was graduating from Reed College, and Neilson's roommate from graduate school lived in town. Tori wanted to stop to see an old school friend, Lucinda Parker. They had these connections, so they stayed and sublet an apartment. Tori, an artist, needed a studio, so she rented a space in the Gadsby building. Initially, they thought they'd spend only a year in the city. Soon, they changed their minds, and they drove back to New York City, packed up half of their furniture, sublet their apartment, and returned to Portland.

In the spring of 1991, Tori and Neilson started looking for real estate. Instead of looking for a house farther out, they decided they wanted to live in a warehouse. In the fall, they found a three-story brick warehouse at NW 13th Avenue and Flanders.

The building was the former Armour Meats building, and in 1991, a brewery. Portland Brewery was building a new facility in the Guilds Lake Industrial neighborhood. The brewery owners needed to get the old brewery off their books. The building had been for sale for two and a half years, and the owners wanted a $350,000 cash buyout.

Neilson sat down with Tony Adams, the building owner, and laid out his offer. He wanted the owner to accept a partial cash offer, hold the mortgage contract, and agree to several other outrageous conditions: The seller "would have to really work with us." Neilson offered 25 percent cash down and a reasonably low-interest rate. Tony rejected the offer. Neilson and Tori spent a week or two of looking at other buildings. A couple days later, Tony called back and accepted the offer.

Neilson had his attorney draw up the contract, it got signed, and the deal closed in December 1991. Tony, the president of Portland Brewery, signed a lease that allowed brewing operations to continue for another eighteen months in the building while Neilson had renovation plans prepared by his architect.

While Neilson and Tori had been dickering over buying the brewery building at 431 NW Flanders, Bruce Forster, a friend of Neilson's, went over to the building to talk with Neilson about renting one of the floors for a new photography studio. Richard Brown, a local architect and friend of Bruce's, had tagged along because he knew Bruce hadn't hired an architect yet. Neilson ended up hiring Richard as his architect. Richard provided plans for the conversion of the building into residential and commercial uses. The third floor was renovated into living quarters and a separate art studio for Tori.

As part of the financing strategy, the building was placed on the National Register of Historic Places. This provided Neilson with tax credits that reduced the overall project costs. For financing, they used their own assets, borrowing against a rising market. In the end, they decided to condo the building and sell off the ground and second floors. Tori and Neilson moved into finished quarters in November 1992.

A year later, Bruce purchased the second floor from Neilson, and Richard became his architect for the build out of his new photography studio. In 1996, the ground floor and basement were sold to Dick Rosenberg, a private investor. He built out office space and rented it to developer Homer Williams. Shortly thereafter, Homer formed Hoyt Street Properties, LLC, and moved around the corner to 1308 NW Everett Street, where some of the fundamental underpinnings for the creation of what became the River District were formulated.

Meanwhile a group of property owners and business leaders had been meeting informally to discuss how to improve Old Town and the surrounding area immediately north of West Burnside. Over time, this group's discussions and ideas would coalesce and crystallize into a bold visionary statement.

12

NORTH OF DOWNTOWN

WEST BURNSIDE HAS ALWAYS BEEN the dividing line between the city's downtown Central Business District and a neighboring commercial area known as North Downtown, which includes Old Town and vestiges of Chinatown. Historically, Old Town was home to a concentration of bars and brothels. After enjoying a drink or two, or too many, some men woke up to find themselves "shanghaied" as new crewmembers on departed sailing ship. As Asian immigrants found permanent homes and established businesses, a micro part of Old Town became known as Chinatown. As time passed, community social services including the Salvation Army and a soup kitchen established a presence in Old Town. The availability of these services and others eventually became a magnet attracting a disadvantaged and indigent population.

To the dismay of Portlanders, groups of homeless people—men and women, young and old, sleeping and sitting or standing and talking among themselves—still congregate along the public sidewalks near the Burnside bridgehead. This public behavior has become an everyday occurrence, less so in the winter months or when it rains. Many view this as distasteful street theater. It has persisted for many decades, and a remedy appeared out of reach to public officials even in the 1980s and '90s. Repeatedly, two questions were raised in the past: is this an immutable situation, and where would the impetus come from to improve things?

WEST BURNSIDE'S IMAGE

Burnside had always been a major arterial roadway in the city. As the city grew, it functioned as an urban highway that connected vehicular traffic from the east side of the Willamette River to downtown on the river's west side and farther outward to the West Hills and the Tualatin Valley. During rush hours, this roadway bustles. Over the years, as traffic volumes increased, segments of the road have become hazardous for pedestrians. When a pedestrian was hit and killed while crossing the street without traffic signals, local officials and community activists became concerned. They began asking for a solution to this problem.

The roadway also delineates the north end of the city's prestigious commercial business core. Before the 1970s, the commercial area north of Burnside had a downtrodden reputation because of the social issues present there. Many of the buildings were older and architecturally undistinguished, and the parade of loitering street people added to this controversial image. A few local business leaders were thinking about what they could do to change this.

In the early 1970s, John Elorriaga, the chairman and CEO of US Bancorp of Oregon, made an executive decision to expand the bank's physical footprint based on the need to house the latest computer technology that had infiltrated the banking industry. He also wanted to build a new commercial office complex in downtown to provide more jobs in Portland. In consultation with the Portland office of Skidmore, Owings & Merrill (SOM) John decided the bank needed a modern operations center and a commercial office tower.

What and where to build? There wasn't any question in John's mind. He wanted to build a forty-story tower. But there were zoning height limitations for office towers downtown. There was an available site adjacent to West Burnside Street near the historic building that housed a US Bank branch. It wasn't the best site, but considering the possible zoning issues, it was the one that offered the most certainty. John hired SOM as the architects to do a feasibility study of the site.

They found acquisition and site issues. Two separate blocks of land needed to be purchased and consolidated into one parcel. This necessitated closing two streets, subject to city approval—Ankeny and Pine between SW 5th and 6th Avenues. The City approved the street closures but required the architects to maintain public pedestrian access along the Ankeny right-of-way between SW 5th and 6th. The resulting site was oddly shaped, due to the intersection of two opposed street grids.

It also wasn't the best location because a future bank tower would have to be built directly across the street from Old Town, the presence of several social agencies, and charities that served indigent populations. These circumstances didn't discourage the bank from constructing the new operations center in 1974 and later the office tower in 1983 on what was essentially a superblock site.

Years later, during an interview about events associated with the construction of this complex, John brought up the efforts of Don Magnusen. Don had been an executive vice president of US Bancorp and chairman of the PDC when the tower was built.

Once the tower—the locals call it Big Pink—was completed, bank executives moved into the thirty-first floor. Don had an office that looked out onto West Burnside. He often mulled over a couple of questions: What should happen on the other side of West Burnside in Old Town and Chinatown? Could the area be improved? These questions rattled around in Don's mind, and he grew more and more concerned with each passing month. Hell, there had been little change on the north side of Burnside over the past couple of decades.

Don couldn't get past the fact that many people still thought of West Burnside as Skid Row. The hobos who used to ride the rails to Portland—a terminal point along the West Coast—were only a memory in the minds of the older generation. Now it was a drug scene; you could buy just about any upper or downer you wanted around Old Town, even the hardest drugs, like heroin. When Burlington Northern ceased use of its rail yards at Union Station just a few blocks farther north, the deserted rail yards also became a haven for drug users.

Don, other downtown businesspeople, and property owners used to meet informally to discuss what to do about the presence of homeless individuals and this growing street drug problem. One member of the group came up with the phrase "the solution is dilution." The idea was to add new activities that would result in more people visiting local shops and businesses. The objective was to reduce the visual concentration of street people and, hopefully, influence them to leave the area as more and more newcomers took over the environment. If Old Town were full of more shopkeepers, shoppers, and, perhaps, tourists; then people who were homeless would go somewhere else because they wouldn't feel comfortable. Instead, homeless people lying on sidewalks, panhandlers and inebriated individuals accosting passersby, deranged persons staggering around or shouting, and the smell of urine in doorways probably intimated many people, who then chose to avoid the area.

THE NORTH DOWNTOWN GROUP

A 1981 report by the Portland Bureau of Planning—*North of Burnside Land Use Policy*—recognized that long-term development of this historic area had been overlooked and was overdue. Plans had been made, and plans had been shelved. For whatever reason, there had been little implementation.

Smart businesspeople don't wait for city officials to act. By the early 1990s, Don's informal group had begun meeting on a regular basis and discussing ways to improve North Downtown. They had talked about the problems, knew what they were, but hadn't come up with an action plan.

Bob Ames was a member of this group. Besides being a banker, he was an active community leader and served as president of the Portland Port Commission from 1988 to 1997. In the past, the port had been a land developer—a big one. The port owned a lot of the land apart from Swan Island and Rivergate. This prompted a decision in the early 1990s by the Port Commission that Terminal One—industrial riverfront land near Old Town—would not be used for any port-related activity in the future. At that point, the port really had to consider the land redundant since it was no longer vital to the port's marine-oriented mission. The port land then should have gone back on the tax rolls to benefit the city's need for revenue. However, there was no sense of urgency to do that.

To find out what land use might be appropriate for this surplus waterfront site, port staff hired a real estate consultant from San Francisco. After arriving in Portland, this consultant went over to the Terminal One site and inspected the property. He also spent time with city officials and others discussing current development at and around Union Station. He also called Bob and scheduled a meeting. They met in Bob's office on the twentieth floor of the First Interstate Bank Tower. At one point, the consultant asked Bob to walk over to the north-facing office window. From that height, the Union Station building, the rail yards, and the industrial area from the Willamette River west were all visible in a wonderful panoramic view. The consultant proceeded, saying to Bob, "Let me tell you what you've got here. I don't think anyone has figured this out yet." He went on and explained that the presence of Union Station, Terminal One, and the large tract of rail yards that had been sold should be rezoned to permit the construction of urban housing.

He really wound Bob up. The port had commissioned this study to get some advice about what to do with Terminal One. Now their consultant had put Bob on notice that it was a bigger deal than anyone realized.

◇ ◇ ◇

So, why did a railroad company sell what for many years was surplus land in Portland? That decision radically changed the scope and scale of future urban development in what had been the Northwest Triangle District. The consultant hired by the Port of Portland had given Bob a sneak peek at what inspired the members of North Downtown group to act.

13

UNION STATION
AND ITS RAIL YARDS

THE BURLINGTON NORTHERN RAILROAD HAD
conducted a national assessment of the company's railway trackage
system back in the 1980s. This survey revealed a huge surplus of
rail yards across the country. More importantly, the assessment
indicated that some of these properties were contaminated with
toxic materials. For years carbon-based materials had leached into
the subsoil. Many of these rail yards were ticking time bombs.

Elsewhere in the USA, oil magnate Fred Anschutz had decided
to buy the Denver & Rio Grande Western Railroad for $500
million. Afterward, he split up the company and its components
and sold the land for $500 million. He had, except for his time
and effort, purchased the railroad for nothing. Burlington and
other national railroad companies now aware of his real estate
deal saw an opportunity to sell off their surplus operational and
agricultural lands.

THE RAILROAD SELLS UNION STATION

Burlington Northern then began making plans to dispose of the
Hoyt Street rail yards. Before this happened, the railroad sold a
separate parcel, about thirty acres of land, to the City. The parcel
included Union Station, a few outbuildings, a fire station that was

located at NW 3rd Avenue and Glisan, and a few vacant blocks of land near the station. The City immediately showed interest in a narrow tract of land that ran parallel to the operational tracks at Union Station. This sliver located between the Steel Bridge and the Broadway Bridge fronted onto Naito Parkway. The City considered the site a prime location for intercity housing.

Chris Kopka, a project manager at the PDC, had procured a purchase option from the railroads in 1985. The purchase price had been set at about $12 million. At one point, the City also considered the property as a site for a new convention center. A new convention center ended up being constructed on the opposite side of the river.

In 1986, Bruce Allen moved to Portland from Tucson, Arizona. Bruce was an architect with a master's degree in urban planning, and he was impressed with the type of urban development that was happening in the city. So, he jumped at an invitation by Chris, an old friend, and the opportunity to work at the PDC.

Initially, the PDC wanted him to manage the Old Town parking garage because Bruce had managed a city garage in Tucson. Bruce wasn't interested in that position. Instead, he was offered a management position to handle the final negotiations for the acquisition of the Union Station property. He closed the deal on Halloween in 1987.

GLACIER PARK'S MASTER PLAN

In 1988, Burlington Northern formed Burlington Resources. This division had seven subsidiary companies—each a separate profit center. Glacier Park, a holding company for Burlington's properties, was the one in charge of all lands.

Marty Sevier, a Burlington project engineer, was assigned to work at Glacier Park. The railroad company needed someone to look at their national land holdings and free up land for potential development. Glacier Park was in charge of $500 million worth of real estate, and Burlington Resources was worth about $9 or

$10 billion in real estate assets. Glacier Park was worth a nickel on that dollar, maybe.

When it came to land development, Burlington didn't have any experience. However, the company could take a piece of land, get the necessary entitlements, and market the property to the national development community. After forming a joint-venture partnership with a development entity, the partnership could then design, permit, and market the land for a specific set of uses similar to what Fred Anschutz had done in Denver.

At the time, Marty was living in Denver managing joint-venture projects. But then the Denver office closed. He was asked if he wanted to move back to Seattle. However, another opportunity presented itself when the railroad employee in charge of the Portland office was fired.

After checking out Portland, Marty told his boss in Seattle, "You know, I shouldn't be moving to Seattle; I should be moving to Portland. Those guys in Portland aren't going to care what this guy from Seattle has to say. But if I'm living in Portland, and I'm on the streets and talking with people there, at least I will have a vested interest in what's going on…I should move to Portland."

On his first visits to Portland, Marty got the vibe: *You're going to move here…You will be part of what we're trying to do…Oh, we're so glad to have you.* His past experiences had taught him "real estate deals are local deals." Every city has a different DNA, and it affects how deals are done. So, he commuted for a year and then moved to Portland in 1989.

Now Marty needed an office. He ended up renting space in one of the buildings Prendergast & Associates owned on Macadam Avenue. As he settled in, Marty got to know Pat Prendergast and John Carroll, both active real estate developers.

As time went on, the North Downtown group became especially interested in what was going to happen to the Hoyt Street rail yards. So, Marty—because he oversaw the disposition of the surplus rail yards—became a member of group. At some point,

Marty was asked what was going to happen to the rail yards. Marty knew he was sitting on a minefield, but he told the group, "I want to go to the City and do a master plan on this entire piece of property."

Marty's idea was to develop the land as an industrial office park. But first, he needed financial projections on alternative development scenarios. Being situated in the offices of Prendergast & Associates, he hired them to make these projections.

Marty then met with Earl Blumenauer, a city commissioner. During their meeting, Earl suggested that the plan ought to include an element of housing. Marty asked him, "How much housing do you want?" Earl's answer was precise: "268 units!" At the time, Marty thought that was a lot.

At this point, Marty began to think this situation might become a "nightmare"; working with city governments could become troublesome. He met again with Earl and agreed to the 268 units of housing. However, his offer was conditional—the City had to assign a staff person to assist him through the permitting process.

Earl told Marty he had to think this offer over. Marty retorted that he wasn't going to invest his time and money if the City wasn't on board with Glacier Park's proposal. Marty suggested that the city staff person should sit in on their weekly planning meetings. In due course, the city decided to take Glacier Park up on their offer. Marty filed a master plan submittal, and the city approved it in 1989.

What's interesting about the Glacier Park Master Plan was City Hall's notion about how much housing should be in the land use mix. As circumstances changed, the numbers changed significantly—268 units became 5,500. This suggests that master plans need a high degree of flexibility to respond to changing economic and market conditions and local politics.

With an approved master plan in hand, Marty now made plans to sell the property. He scheduled a meeting with Pat LaCrosse, the director of the PDC, and Larry Dully. Marty had hopes the

City would want to buy the rail yards since they had previously purchased a smaller parcel. Pat was interested. Since Larry knew the site was contaminated, Pat only offered to take the property off Marty's hands and relieve Burlington Northern of burdensome and expensive cleanup costs.

◇ ◇ ◇

The Last Place in the Downtown Plan had envisioned a business park development on the Hoyt Street rail yards property. Glacier Park had obtained an approval to build a business office park. However, another real estate deal would arise—a deal that replaced the vision of a business park with a better vision.

14

THE LAND SWAP

TWO LOCAL DEVELOPERS WERE ON the verge of making a great real estate deal. The eventual sale of Hoyt Street rail yards dramatically changed residential development game in the Northwest Triangle. Converting old warehouses along NW 13th Avenue had resulted in new loft-style housing units. Construction of new structures—condominiums and apartments buildings—along NW 10th and 11th Avenues was an obvious choice when vacant land became available. New buildings began sprouting like toadstools over the coming decade.

Prendergast & Associates bought the rail yards. Pat had been a builder of commercial office spaces before the 1980s. But as Oregon's lumber-based economy slid into a decline, he discovered the emerging demand for flex space. This new real estate product commonly was a modern variation of a one-story industrial building with a strip of office space tacked onto the front of the structure. Pat was a merchant builder—a developer who doesn't build for the long haul. They plan, construct, stabilize a development project, and then sell it usually to a group of investors or via an arrangement with the primary tenant. It's a short-time play. Pat never had an extensive portfolio. His view was to follow the market and sell at the appropriate time and take profits.

Like all successful developers, he was a calculated-risk-taker. His son Todd remembered Pat always attempted to "one-up" his last project. He wanted to do something different and better than what he had just done. He wasn't the kind of guy that was satisfied doing the same thing over and over. Pat wanted a challenge. His mind-set was to look beyond the immediate horizon. His focus was so singular that he would even break up a business partnership to do what he wanted.

John Carroll was Pat's partner. John's childhood had been nomadic, but his family had finally settled in Portland. After graduating from Lincoln High School, John went to work for the Pendleton Woolen Mills. He worked in the cutting room laying out materials. After a while, he was asked to work in the plant's industrial engineering department. This involved conducting time-and-motion studies, setting up production lines, and laying out materials and patterns in an efficient way.

This experience gave him insights into manufacturing processes that John later adapted to building renovation and construction. There's not much difference between the basic process of making shirts and that of building structures. You take materials of various kinds, fit the pieces together as in a construction process, and get them working efficiently as a whole, and you end up with a Pendleton shirt or with a building. Once John realized the overall process of making a shirt or producing a building reflected similar incremental processes, he was on his way toward a professional career as a developer.

John met Pat at a neighborhood-planning meeting, and they quickly struck up a conversation. At the time, John had been working with Zidell Industries in Portland. That first conversation blossomed into a friendship, which led to John going to work for Prendergast & Associates. John quickly picked up the requisite expertise a developer needs about land acquisition, site construction, and property management.

PLANNING WINDLOPH FARMS

Prendergast & Associates had been close to forming a partnership with Nike, then just a local shoe manufacturing company. Pat had become involved with Nike in the 1980s when his company built Nike's research and development facility on Nimbus Avenue. Nike now wanted to plan and expand its campus on a sprawling seventy-five acres of land.

At the same time, Pat and John were working with Glacier Park. They had signed a joint venture agreement to develop 150 acres, called Windloph Farms, adjacent to Nike's property. This venture led to the formation of the Walker Road Limited Partnership.

As Prendergast & Associates went into planning mode, they needed a planning consultant, so they hired Wilsey Ham, a local engineering and planning firm. Tom Jones, a landscape architect with Wilsey Ham, was assigned to work with Pat and John. Tom visited the Windloph Farms site and was impressed with the property—it was pastoral with groves of large oaks, Douglas fir trees, Ponderosa pines, and rolling hills. He envisioned a large-scale office park nestled in the woods. By contrast, John wanted an auto mall, and Tom had prepared a layout plan for this auto mall. The plan was submitted to Washington County, but it was denied because of site issues around the proposed traffic access point where Nike's main entrance was built.

In the middle of this site planning effort, Marty over at Burlington Northern got a call from a senior colleague. This individual told Marty he had some "bad news and some worse news." Marty wanted the bad news first, and he was told the railroad was not going to do any more joint ventures in Portland. Marty asked him why not, and he received the worse news. Burlington Northern was shutting down Glacier Park.

Burlington Northern had hired Morgan Stanley Realty to assist in the disposal of all nonessential and obsolete rail properties nationwide. Remember that Glacier Park was only worth a nickel-to-a-dollar in value as compared to Burlington Resources' national landholdings portfolio. And in 1989, land values were depressed across the nation. Marty was told to put together a pro forma for all the Burlington Northern property under his management. He was also told that Morgan Stanley would handle all future deals.

Marty then called Pat and John. They met, and Marty told them the Walker Road joint venture was dead. He added that Windloph Farms had been put up for sale at a price approaching $5 million. When advised of this situation, Pat and John's legal counsel told them their agreement with Burlington Northern was valid and couldn't be dissolved unilaterally by one party. Glacier Park was now in a bind. Their agreement with Prendergast & Associates prevented them selling the Windloph Farms on the open market.

THE LAND SWAP

Things grew more complicated because Pat and John's tentative deal with Nike fizzled. Prendergast & Associates were under a contract with Nike, and there was a non-compete clause. Nike contacted Pat and John told them Nike wanted to buy the 150-acre farm property.

Pat and John were sitting pretty. They worked out a deal. They bought the Windolph Farms property from Glacier Park, sold one hundred acres to Nike, and then sold the remaining fifty acres to Sequent Computer Systems. To forgo any capital gains taxes, Prendergast & Associates purchased the surplus rail yards—the property now formally referred to as the Hoyt Street Yards—from Burlington Northern using a 1031 tax-deferred exchange. This serendipitous event was finalized in late 1990. It was a hurried sale, but a done deal. Besides the forty-acre property, Pat and John acquired additional property near the rail yards, bringing their total ownership to fifty acres of land in a most favorable location next to downtown.

The additional ten acres was located immediately north of the Fremont Bridge and had been owned by an entity called Front

Street Partners. After this acquisition, Prendergast & Associates sold most of it since the development pattern of separated land parcels didn't appear to work for their tentative plans. Historically, the property consisted of remnant parcels the railroad had declined to sell to tenants that they'd had since the late 1930s. Prendergast & Associates contacted every individual tenant and gave each a window to acquire various bits and pieces of the ten-acre parcel. After liquidating most of the ten acres, Pat gifted the remaining land to the Childpeace Montessori School for expansion of their Northwest Portland facility.

One of the mini land parcels was sold to Ken Unkeles. He had purchased the US Steel building on Front Street and needed additional parking space. Ken had sold the family's Carton Service building on NW 13th Avenue and moved the family's commercial carton storage and sales operations to Front Street.

Pat and John had done rather well by acquiring the Hoyt Street rail yards. But there was a degree of risk. They had no explicit knowledge about the level of toxicity in the soil. Burlington Northern had known they had a brownfield. They had even begun to clean up the site. However, as Pat and John began to think about replacing the Glacier Park Master Plan with a new plan of their own, the issue about who was responsible for cleaning up all the toxic soil entered the picture. Over time this unsettled issue became a contested legal issue and would end up in a court of law.

Most of the old industrial-manufacturing businesses had moved out of the Northwest Triangle and relocated to suburban business or industrial parks or faded into history. A few remained. Now the vision of a mixed-use neighborhood with in-town residential living—the River District—awaited the spotlight. The rail yards land sale and swap had finally unlocked the promise of redevelopment long envisioned by past planning studies.

PART THREE
THE RIVER DISTRICT

PLANNING AND BUILDING A NEIGHBORHOOD

1992-2001

THE RIVER DISTRICT TIMELINES

Planning And Building A Neighborhood

1991	Pearl District Neighborhood Association is established
1992	The North Downtown Consortium publishes the *River District Vision*
1992-1995	Early planning work for a streetcar system and financing in the district begins
1994	John Carroll sells his interest in Hoyt Street Properties to Homer Williams
1994	Tiffany Sweitzer goes to work for Homer as an intern
1994	Pat Prendergast builds the first new construction project Pearl Lofts
1994	City Lofts becomes the first conversion of a warehouse to condos
1995	The City approves the River District Development Plan
1996	Pat begins renovation of brick railroad freight houses into condos
1996	Pat sells his interest in Hoyt Street Properties to Clay Fowler and Roy Disney
1997	Wiedon+Kennedy acquires the W. P. Fuller Paint building
1997-1999	There is a Master Development Agreement between the City and Hoyt Street Properties
1998	The River District Urban Renewal Area is created with tax increment financing
1999	The City demolishes the Lovejoy Viaduct
1999	The Brewery Blocks are sold to developers Gerding Edlen Development
2000	Wiedon+Kennedy move into their new corporate headquarters
2001	The Portland Streetcar begins operation
2001	Ecotrust occupies the newly renovated McCracken warehouse

15

WHAT DO WE DO NOW?

AS SOON AS PAT PRENDERGAST and John Carroll took possession of the rail yards, they asked themselves, "Now that we have this land, what do we do with it?" They were aware of the fact the City has already approved a master plan for the property. The plan envisioned a business park with industrial land use. Pat and John both thought that wasn't the best use for old train yards. What they really had was a piece of contaminated ground, and they didn't know what it would cost to clean it up.

Another issue was the presence of the Lovejoy Viaduct. It was a physical barrier that constrained the overall redevelopment of the property. Furthermore, the underside of the elevated roadway depicted a scene from Portland's underbelly. The landscape was seedy. Homeless people camped out there. Drug dealers favored the area, and there was active drug use. Someone during one of my research interviews commented that some people thought it was a great place to go when it was raining. They could hang out undercover and watch the activity at the roundhouse. Who were these people?

WHERE DO WE EVEN BEGIN?

For a while, nothing happened at the rail yards. The physical appearance of this industrial landscape remained unchanged.

Boxcars sat on rails awaiting assignment because the railroad had negotiated a short-term lease back from the new owners. Conspicuously the rail yards were divided in half by an elevated roadway, the Lovejoy Viaduct. This seven-block heavily trafficked stretch of roadway was elevated from NW 14th Avenue eastward to the Broadway Bridge. North of the viaduct, there were a few small railroad maintenance sheds, the rails, and a roundhouse. The roundhouse sat like a lonely, oversized oilcan. Tracks covered the ground like snail's trails. Many of the boxcars had been "bombed" with graffiti. The unresolved question was: where does one begin redevelopment efforts?

The southern half of the rail yards contained two long rows of old storage sheds that extended north to south from Lovejoy Street to Hoyt Street. Each row consisted of four detached buildings, three of which were one-story wooden freight warehouses. A pair of two-story brick buildings—the historic North Bank Station Buildings—terminated each row at Hoyt Street. They had been the east and west freight houses of the Spokane, Portland & Seattle Railway. Both freight houses had elevated first floors with loading docks, although the corner of the east building had a ground-level entry since it had seen service as a passenger terminal.

Shipping crates and other materials were scattered along NW 12th Avenue in groupings. They awaited shipment or retrieval by local customers. A singular structure anchored the corner of NW 12th Avenue and NW Hoyt Street. The remainder of the landscape served as a parking lot for cars and small trucks. The railroads had used this land as a shipping and distribution center for decades.

The partners quickly realized they had limited opportunities to convert these existing structures into new uses, as had happened along NW 13th Avenue. Pat contacted Wilsey Ham again and began brainstorming conceptual ideas for new construction with Tom Jones. Tom suggested mid-to-high-rise residential development similar to what had been built along the South Park Blocks in downtown. He also recommended integrating pocket parks.

Pat wasn't very enthusiastic about those ideas. Out of necessity, Wilsey Ham prepared a new master plan for the Hoyt Street Yards. The plan focused on a mix of residential, commercial office, and ground-floor retail uses.

Meanwhile, the City had approved new development density requirements for any future housing on the Hoyt Street Yards. New residential use had to meet a minimum density of fifteen units per acre. The prevailing thought about building heights was that new residential structures should be three to six stories with a vertical profile that stepped down toward the river.

By now, John was beginning to have second thoughts about how to develop the property. Pat, being a merchant builder, just wanted to build—build it and move on. Both he and Pat had strong personalities. Now there was disagreement about what exactly they should do with Hoyt Street Yards.

Separately, each of the partners approached Homer Williams, the local developer, to see if he wanted to purchase their share of the partnership. Pat talked with Homer first because he'd had a history of working with Homer. Nothing came of either conversation. By 1993, John had decided to take a year off to contemplate his future.

However, lacking an immediate development strategy, the partnership still needed cash flow. An inspection of the wooden freight warehouses revealed they had been constructed on the standard bay module that measured twenty by fifty feet. Pat called his son Todd, who was a real estate agent, and directed him to start leasing space in the westerly row of sheds to bring in extra revenue. Those bays were ideally suited for use as barebones studio spaces. The spaces rented for $200 a month. At first, one could only wonder what kinds of activities would or could happen in these bays.

HAPPENINGS IN BAY 38

Artists loved the bays. Marty Houston, an architect in his early twenties, had arrived in Portland in 1992. Looking around for a cheap studio space, Marty rented a bay for his model-making business. Marty has fond memories of this period in his life. Over a beer decades later, he said, "It was an awesome time to have a one-thousand-square-foot space to do anything you wanted to do…really amazing."

Others rented workspaces, and some renters lived in their spaces. Fortunately for them, one of the old manufacturing buildings along NW 13th Avenue had been renovated into a Gold's Gym. Many joined Gold's Gym to have a place to shower.

A young woman named Nan Curtis rented the space adjacent to Marty's. She was a sculptor—a welding fabricator. Six bays down the row, their friend Mary Hughes had a studio. And there was Noelle, another friend, who hosted band events and other "art performances" in her space. Together, the bay residents represented a micro subculture—an extension of the art community that pioneered the Pearl.

Nan and Marty came up with the idea of creating an unconventional art gallery in his bay. They called it Gallery Bay 38. They wanted to create a space where they could host odd events and performances to give emerging artists exposure. A place for artists and lovers of art to see what art could be, beyond what was available in commercial galleries. This was a guerrilla art scene. They had several shows, but the gallery's opening show, World's Heaviest Show, and later the Skill Saw Cockfights illustrate the creative energy at play in Gallery Bay 38.

World's Heaviest Show was about the objective term *weight*. Instead of using subjective terms associated and understood within the art world, they wanted to use and feature something utterly objective in nature to allow anybody to be part of the show. The show was organized as an open competition, and all the submissions were judged on an objective criterion. People were invited to bring in the heaviest piece they could assemble, and no restrictions whatsoever were placed on the use of materials.

Marty found an old freight scale that measured about eight feet on each side, acquired it, dismantled it, and moved it piece by piece to Bay 38. Formerly the scale had occupied a pit that was eight feet deep. At his studio, Marty and his friends had to dig a hole three feet deep and build a supportive steel structure to house the scale. It was also necessary to build a thirty-foot-long, four-foot-wide ramp so people could bring their submissions into the gallery.

A welder brought in his shop equipment and all his scrap metal. A rock-and-roll band showed up with all of their equipment. Someone else laid a feather on the scale. Nan and Mary acquired several big blocks of ice and strapped them to a wood palette that formed a four-foot cube. They drove it up and into the gallery and placed it on the scale. It was the heaviest piece. Two weeks later, it weighed nothing, *nada*!

The skill saw event was also a competition, a fight between machines. The winner was the last one hanging—instead of standing. Duchamp's artwork *The Bachelor Machine* was the inspiration for the event. Marty's interpretation of the artwork was that of a machine, which through its own functioning, creates its own destruction. It was an idea he and others had played with throughout architecture school. To pull this event off, Marty had help from three close friends: Marcus Straw, Jamie Hurd, and James Kaczmarowski. James and Jamie were old buddies from architecture school. They had moved to Portland a year before Marty arrived.

Marcus and Marty decided to create that cockfight between machines. These guys were in their early twenties. They simply wanted to have some fun. They built a wooden bowl—a half-spherical structure framed with two-by-fours on the underside and sheathed with oriented strand board. They also built a cover using chain-link material, creating a dome-like structure.

Within it, they hung several electrical powered machines—like circular skill saws and power drills. Each device hung down from the dome by its power cord that had been reinforced with two layers of garden hose and duct tape. This extended the battle time. The on and off switches had been by-passed, and once powered up, the machines moved about in jerky motions. The chain-link cover was necessary to contain large flying materials to avoid injury to spectators.

The event consisted of several one-on-one battles or rounds. There were about twelve of these individual rounds. For a finale, they put about eight saws into the dome together and had a last-machine-standing round.

They also hung a washing machine motor with a big circular saw blade on it. But it didn't twist, jerk, or bounce around a lot—it was too heavy—and the made-up machine ended up cutting into the wood surface of the bowl. The drill machines were the best. They were awesome. They were so light that when they hit something, they bounced away due to the torque of the machine. They went spinning and jumped around in wild, random patterns.

All the spectators had to sign a disclaimer and waiver. This attested to their recognition that this activity was inherently dangerous, and they held the event sponsors harmless from any problems or injuries that might occur.

Marty also associated what he called the "smell of blood and beer" with the ambiance of the district. Wilbur-Ellis had operated for fifty years at a site on NW Marshall Street. They produced bone meal and blood. Rail cars delivered the offal and remains of animals—pigs, cows, and chickens—all of which were used to make pet food. An awful odor wafted out from Wilbur-Ellis and, often as not, mingled with the smell of hops from breweries.

By now the City was committed to establishing a comprehensive, community-based planning process for the newly formed River

District. Key to the process was the Portland Design Review Commission's desire to have a neighborhood association that could review and comment on draft planning documents and building permit applications for proposed projects within the new district.

16

ESTABLISHING THE PDNA

AS THE DEVELOPERS PAT PRENDERGAST and John Carroll were formulating a development strategy for Hoyt Street Yards, City officials and staff were thinking about how the Design Review Commission would deal with developers' future project submittals. The City typically solicited comments from recognized neighborhood associations that had oversight over what happened in their communities. The emerging River District now needed an active neighborhood organization.

FORMING A NEIGHBORHOOD ASSOCIATION

The Pearl District Neighborhood Association (PDNA) was formed in 1991. Encouraged by the City and supported by pioneer residents, this organization became another set of eyes on the neighborhood. Many residents—following in the footsteps of Jane Jacobs—wanted to be active participants in all the city decision-making processes that would affect their neighborhood. They wanted to be knowledgeable about what was being proposed and how they could exert influence over decisions about what was going to be built in their neighborhood. As such, they were concerned about the ongoing city planning process, the visual quality of development and the livability of the changing district. Several subcommittees were formed to monitor prospective projects, and all projects were put under their microscope. The early focus of PDNA was to make sure developers "kept a sharp point on their pencils." Unlike many other neighborhood associations, the PDNA was not overly critical or nitpicky when they reviewed new development proposals. It has been said, members wanted to avoid design-by-committee buildings as the district grew.

The association made positive contributions to the district. The members championed the idea of a thirty-month homeless shelter on a vacant piece of property adjacent to the horse patrol site near the waterfront. Another time, at a public meeting, someone objected to outsiders—people from the suburbs—taking over Jamison Square. The individual had referred to the square as "our park." He was quickly reminded that the square was a public park under the jurisdiction of the Bureau of Parks and Recreation. It belonged to the public at large. It was not for the exclusive use of the emerging River District Community and later the Pearl District.

The resident population in the Pearl diversified as more condominiums and apartments were built. As the district grew, a noise issue arose. People began to complain about the train noise, especially at night or in the wee hours of the morning when people were sleeping. By federal law, train engineers were required to blow their horns as a warning when approaching all street-rail-grade crossings. One response to the issue was that the trains were here first. Residents were reminded that they knew that when they moved in. They were advised to "get used to it." This only increased the level of frustration and anger felt by residents.

Another response was to establish a quiet zone. Sounded simple. However, installing specialized equipment was estimated to cost from $30,000 to a million dollars per crossing. The railroad companies disliked and resisted this solution. Yet, in the Pearl, a quiet zone was established using both private and public funds. In negotiations with Portland Terminal Railroad, the association settled on a simple solution: ringing a bell in place of blowing a loud horn.

Pile driving became another serious issue. Most of the new structures in the Pearl required pilings due to soil conditions. The constant banging of metal-on-metal for weeks or longer became a primary source of irritation for residents. In a few situations, the developer used an alternative method. Pilings were basically screwed into the ground, giving neighborhood residents relief from a very irritating, repetitive sound.

During my conversations with Carol Smith-Larson, I learned she had been active in the neighborhood organization. In fact, she helped start the organization because she believed the association needed to be a strong voice in the overall planning of the Pearl District. Jolene Jenson from Neighbors North/Northwest—a coalition representing nine neighborhoods—had advised the PDNA on how to organize in response to the city's need and request for a neighborhood association to represent the neighborhood residents' point of view in the design review process since a zoning design review overlay had been placed on the district. Some entity had to represent the neighborhood when development applications came up for review by the City—PDNA was given that task.

Carol became a walking, talking signboard encouraging everyone she ran into to join the association. A few years later, as the president of the PDNA, she served on the River District Steering Committee.

◇ ◇ ◇

Meanwhile, that ad hoc group of community leaders concerned about the future of the North Downtown began to think of their group as a consortium. And they wanted to crystallize their ideas into a concrete plan for action.

17

A BOLD VISION

THE CONSORTIUM WANTED TO CHANGE the public face of Old Town and the surrounding urban fabric. Being business-people and community leaders, they wanted a strategic approach and a plan that would redirect the City's planning efforts.

A year earlier, the City had published a report titled the *North Downtown Development Program*. This was a collection of development ideas taken from earlier planning efforts like the 1983 R/UDAT study and the 1988 update to the Downtown Plan. Primarily a product of the Bureau of Planning and the Portland Development Commission (PDC), the report summarized and documented an array of projects ranging in various stages of development in and adjacent to Old Town. The report recognized and confirmed a multitude of redevelopment opportunities associated with approximately 150 acres of land immediately north of the downtown core. Specific attention was devoted to the renovation of Union Station, an anticipated master plan for Hoyt Street Yards, and improvements to the North Park Blocks and several riverfront properties. Other highlighted program elements included the need to remove the Lovejoy Viaduct because it posed a physical barrier to redevelopment efforts and the provision of a mooted vintage trolley line.

The commission had also published another report titled the *Union Station Task Force Development Plan and Implementation Program*. Lots of planning had gone on before Pat Prendergast and John Carroll had gotten involved in the Glacier Park deal. Years later, Don Magnusen—he had been the chairman of the task force—told me, "There had been lots of competing parties in the pre–Pearl District times; people had different views of the world and different views of local history."

FORMING A VISION

Some of those views had been discussed and shared among an informal group of downtown business folks and downtown property owners that comprised the consortium. Besides Don and John, other members of the group Roger Breezley from US Bancorp, Bob Ames, a past president of First Interstate Bank, Jim Edwards from Hillman Properties Northwest, Paul Hathaway of the Chamber of Commerce, Bill Naito from Norcrest China Company, Bob Ridgley from NW Natural Gas Company, Mike Thorne from the Port of Portland, and Doug McGregor from the PDC. Now, they all realized they needed professional assistance to come up with a new course of action.

The creative expertise the consortium needed came in the form of Zimmer, Gunsul, Frasca Partnership—ZGF Architects. Selecting this firm was an easy decision. Greg Baldwin was a senior partner at ZGF, and he had been present at many of the consortium's meetings. Both ZGF and Greg had strong positive reputations.

Bob knew Greg personally too. They had raced cars together at Portland International Raceway. Bob had told me Greg "was a visionary. He does a nice job. He is one of the few people that can handle these cats [politicians, bureaucrats, and others, my words] and herd them without them ever suspecting they are being herded."

According to Don, Greg "kept our institutional memory." When one of them came up with an outlier idea, Greg "would tend to keep the original vision together."

Paddy Tillett, another principal and senior architect at ZGF, had been involved in the early stages of the firm's work with the North Downtown group. Paddy told me the group "wanted a concept that went beyond what was in the 1988 Central City Plan,"

By the early 1990s, Portland residents enjoyed an urban quality of life that was based on the idea of a livable city. Cognizant of the fact the population of the city was growing, ZGF Architects had realized the redevelopment of the Northwest Triangle presented a timely opportunity to accommodate future residents and community services by planning a new inner-city neighborhood. As they formulated and refined their conceptual approach, they proposed "a strong, new sense of direction," which made "better, more intense use of existing resources in the Central City."

Greg knew the planning context was vital, so he had put together a series of past plans that had been proposed for the North Downtown and showed them to the consortium. After several meetings and numerous presentations, the group reached a consensus about a final plan of action. The private sector took the initiative with Greg fueling the fire. The consortium went to the City and said, "We don't want to do your plans; we want to do this." This portended a paradigm shift about how a major development proposal would be handled by the City.

A Vision For Portland's North Downtown—a document that outlined a broad scale development concept and rationale for what ZGF Architects termed The River District was published on March 11, 1992. It lit a fuse and triggered a discussion with Mayor Vera Katz and City Hall on how best to accomplish the document's goals and objectives. The document described the concept and rationale for the River District Vision.

THE RIVER DISTRICT VISION

ZGF Architects together with Shiels Obletz Johnsen (SOJ), an urban design development and management firm, had proposed and articulated a visionary approach based on the idea of creating a new mixed-use residential community with supporting retail and commercial services. The new housing would be of varying densities and service a variety of income groups. Most importantly, the new district advanced one of the central tenets of the 1988 Central City Plan—reorienting downtown development to the Willamette riverfront.

The plan advocated waterfront improvements along a stretch of riverfront between the Burnside Bridge and Terminal One, property owned by the Port of Portland. Since the proposal referred to a "River District," new development had to connect to the Willamette waterfront. However, there was a big impediment. Front Avenue, a major arterial roadway, limited points for pedestrian access to the river. Greg knew the vision had to include several bold ideas to get people's attention. One of the big ideas was to build two boat basins connected to the Willamette River. Building the basins meant biting into the shoreline and extending the basins underneath Front Avenue and adjacent railroad tracks to provide grade-separated pedestrian connections allowing access to the river.

The plan also recommended new recreational open space along the waterfront and the construction of riverfront housing on the Terminal One site. Constructing both market and affordable housing units on the forty-acre Hoyt Street Yards property was viewed as pivotal; it was the potential heart of the district.

In consultation with the consortium, these consultants decided to seek an out-of-the-ordinary relationship with City Hall. Greg knew that the usual procedure was to put together a draft plan proposal and interact with the various city bureaus, middle managers, and staff, and then submit the proposal to the city. This was time-consuming and sometimes led to difficulties when there was disagreement between the bureaus on a particular topic or issue. John Thompson, a senior architect at ZGF Architects who had worked closely with Greg on the creation of the vision, has said, "The idea was to come up with a vision and an economic plan and go directly to the mayor. It would be a top-down process instead of a traditional staff bottom-up process."

Greg was aware of the tendency in Portland for major development proposals to get mired in endless bureaucratic reviews and requests for program and design changes. And heaven help the applicant if the project turned "political." If that happened, a bold idea often died a slow, agonizing death or ended up reduced to a palatable solution that was acceptable to the whims of a cadre of select decision-makers and interest groups.

As ZGF Architects refined their approach for the consortium, Greg was conscious of the need to inspire support for the vision. Speaking at the Portland City Club in 1992, he said: "The River District has identified aspirations which would enrich the potential of its neighbors but has yet to confirm a strategy for realizations." During the early planning stages, Greg envisioned and noted in a personal journal that the River District could be: "a community of places—a place for people to live, work, visit, and play." He felt the district could be "at the heart of the city and at the heart of a metropolis and would be a place to exemplify how the metropolis communicates, assumes responsibilities, aspires, inspires and grows."

PREPARING A DISTRICT DEVELOPMENT PLAN

Having a central idea and vision about the future was important, but developing a plan that could be implemented was the next crucial step. The architects had to create a skeleton framework plan and put flesh on the vision.

Accomplishing this task involved a lengthy, complicated process that eventually required the formation of a steering committee to ensure city bureaucratic coordination and public input to the planning process. While ZGF Architects coauthored the visionary concept for the district, they were also responsible for much of the detailed urban planning and design work that needed to be done.

On May 13, 1993, a diverse group of planning professionals and public officials from the Port of Portland and the Bureau of Planning assembled to review what had been accomplished so far for the River District. The workshop's agenda focused on the port's riverfront Terminal One property, previously approved alternative master plans by the City, a plan amendment for Glacier Park, and three optional master plans that had been prepared for Hoyt Street Yards in 1992. The group had explored the idea of daylighting Tanner Creek to create an open-air channel for water flow previously transported in underground piping. The concept also included creating a major open-open space corridor along the watercourse route, providing boat basins along the riverfront, and an integrated local street grid design for the new district. A key consideration was the demolition of the Lovejoy Viaduct.

An essential outcome of this workshop was the acknowledgment that the new vision repudiated the notion of having a business park as the dominant use on the Hoyt Street Yards property. Instead, one of the outcomes was a recommendation to plan for a high-density residential community with ground-floor commercial and retail uses with a strong pedestrian presence at the street level.

The City had also been investigating the feasibility of building a reservoir to handle the outfall of the combined stormwater and sewer overflow to the Willamette River near the sites for the proposed boat basins. Had the reservoir been built, this would have required demolishing Centennial Mills, a collection of historic buildings on the waterfront, for construction of a reservoir site. This was part of the City's rationale to acquire the Centennial Mills property in the first place.

The boat basins concept was a stimulating idea. To determine the viability of the idea to daylight the creek, the City instructed the Bureau of Environmental Services to undertake a feasibility study. Subsequently, an upstream catchment study, the Tanner and Nicolai Basin Diversion Plan, determined that there were insufficient perennial stream flows—only about fifty cubic feet per second at most—and that the creek could even be dry during summer months. More importantly, heavy rainfalls might result in potential toxicity in the creek due to upstream surface runoff and irrigation waters. Unfortunately, if Tanner Creek had to remain in a pipe, people questioned the boat basins concept.

As the architects refined the conceptual riverfront designs, the associated cost considerations became a major factor. The riverfront concept plan was revised to reflect a single basin. Other investigations and discussions then revealed the presence of a large sewer line under Naito Parkway. A disruption to this service utility line in combination with the politics and costs associated with having to construct an overhead bridge to maintain an existing railroad line and Naito Parkway over a boat basin eventually contributed to the elimination of the basins concept from further consideration.

It was easy for the City to get behind a new plan for the River District plan because no businesses were being displaced. No jobs were going to be lost. In fact, more jobs, lots of them, would be needed to build out a new neighborhood once a plan was in place. A future River District also foreshadowed a new tax base for the county.

The planning emphasis now focused on how to extend and use existing infrastructure to construct upward of five thousand urban housing units. The City now in partnership with the private sector established a community-based planning process that integrated comprehensive civic input and public participation. Not everyone realized how detailed and lengthy this process was going to be as the River District Steering Committee and a companion technical advisory committee was formed.

As the planning process for the district proceeded, the development concepts embodied in the River District Vision began to percolate through the community's consciousness. ZGF Architects were now positioned to provide services to both private and public sector clients. During the remainder of the first decade of the 2000s, this architectural and planning firm provided urban design services to Prendergast & Associates as well as the City of Portland.

As ZGF Architects became involved in this ongoing planning process, the firm adopted an innovative transit-oriented development model in the 1990s. This approach was based on a design program focused on diversity and balance among the mixed land uses and services that would be necessary to support a new urban neighborhood.

By fall 1993, there was enough interest to do an economic study and a master plan for Hoyt Street Yards. OTAK, a Portland-based interdisciplinary design and planning firm, had been integrated into the planning process. Their primary task was to prepare an economic cost analysis and a land-use assumptions map. The intent was to demonstrate financial feasibility for the project. A report, the *River District Development Plan, A Technical Memo #2*, listed a development program and assigned uses and conceptual budgetary costs to every block within the proposed River District. The plan assumed construction of 6,480 housing units with estimated costs totaling $560.5 million. The projected total cost for all combined project improvements was almost $840 million. The City was looking for a "handle"; the City needed a strong financial strategy to support and fund the project.

The OTAK study laid out the need for both private and public improvements. What side of the ledger did costs fall on—private or public? What would the City's contribution be? The study created a preliminary sense of cost accounting for future improvements, and put forth the question, if a private-public partnership could be put together, who would be responsible for each of the component cost items?

About this time the local development market brightened. Previously it had been dead for ten years. Now there was huge pent-up demand. Everyone was looking for a way to get invested in the River District by 1994. People from Los Angeles were coming to Portland to scout opportunities. It was a unique moment with a high level of excitement. Properties were beginning to change hands. Portland was on the verge of a communitywide effort focused on urban redevelopment at a scale previously unseen in the city. It would be a big experiment.

At ZGF Architects, Greg Baldwin and Charles Kelley directed much of the urban planning and design work on the River District. To strategize they used a semi-charrette format as a planning tool in meetings with selected "stakeholders." These events were simple work sessions geared to discover shared ideas and values. The architects were looking for common ground to build an approach with a stated goal or set of objectives. About this process, Charles has said, "When it comes to taking on an urban design project, you're not just doing a project; you are building a community to support the project along the way. If you don't bring the community along the way as the project is conceived, they can disown the project—throw it back at you later. This is pragmatic planning; you are doing it this way to minimize risk." This is a way to "front-load" the process—a kind of mitigation to avoid future problems in the process. For the architects it was a way to avoid redoing parts of the process and eating up fees. The approach was necessary because the financial resources associated with the communitywide process were limited. The architects had found a way to work with project budget limitations while also giving the stakeholders a sense of ownership in the project.

One of the techniques Greg used in these work sessions was to draw up his design idea cartoons in ghost fashion—he outlined the drawing in light pencil—and then filled in the sketch with a black Pentel pen as he presented an idea. Charles thought of this as a hallmark of what he called "real-time design." This technique allows a designer to get immediate feedback from participants in a meeting or design workshop. It sometimes enables one to encapsulate the aspirations of a group. In the charrette format, you set a time limit, ask questions, and generate as many ideas as time allows. But in the beginning, you have to state what the "outcome" needs to be. This assigns responsibility to the participants to work toward that outcome.

The designers translated the conceptual ideas into drawings as they were voiced. These provided a basis to build a conversation and a discussion around the project. Greg sometimes simply asked the client, "What do you want to do?" Then he would create a story about how to do it.

The principal product of this effort was the *1995 River District Development Plan.* The document summarized the evolution of the district over the past twelve years. It outlined a program for infrastructure improvements including transportation, parks and open spaces, and utilities. The primary goal of the plan was to provide 5,500 new housing units with supporting commercial office space and retail facilities. To facilitate implementation, the plan recommended creation of an urban renewal district and a private-public partnership agreement as well as the preparation of city guidelines that would apply to four distinct neighborhoods— Union Station/Old Town, Terminal One, Pearl District, and Tanner Basin/Waterfront. Other products from this effort included new right-of-way and street design standards for the district, the design of a streetcar corridor, an update for the expansion of the North Light Rail Transit Mall that connected the downtown core to Union Station, and a specific development plan for Hoyt Street Yards now owned by Hoyt Street Properties, LLC.

Up until this point in time, most of the new residential development in Portland had been built in the outlying suburbs. The City of Portland had now embraced a new policy of having developers construct more urban housing units in and around the downtown core.

DOWNTOWN HOUSING

HAVING MORE INNER-CITY HOUSING IN downtown Portland was an established core goal of the River District Vision. Some of the groundwork for this idea can be attributed to the recognition that the enactment of a local urban growth boundary had restricted the construction of new homes along the perimeter of the metropolitan area. Portlanders had also been introduced to the concept of urban living in a livable city. So how did city officials and the development community determine the number of housing units that were feasible to build?

The consortium had been privy to research on condominium construction in downtown Portland by a local consultant, E. D. Hovee & Co. In the early '90s, astoundingly, there were only about sixty condominium properties in the whole downtown core. Constructing thousands of new housing units in the River District didn't seem like a good idea.

However, a demographic shift was underway locally. More people, including a lot of young people, began moving to Portland. This new population together with the emerging popularity of an urban lifestyle would drive up the demand for housing and make condominium ownership viable. When a development vision that embraced lifestyle choices and economics came together, residential development took off. Those elements weren't together in 1992–93, but they came together at the end of the '90s.

FUTURE GROWTH FOR PORTLAND

The 1990s witnessed the early planning work for Metro's 2040 Growth Concept. This plan set a regional framework and commitment to growth management in the metropolitan area. The plan allocated population target figures—thirty thousand for Portland. However, the City objected to this allocation. They wanted the figure to be one hundred thousand, and the City wanted thirty thousand to be in the central city alone. This statement changed attitudes. Previously these numbers were abstractions. Now the City had to find a way to accommodate this goal. In 1988, the stated housing goal had been only five thousand new residents for the central city. In 1995, the goal was thirty thousand.

By 1995, the City had also completed the Central City Transportation Management Plan. This plan's mission was to get rid of the parking lid that had been imposed on the total number of parking spaces allowed in the city. The only way to get rid of the lid was to make environmental improvements.

In response, the City decided to model the central city to reflect a full built-out for the projected population. Shiels Obletz Johnsen (SOJ) was hired, and they added the planned densities to the model to see what would happen. There were ninety-five thousand jobs in the city, and they added another seventy-five thousand jobs to the model. The modelers came back and said, "This created a horrible imbalance."

The response was to add housing to compensate for the increase in employment. An estimate of fifteen thousand downtown housing units was added to rebalance the model after checking to make sure there was enough available land to do this. The result was that the fifteen thousand units had more of an impact on reducing traffic travel in the region than the entire light rail transit system. These made-up numbers spurred a revision to the City's in-town goal for new housing units. This became the basis for supporting new housing policies and goals in downtown Portland and the proposed River District.

◇ ◇ ◇

As the urban design process for the district proceeded, the development concepts embodied in the River District Vision were refined. Attention was now focused on the physical infrastructural improvements that were needed. The rail yards property was going to need a street grid. More specifically, investigations were needed into what form the street grid would take as well as design guidelines for future street rights-of-way.

Portland's experiences in planning and designing the public realm and streetscape as exemplified by the downtown bus mall and light rail transit system had proved successful. The City wanted the same attention given to the proposed River District.

19

DESIGN FOR THE PUBLIC REALM

IF THE PUBLIC REALM WAS important, what did the realm consist of? Obviously the streetscape, but the public realm also extended into other accessible places where people could walk and be engaged in their surroundings like parks, interior open spaces between structures, surface parking areas, and forecourts to buildings. These are all public spaces architects tend to think about as spatial zones where people can see, touch, and feel.

These outdoor spaces tend to have an intangible ceiling at about thirty feet above ground level. People don't seem notice what's going on above that height, unless they look up. They are active participants in the public realm whether or not they realize it. The public realm is where the color, the texture, and the vibrancy of public life occur on a daily basis. Urban designers think of the activity that occurs in the public realm as "urban theater." So, the architects and other designers who worked on development plans for the district wanted to design a framework for urban theater—the experience of urban living.

INFRASTRUCTURE

As planning for the new district proceeded, attention had to given to the physical infrastructure needed to support the construction of any and all new buildings. One of the first questions was about what street grid to overlay on the rail yards. The street grid would impose limitations and restrictions on what form the urban design would exhibit in the long-term. The selected grid pattern was going to be of the utmost importance to the scale of the public realm.

The existing downtown street grid in Portland consists of short blocks that measure two hundred feet by two hundred feet. Portlanders have generally felt that early leaders were insightful when they decided the short-block grid had advantages over long, rectilinear blocks. They had wanted to maximize the number of retail shops at corner locations.

Past expansion of the downtown street grid usually reflected that two hundred square-foot grid. But the local architectural community knew from experience that this grid had imposed limitations when designing parking facilities within or under most new buildings. Therefore, an alternative grid of 200 feet by 220 feet was examined. A lengthened block presented a better and more efficient interior parking arrangement for future development. However, the City did not support this idea. The square grid was sacred. The street grid in the River District would use the square grid.

ZGF Architects first explored alternative street grids as they developed the Tanner Creek and Boat Basin scheme. They concluded that the extension of the existing street grid of 200-foot blocks and 60-foot rights-of-way across the rail yards made the most sense. The design team then developed specific street design guidelines and standards for the proposed River District because, at that time, city standards were vehicle oriented and conflicted with new ideas the team was exploring, including the provision of stoops at residential buildings. Another idea was to convert segments of Irving and Kearney Streets into mini-parks because the I-405 freeway to the west and the U.S. Postal Service property and rail tracks to the east restricted traffic movement on both streets. Those discussions gave rise to the idea to close portions of NW Irving and

NW Kearney Streets and design these rights-of-way as exclusive pedestrian ways in the form of a linear mini-park. However, there was still a need to maintain a twenty-foot functional access for fire trucks, emergency vehicles, and controlled access to private vehicular parking associated with adjacent development. These small parks added a special amenity quality to the Pearl District.

This decision created a special design opportunity for the development of abutting private property. It allowed private property owners and developers to entertain the idea of different architectural facade treatments that fronted onto these pedestrian-oriented spaces. You could have more extensive window treatments facing the adjacent open spaces instead of blank walls for privacy reasons or to reduce the noise from vehicular traffic. These micro open spaces became delightful green oases of calm in the city.

As urban designers, ZGF Architects were thinking about the form and massing of vertical architecture in the future, the design of the horizontal ground plane, and the underground utilities, all at the same time. The way a designer handles public infrastructure can add value and delight plus meet the functional requirements of a given situation. It's about identifying opportunities, not over-prescribing, with the understanding that there can be creative solutions outside the norm.

HOUSING AND PUBLIC ACCESS TO THE RIVERFRONT

As planning for the district progressed, the City decided to build a mixed-unit housing project on a sliver of land they had purchased in the past adjacent to Union Station. The site consisted of a long sliver of land sandwiched between the station's active tracks and Naito Parkway. A request for proposals was issued and evaluated, and GSL Properties was selected as the developer for the Yards Project in 1997. GSL hired ZGF Architects and OTAK, Inc. to prepare a master plan. This housing project, accomplished in four phases, was completed in 2011, and it brought six hundred affordable and market-rate units to the marketplace.

In 2000, ZGF Architects was commissioned to design a pedestrian bridge. This allowed pedestrians to walk from Union Station to the nearby waterfront. The bridge began at the south end of the railway station, spanned the operational railroad tracks, and landed in a courtyard at the Yards housing project. The public walkway continued and crossed Naito Parkway. The architects, working with the Naito Development Group, threaded the walkway through the McCormick Pier apartment complex eventually connecting the walkway to the Willamette River Greenway Trail. Pearl District residents now had a direct means of access to the riverfront.

FINISHING A DISTRICT DEVELOPMENT PLAN AND GUIDELINES

ZGF and OTAK completed their work on the River District Development Plan in 1995. The Portland Bureau of Planning subsequently updated the earlier 1988 Central City Plan, incorporating the work that had been done by the consultants on the River District. The language of the adopted ordinance called for "downtown development throughout the River District that is highly urban in character with supporting jobs, services, and recreation." More importantly, the City established a mandatory design review process for all future development proposals within the district.

In 1996, the Portland City Council approved the *River District Design Guidelines*. This document, prepared by the Bureau of Planning, integrated the new planning district with the more comprehensive planning framework of the Central City Plan.

With a plan in hand, the city turned its attention to implementation and financing. Created in 1998, the River District Urban Renewal Area provided public capital in the form of tax increment financing for the envisioned development. The urban renewal plan for the district continued the work begun by the steering committee, while also building on the River District Development Plan and a Strategic Investment Plan. By priming the pump, the City reduced the uncertainty associated with the questionable availability of private or institutional financing.

The Pearl District was not born fully formed. There were those "deep roots," the vision of a riverfront-oriented community, and lots of community and public agency input. There was also a strong urban design philosophy that gave guidance to the contribution made by ZGF Architects.

20

DESIGN PERCEPTIONS

GREG BALDWIN WAS A LEADING force from the inception of the district vision in 1992 to the *Pearl District Development Plan*, which was published in 2001. Greg, ever the architectural philosopher, during a 2003 interview, began to think about how projects could lead to other projects. He called this the "concept of establishing the fertile project." What he began to see happening in Portland was "the project that begets the next project which, in turn, begets the next project."

URBAN DESIGN ETHICS AND VALUES

Greg had expanded his thoughts about what he termed the fertile project. He felt this idea reflected an ethic that was a useful principle when applied to urban planning and design. The principle had four parts: The first was "the value of a good idea and the good deal. We had lots of good ideas in the 60s, but in the 70s, we asked each to be a good deal."

The second was "the utility of the fertile project." Greg explained this idea as that which "creates an environment that causes individual initiatives to coalesce and complement each other." He felt this enriched and expanded the human condition.

The third was "the efficacy of contingent relationships." This was all about planning to create conditions that produced a desired or intended result. He'd seen this concept mature in the '80s when private-public partnerships in Portland became more sophisticated. As local businesspeople and public officials begin to understand each other's business, their partnerships produced better results. This led to a development agreement and complementary relationship between Homer Williams as the president of Hoyt Street Property, LLC and the City of Portland. That partnership guided development of Hoyt Street Yards.

The fourth was simply "common sense." Greg saw this as a "fundamental nineteenth-century agrarian deal." He was speaking about the cultivation of land for purposeful ends. When people used common sense to guide their behavior, they tended to come up with reasonable solutions to their problems.

Greg operated with a value system based on doing civic good and great design. He wanted civic design that came out of urban design fueled by a heavy touch of morality. Brian McCarter, a colleague at ZGF, had a different perspective on what he termed Greg's notion of "morality in design." Brian felt Greg's morality was always a subtext to the overall conversation. He remembered how Greg liked to prod both the public sector and developers into "contingent relationships"—Greg's phrase for enlightened development agreements.

As an example: If there were several develop proposals on the table, the City would be better off identifying which developer had the means and the passion and whose project could have the best catalytic effect on other future projects. Greg felt it was a better bet to maximize the investment of public support on one project than to spread the money among several projects, in effect diluting the impact of the investment. He also felt this approach could be used as leverage to raise the design quality of city-supported development projects. In this kind of situation, he would approach a private developer and say, "You are asking for publicly funded improvements and other assistance. You should demonstrate your commitment by showing us the quality you will put into your project."

Greg also had a notion that one plus one can equal three. People referred to this as Greg's Stone Soup. He believed and functioned under the assumption that if you put two people or two groups together that had opposing views, there was always the possibility of arriving at a position through cooperation and landing on another option that neither party had considered embracing before.

THE SECRET SAUCE

Lots of people have traveled to Portland seeking the Pearl's holy grail. They hoped to discover the secret sauce behind the creation of this amazing neighborhood. They talk to local politicians, planners, architects, and especially the developers and ask questions about the vision and its implementation.

That vision: Well, it wasn't a singular vision that could be assigned to a single individual. It was a plurality and aggregation of complementary visions that overlapped over a specific continuum of time. Some of the visions were expressions of individual commitments, while others were group efforts to improve the state of civic affairs. The story of how the Pearl District evolved is about how all these efforts, when viewed as building blocks, were integrated to produce an urban environment that added a dynamic vitality to Portland's city core.

That secret sauce, if it has a heart, might just be the Portland Way. This was an approach to city planning and problem-solving that flowered in Portland as an intangible form of collective consciousness that flowed beneath the city's social surface. Enlightened community leaders, businesspeople, politicians, bureaucrats, and professionals of all stripes that appeared to think and work together in ways that benefited the public interest, not just their self-interest. But did it have an expiration date? Or maybe...

besides this local consciousness it was the addition of Greg's civic and personal consciousness.

That central vision for the Pearl District included incorporating localized public transit service to and through the neighborhood. A Portland newspaper reported at one point: "Those new rails for the future streetcar, laid between muddy blocks of undeveloped land, heralded what was to come."

21

THE STREETCAR RETURNS

PORTLAND ONCE HAD THE MOST extensive streetcar system on the West Coast. Streetcars were introduced into the city in 1872. Then, horses and mules provided the go power. Almost two decades later, in 1889, electric power replaced the muscle power. By 1950, the use of streetcars ceased locally. The city then waited five decades for streetcars to return to Portland.

There had been discussion in the mid-1980s about connecting the downtown and the eastside business district with public transit. In 1987, Commissioner Earl Blumenauer stepped forward and said, "We should build a streetcar loop." Downtown businesspeople asked: Why would we want to do this? The answer was simple: it will bring in new customers! Earl elevated this idea by saying, "A streetcar loop should be built to connect all the districts" in the inner city. This loop concept then became a crucial component in the 1988 Central City Plan.

The idea of having a streetcar in the River District had been discussed during one of ZGF Architects work sessions with the North Downtown Consortium. One of the members had said: "What if a streetcar went through the Pearl District?" In response, one of the architects had rolled out some tracing paper on a map and started drawing. The idea for streetcar ended up stimulating development. It became an urban design tool.

VIC AND VICKY

There's no official date for when the Portland Streetcar Project began, but both city engineer Vic Rhodes and Vicky Diede played important roles while overseeing the Streetcar Development Study in the early 1900s. Vicky was interesting because she was a nontraditional hire and employee in the Bureau of Transportation. Previously, Vicky had worked in sales for the Boise Cascade Company.

Asked why he hired Vicky, Vic said, "We had moved away from hiring engineers as project managers. Instead, we were hiring marketing people like Vicky and others." Vic explained that the City needed new hires with good communication skills. He wanted people who could sell ideas. Managers with sales experience were naturals to sell transportation improvements to the public.

Both Vic and Vicky viewed the streetcar line as a means of opening up Portland's Westside Downtown between 10th Avenue and I-405. When built, the streetcar would foster new development on both sides of West Burnside Street as the Pearl District took shape. The Westside has seen little new investment and development during the past twenty years.

When the talk about forming a nonprofit venture to start up a streetcar system became serious, Vic and Vicky paid attention. Both were supportive and liked the idea. They were thinking about a public-private partnership, and so they posted a request for proposals. The notice was intended to entice a company to design, build, and operate a streetcar in Portland. They thought a firm like Bechtel—a nationally recognized leader in engineering, construction, and project management—might be interested in this type of project since the firm was already involved in an upgrade and expansion project at the Portland airport.

Unfortunately, the City didn't have much to bargain with; all it had was the land for a deal. But there was a larger problem at play. None of the big transportation-oriented engineering firms responded to the request for proposals. In fact, no one submitted a proposal.

A NONPROFIT TAKES THE LEAD

The fact was that no national firm had any trolley expertise in the United States. Instead, a nonprofit headed by Roger Shiels responded to the idea of reviving streetcar usage in the city. Portland Streetcar Incorporated was a nonprofit organization with a singular mission: to implement a modern streetcar system in the River District. The organization was composed of very credible, local businesspeople including Don Magnusen, John Carroll, Roger Breezley, Mike Powell, Al Solheim, and Tiffany Sweitzer. They were all bona fide, no-nonsense businesspeople, not trolley jollies, and together they formed a tight-knit networking group who zeroed in on promoting the idea of bringing back streetcar service to Portland. All of them saw the opportunity to give people another option for moving around downtown. They were also convinced that the streetcar would initially serve as a development attractor.

As the project moved forward, it became a private-public partnership. The nonprofit oversaw hardware design and the streetcar manufacturing process while the City coordinated infrastructure improvements, including street right-of-way issues, provision of utility services, and construction activities. To accomplish this, Vic and Vicky thought, "We're not going to reinvent the wheel like TriMet [Portland's public transit agency] did for light rail transit vehicles." Their approach, according to Vic, was "We're going to go buy something from Fred Meyer—a local business. We want it off-the-shelf." However, acquiring streetcar vehicles would become a complicated affair.

To Vic, the idea of having public transit as an integral part of the city's transportation infrastructure was a fundamental necessity. From a transportation perspective, public transit was a winner, and Vic became a vocal advocate for the streetcar. He had a speech he always gave:

> If you look at the history of Portland's transportation system, you'll remember that back in the 1970s, there was a Portland-Vancouver Transportation Study that produced a plan map with an extensive grid of freeways all over the metropolitan area. The 1970s were about moving people long distances with a high-capacity road system. By the late 1980s or early 90s, if you went to an Earl Blumenauer breakfast roundtable, Earl was talking about public transit, not freeways. And the illustrative plan map he put up was a system diagram of proposed light rail transit lines. We had gone from trying to build endless systemic capacity with freeways, but we're still trying to move people from one end of the universe to the other end. And then if you fast-forward to Metro's 2040 plan, you were talking about proximity to live, work, and play. This was about walkable neighborhoods and town centers.

Public transit had become a critical transportation mode that complimented the notion of a livable city.

The agency's middle management was dedicated to Portland's system-wide emerging regional light rail transit service. Before the trolley concept, the first idea was a loop of the MAX line from the Steel Bridge through the River District was proposed connecting it to downtown. However, scale, efficiency, and cost made this a poor choice. When the trolley concept became a popular idea, they made it clear they were not interested in invested in another mode. They viewed a streetcar line as a distraction.

TriMet eventually came around and became a proponent for the streetcar. Vic had reminded the agency that the new neighborhood needed some form of public transit. Having a streetcar service meant TriMet wouldn't have to provide new bus lines or reconfigure existing routes to service the River District. The primary reason the streetcar project got done was because supporters organized it as a nonprofit.

SELECTING AN ALIGNMENT

Now everyone jumped on the streetcar bandwagon. The question became where to locate the streetcar alignment. Good Samaritan Hospital was interested in having the streetcar come to the Northwest Neighborhood. The hospital donated a million dollars for the project as well as gave up a lease for property under the I-405 freeway. This allowed the construction of a streetcar vehicle storage and maintenance facility under the freeway at NW Northrup Street.

The City initiated a Streetcar Feasibility Study and established the Central City Streetcar Advisory Committee in 1990. Shortly after that, the committee became the Portland Streetcar Citizens' Advisory Committee, with John Carroll as chair. The committee—together with input from the nonprofit, city planners, ZGF Architects, and local business owners—began studying streetcar routes.

Considerations for the streetcar alignment experienced a tectonic shift in 1992 when the *River District Vision* was published. The proposed route along NW 13th Avenue was discarded as the idea of refashioning the Hoyt Street Yards into a high-density residential neighborhood took hold.

One alignment option was to use NW 9th and Park Avenues, but Atiyeh Bros. company didn't like this option because they believed it conflicted with loading and unloading activity at their retail stores. Other alignments included either NW 2nd and 3rd Avenues or Broadway. However, the business community did not support either of these options. In the end, the advisory committee recommended an alignment on NW 10th and 11th Avenues with the view the future streetcar line could service the downtown west end that was ripe for redevelopment.

The presence of Powell's Books along the preferred route was also a factor. People recognized that Powell's would be a popular mid-anchor retail destination on the streetcar line. The bookstore was and remains a major tourist attraction.

Earl Blumenauer, the politician, and Roger Shiels, the architect-turned-management-consultant both believed that connecting things was the underlying reason for having a streetcar in Portland. To describe this connection, Roger referred to Portland's streetcar system as "the dumbbell," although others had called it a "barbell."

The streetcar line, when built, connected the Good Samaritan Hospital in the Northwest Neighborhood to Portland State University. Later, the streetcar line was extended to the South Waterfront District. Additionally, this streetcar line provided multiple stops in the Central Business District and Portland State University. Having public transit service to South Waterfront was a tremendous benefit because this waterfront neighborhood community had limited vehicular accessibility.

Tiffany Sweitzer—she later became president of Hoyt Street Properties, LLC and had served on the TriMet Board—had a different opinion and perspective on the streetcar's contribution to the Pearl District. She said:

Of all our negotiations made with the city, [the streetcar] has been one of the most significant pieces. We knew that transportation was so important to getting people through our property and to other parts of the city. I call the streetcar a horizontal connector because one can use the streetcar to take you to the next mode of transportation. The streetcar gets you downtown to MAX, and MAX gets you to other parts of the city and the suburbs. So it's probably been the biggest piece of infrastructure and the most important component for this entire development [the Pearl District].

◇ ◇ ◇

The alignment and routing for the proposed streetcar had been settled. Now the nonprofit needed vehicles—actual streetcars, not trolleys. Vic wanted to buy a streetcar off-the-shelf. Who stocked streetcars for sale?

22

ROLLING STOCK

ADVOCATES FOR THE STREETCAR DIDN'T want to reinvent the wheel, but the local grocery store wasn't stocking streetcar vehicles among the groceries, hardware items, and household notions. One of the first issues was to figure out where to acquire rolling stock, and not any old kind. The members of the Portland Streetcar Citizens' Advisory Committee didn't want picture-postcard old-style trolleys. Everyone wanted a modern public transit system, not a tourist attraction.

TIME TO GO TO EUROPE

No company in the USA was manufacturing streetcars in the 1990s. Therefore, Portland-based engineers were sent to several European cities with modern streetcar systems to evaluate every aspect of operation, maintenance, and associated costs. After reviewing these assessments, committee representatives flew to the Czech Republic to inspect and, they hoped, buy streetcars.

They had selected the Czech Republic because they had built locomotives and railroad cars for the Union of Soviet Socialist Republics. In the Soviet economic system, each country had a designated role. What had become the Czech Republic used to be the USSR's official builder of railway equipment.

Construction was basic, but the people were good at it. They simply taped out the form of a streetcar on the floor of a warehouse and started banging on metal. They had great steel—especially useful in making durable rail car wheels—and excellent engineering capability, and most importantly, they needed American dollars because the Soviet Union had collapsed.

The initial deal was for $500,000 per car if Portland took the vehicles as they had been designed in Europe. However, changing the vehicle specifications to satisfy US vehicle test requirements became necessary, and the Czech manufacturer Skoda raised the unit cost to $700,000 per vehicle. Portland's representatives wanted double-ended, double-sided, air-conditioned cars. And they wanted the original window mullions removed to have unobstructed outside views, and bigger seats placed in the cars. The streetcars ended up costing close to $2 million each.

The manufacturer put together a proposal and gave it to Roger Shiels, who was on the representative team. Roger noticed a line item that seemed odd. He asked what it was for, and he was told it was for engineering.

Roger responded by telling the Czechs that the proposal costs were over Portland's budget. He informed them the proposal was unacceptable, and Portland was going to sue the manufacturer because they had changed the proposal from what had been originally agreed to by Portland. That extra charge was dropped.

The Czechs finally delivered five cars to Portland. Later, Portland got involved with Oregon Ironworks. They designed a prototype vehicle under a federal grant arrangement. The streetcar project created a new business in Oregon. The company ultimately supplied the project with fifteen streetcars, although there were a few production problems that had to be weathered.

INSTALLING THE TRACKS

OTAK—they led the design and managed the overall construction phase of the project—and the City chose an innovative way to install the streetcar tracks. They found a company in San Francisco that could install streetcar tracks by excavating only about a foot deep.

Because of this, the City didn't have to remove and relocate any existing utilities as was typical during the construction of Metro's light rail transit corridors. The contractor for the streetcar project excavated a trench approximately 14-inches deep and 8-foot wide. Afterward a continuous reinforced concrete ground beam designed to support loaded streetcars was cast in place along the streetcar line. Skeptics questioned the unique structural slab system used in laying the streetcar rails, but the system minimized damages to existing streets during construction. This allowed rapid installation while causing relatively short-term disruption to existing businesses along the streetcar route.

The first streetcars arrived in Portland in the spring of 2001, and service began on July 20, 2001. The streetcar project was a trailblazer in the real sense of the word. It exemplified the notion of taking good ideas and making them real.

WRAPAROUND COLOR

People are always struck by the paint colors on the streetcars and the lack of advertising. By contrast, the exterior of the city's light rail transit trains is adorned with advertising imagery and text. The advertising brings in revenue to the city's coffers. The exterior finish on the streetcar was different. Al Solheim had spoken with Roger Shiels and Greg Baldwin. All three agreed that no advertising should be allowed on any of the streetcars.

The color scheme for the vehicles is a wraparound concept. Two different bold colors are used on each streetcar. One color is painted on each vehicle's side with the same color wrapping around one end of the vehicle. The wraparound idea originated when Roger, Greg, and a guy who worked in Commissioner Charlie Hales' office first discussed the idea. The selection of bold colors was about making the cars highly visible in the street environment. Greg saw the streetcar as an active feature of the city's urban theater.

The European manufacturer that Portland eventually worked with on producing the streetcars was very unhappy when they first saw the color wrap. No one in Europe had ever seen this approach before. Roger said, "They were going to be very happy in being unhappy."

The streetcar project began with a budget of around $30 million. At one point, the City and nonprofit looked down the barrel of $50 million or more in cost. Would even that be enough?

23

FUNDING THE STREETCAR

THE SUCCESS OF THE STREETCAR Project was dependent upon lots of deal making. Success depended on everyone knowing what had to be done, how it could be done, and who would do it. On that last point, everyone was relying on the principle of "you take care of your end, and I'll take care of my end." There was a clear sense of trust and respect among the parties involved in obtaining the funds to build the streetcar system.

In 1992, The *River District Vision* report suggested, "Replica Council Crest streetcars would operate at 15-minute frequencies carrying people from the River District waterfront to residential areas to the downtown commercial core." That same year, Roger Shiels tapped the Portland Vintage Trolley project monies, obtaining $25,000 to support the initial work on the streetcar project. The City then applied for a grant from the federal Department of Housing and Urban Development (HUD). HUD responded by offering a $500,000 grant that required a matching amount from local resources. The City matched the grant funds with revenues from increased parking rates in the City-owned downtown SmartPark garages. Some of that revenue generation rolled back on the business community in the form of parking validation for downtown shoppers. That revenue plus 20 percent of the capital costs given up by people in the local improvement district that were within four blocks of the streetcar line helped pay for the streetcar project. Funding the project was complicated, but there was tremendous support for the project from the business community.

To secure more funding, the City and ZGF Architects decided to schedule a meeting with Senator Mark Hatfield. Mayor Vera Katz, Bob Ames, Greg Baldwin, and Bob Frasca attended the meeting that took place at the Albers Mill building in Portland. The outcome of this presentation was a $5 million earmark for the streetcar project in a federal transportation appropriations bill. When officials at Metro found out about this funding allocation from the feds, they were upset. There was a concern at the regional level that city officials were considering and endorsing competing public transportation modes. Some officials thought: "What the hell are you guys doing with this streetcar thing?" Finally, an informal agreement was worked out conditional upon the streetcar advocates pursuing the project with nonconventional transportation funding.

The senator eventually procured the funds for Commissioner Earl Blumenauer. Unfortunately, the nonprofit group couldn't use the money as the funds went to TriMet. What to do? They had to do a "switchy-switchy"—a local administrative maneuver. The region and Portland came to an agreement to maintain peace, so they could all obtain federal funds for future projects. This was part of the local notion of trusting that people would do the right thing for the public good. The Portland Way was working.

The switchy-switchy tradition originated in the 1970s after several high-level projects were shut down due to cankerous attitudes. Major players like Mayor Neil Goldschmidt and Glen Jackson, a local power broker, were determined to reverse this attitude to move major civic and public projects—many of them transportation-oriented—through the planning and funding process efficiently. To accomplish this goal, everybody had to be in the "club," thereby creating a sense of "regional accommodation" for the better good. The switchy-switchy was a strategy that allowed funds to be moved around to get by limitations on how you could use the money on specific projects.

For example, TriMet could get $5 million and then give the streetcar project $5 million. Something could be built even if TriMet didn't particularly like it. The idea was "if it doesn't hurt you and it's a fair deal, you can support and go along with it even though you are on a different path."

The reason for this behavior was to organize the local agencies' communication with the feds. This meant there would be a single voice and script emanating from the region. The Mt. Hood Freeway established this tradition when $600 million in federal funds remained in the metropolitan region and wasn't lost. These funds were available over fifteen years, and the federal dollars brought people together and fostered the notion that cooperation was vital to preserve access to this "pot of gold."

What helped make streetcar mode attractive was the cost for the light rail transit improvements was escalating. The Banfield Light Rail Transit corridor cost $125 million, and the west side corridor construction cost was about $1 billion. The cost comparison was about a dime to a dollar for the streetcar versus light rail. The initial cost for the streetcar was about $10 million per mile while the light rail cost about $100 million.

The River District Association, with Roger at the helm, formed in 1995. The association's mission was to come up with an infrastructure financing strategy as the Pearl District evolved over time. The association had supported the proposal to raise parking rates in garages throughout the city. The outfall was that the City bonded $28 million plus some reserve funds for the streetcar project.

Early in the process, the board of directors of the nonprofit Portland Streetcar Incorporated informed property owners located along or close to the alignment that their property taxes would go up. All the property owners agreed to be taxed in the future. This allowed the nonprofit to self-bond against the limited improvement district that was formed.

The provision of streetcar services in the district significantly reduced the need for expanded bus service. This allowed Vic Rhodes to broker a deal with TriMet. The transit agency funded two-thirds of the streetcar's operating expenses initially. The formula eventually changed, but in the beginning, this made the streetcar project financially viable.

When the streetcar finally began operation, the estimated cost of $30 million to build a line from Northwest Portland to Portland State University totaled $57 million. It has been estimated that this public transit service has leveraged nearly $250 million in urban development between then and 2018. Most Portlanders consider this a pretty good deal financially.

Daily, thousands of Portlanders enjoy a myriad of benefits provided by the streetcar system. Vic said that once the streetcar line was operating, the City gave the Les Schwab Tire Center free tickets, as they did for all businesses along or near the streetcar line. Les Schwab suddenly benefited from a big jump in business. Downtown workers could drop off their vehicles early in the morning and take the streetcar to work and then take it back again at the end of the day to pick up their vehicles.

By 1992, two years had passed since Prendergast & Associates had taken possession of Hoyt Street Yards, and the two developers hadn't built anything on their new property. They were still waiting because they weren't quite sure what to do first. And both had had thoughts about selling their interest in their vacant property.

24

URBAN HOMES

PAT PRENDERGAST WAS A BUILDER. Builders build, so in 1992, he formed a new company, Urban Homes, Inc. Under this company's banner, in 1993, he developed the Virginia Avenue Row Houses in the Johns Landing neighborhood.

Pat was getting anxious. He wanted to start building on the Hoyt Street Yards property, but he and John Carroll were having disagreements. Their partnership was in trouble. The partners were still trying to figure out what to do, and John was about to take time off to go traveling.

Still a bit anxious, Pat decided to build a residential project on the property. He had lots of land but few options as to where to build. It didn't make sense to build in the middle of a contaminated brownfield. He looked over the vacant landscape and decided the south edge of the property along the north side of Hoyt Street was the best place to begin. The Low Brow Tavern and a few other businesses lined the other side of the street, and available underground utilities made for easy hookups. His concept and plan was to build along Hoyt Street and expand to the north, increasing the development footprint on a block-by-block basis.

The local real estate market appeared tenuous at first. Thankfully, there was an increasing number of inquiries by people who were attracted to the idea of in-town living. At the time, you couldn't sell anyone an urban living space unless they'd already made up their minds. Many had already made the decision: "I want to live downtown, but I can't find anything to buy." This was every developer's dream; people looking to buy something that wasn't available in the marketplace. Someone just needed to supply the product.

Financing the project was a big problem that Pat had to solve. The local banking industry had no interest in financing condominiums, especially in an area that was unproven after a decade of no new construction. Pat spoke with Roger Breezley at US Bank and was told: "You guys will have this built before I can run it through our loan department and get it approved, if I can even get it approved."

Pat came up with a financing strategy based on two self-imposed requirements. First, he would limit the number of units and keep the price relatively low so as to appeal to a broad market audience. Unit prices ranged from $79,000 to $159,000. Second, he had to presell at least 50 percent of the units. With no conventional financing available, Pat scraped together a few investors and formed a limited partnership. Buyer takeout financing was accomplished by qualifying the project for financing from Fannie Mae.

Pat had told me that people would come into the office on the weekend, look over the drawings on the wall, and put down a deposit. His challenge was to make sure they understood that there were no guarantees that the recently approved River District Development Plan would be implemented. His salespeople couldn't represent to buyers that improvements like new streets, parks, and a streetcar line would really happen. Buyers had to commit to a sale not knowing what infrastructure would actually be built over time. But potential buyers weren't deterred; they were eager urban pioneers.

BREAKING GROUND

Urban Homes' first project in what became the River District was a twenty-seven-unit, two-story brick building called Pearl Lofts.

The structure featured two rows of condominium units that faced onto an open-air, landscaped courtyard. Amazingly, nearly all the units were sold before construction began.

Construction had begun in 1993 at NW 10th Avenue and Hoyt Street on a half-acre site. The building footprint, which occupied 18,719 square feet of space with a construction cost of $68.44 per square foot (excluding site improvement costs), was a small step toward the ultimate build out of a forty-acre landholding. When completed in 1994, these condominium units were the first constructed in the city after a ten-year downturn.

Based on the success of Pearl Lofts, Pat and his limited partners next built Hoyt Commons in 1995, also under the Urban Homes banner. The building was constructed on NW 12th Avenue at Hoyt. This time US Bank financed the project. The project was built at the cost of $110 a square foot, a high watermark then. Hoyt Commons was a mixed-use project with ground-floor retail and housing above. Admittedly, the retail spaces weren't vast because there was a high degree of uncertainty about whether the embryonic River District could attract a diverse resident population.

Initially, the City didn't require ground-floor retail use in the district; it was voluntary. Later, officials decided to require street-level commercial uses within the new district. The River District Development Plan, as adopted, required retail or commercial use of at least 50 percent of all new street-level real estate on NW 10th, 11th, and 12th Avenues within the district.

Hoyt Commons was a four-story brick building that added forty-eight condominiums to the housing supply. The project received a platinum Leadership in Energy and Environmental Design (LEED) award for Green Neighborhood Design, reflecting the fact that the City was advocating smart growth policy, sustainability, and design principles associated with green building practices. Giorgio's Restaurant—it was the first dining establishment in the new district—found a home on the ground floor of the Hoyt Commons. Many more restaurants, cafés, and bars followed Giorgio's lead.

RENOVATING THE RAILWAY FREIGHT HOUSES

Pat now turned his attention to the existing North Bank Station freight houses that were sandwiched between the Commons and the Pearl Loft projects along Hoyt. He called his renovation of these historical structures the Pearl Townhomes. Both brick buildings were converted to condominiums between 1996 and 2000, again under the Urban Homes banner.

After Pat announced the conversion of the first of the two warehouses, the project immediately ran into trouble. The construction cost estimate ballooned in part due to the building's brick masonry construction. The building didn't meet City seismic regulations. The City required the application of gunite, a type of mortar, which could be pneumatically sprayed onto vertical surfaces to improve structural stability. But it was expensive to apply. Pat thought he might have to abandon both buildings, maybe even tear them down. Unsure, he had to mothball the project for several years.

Gordon Davis had reserved a unit when Pat announced he was converting one of old freight houses into condominium units. After Pat shut down the project, Gordon canceled his reservation. However, he continued to monitor Pat's efforts. Pat—after he restarted the Pearl Townhomes project—contacted Gordon and suggested he look at the end unit next to Hoyt. This corner unit was atypical—it was twenty-five feet wide compared to the other units that were only seventeen feet wide, and the entry was at ground level. In 1995, Gordon bought what was really a shell to custom design. Gordon, an architect, renovated it, acting as his own contractor, and moved in during August 1997.

These brick two-story structures were visually attractive, owing to their historic character and brick facades. The buildings were also unusual because the first floors were elevated. The structures appeared to perch above the street level.

Pat had hired ZGF Architects to advise him on the conversion of the freight houses. He wanted to know how to handle the transition from the street level to unit entries that were three feet above the street. And there was another consideration: Both Pat and the architects were well aware that the area between the two brick structures had to become a new street in the future. Therefore, the challenge was to design a special semiprivate/public streetscape theme.

Greg Baldwin immediately saw an opportunity to create raised patios in front of each building entry with projecting concrete steps. He envisioned a look similar to the old brownstone townhouses found in New York City and Brooklyn. Today, a series of landscaped terraces adorned with potted vegetation—shrubs and small trees—along with handsome planters overflowing with ornamental foliage grace each semiprivate patio just outside the main entries to the condominiums. Decorative metal railings and handrails further embellish the charm of these historic building. The idea of having "urban stoops" led these urban designers to develop an enhanced pedestrian experience as a "gateway street" for the River District.

The first freight house building conversion was configured into ten units with private, secure, off-street parking behind the structure. The developer provided several alternative floor plans for a typical two-thousand-square-foot unit. Eight of the ten units sold for $319,000 while the remaining two units sold for $339,000 and $349,000—the latter being the condominium with an entry at grade level.

Pat would later convert the other building in a similar fashion. In 2020, one of these customized condominium units had a resale price of around $2 million.

◇ ◇ ◇

Urban Homes had one more project left to do. Pat built the Irving Street Townhouses in 1996. Closing off portions of Irving Street to through traffic allowed the construction of condominiums at street level. One end of Irving Street was planted with trees and shrubs that blocked vehicular access. The other end of the street had a double row of trees spaced twelve feet apart that allowed the passage of an automobile or small pickup truck to a private resident parking lot. The project created fourteen townhomes with private entrances in a semi-secluded, landscaped, garden-like setting.

On a sunny day, residents and visitors to the district often find a welcome retreat from the hustle and bustle of this busy urban neighborhood on either Irving or Johnson Street. Both are pedestrian-oriented streets that function as pocket parks. Among the ornamental shrubbery and under the tree canopy, homeowners, residents, and visitors can enjoy sitting on a bench chatting with a neighbor or a friend, reading a book, or eating lunch.

TIME TO TAKE PROFITS

In 1996, Pat realized it was time for him to liquate his interests in Hoyt Street Yards—the time to harvest profits. He'd had a good run. And it'd been a bit riskier than the projects he'd been involved in before. It was also time to sell the remaining land he owned.

Homer Williams wanted to buy what remained of the rail yards. However, this required more capital than he had. So, Homer brought in Clay Fowler, an East Coast businessman who owned Spinnaker Real Estate, and Apogee, a California company owned by Roy Disney. Clay and Apogee purchased what remained of Hoyt Street Yards from Pat.

Pat never regretted selling his assets. However, as part of the deal, Pat kept a couple of properties out of the original Hoyt Street Yards holdings. His plan was to do one more project immediately, then wait until the marketplace settled down. He'd let others test the depth of demand for units to rent or buy.

Pat developed Pearl Court Apartments, a mid-rise 199-unit housing tower, in August 1997. It was one of the first affordable housing projects in the district. About half of the units were medium-income units. To qualify for the special rental rates, a resident had to earn between 40 and 60 percent of the area median income. Six months after construction completed, the building had full occupancy. This apartment building was built with virtually no parking. There were only thirty spaces on the adjacent side streets when it opened.

All this was risky because the rental rate Pat needed to achieve was $170 per foot. This rate had never been reached before in Portland. Ultimately, Pat realized more than $170 per foot. It leased out nicely because it had been the beneficiary of an urban tax abatement program for multifamily housing for ten years.

Pat waited until 2005 to build his last project, the Burlington Tower. It became a longtime investment hold for him. The yields on apartments can be low in the early years but stable over the long run because you don't have the recapitalization costs that are usually associated with office buildings. The Burlington once had a very unusual feature. During the project's lease-up, it was the only apartment building in the River District that had a doorman.

Hoyt Street Lofts had wanted to convert an old warehouse into loft-style condominiums back in 1984. By the early 1990s, City Lofts was the brainchild of two Portland businessmen. They thought they could succeed where Hoyt Street Lofts hadn't.

25

LOFT CONDOS

THE HOYT STREET LOFTS INVESTORS had placed their bet back in the mid-'80s. Nearly a decade had passed. It was 1993, and they hadn't achieved their goal of converting the Gadsby building into condominiums. Now one of the investors wanted to sell his shares.

The investors were tired; their interest in the project had dulled. Their common bond had unraveled. Personal circumstances now ran counter to their original plans. As owners and shareholders, they met, voted, and agreed to sell the building. It didn't take long for a local buyer to appear. Businessman Rick Michaelson led an investor group known as Inner City Properties. They bought the building and began an incremental program of building upgrades. After the tax deferment on the structure had run its course, the group changed their business model and attracted a higher-paying clientele.

Before 1994, no developer had successfully converted an existing warehouse in the old Northwest Triangle District into loft condominiums. That year Rich Ford and Terry Brandt bought a warehouse that had been the corporate headquarters for the Eoff Electric Company. The developers renovated the building, which was located at NW 10th Avenue and NW Glisan Street and called the building City Lofts.

Rich had previously worked with Al Solheim on real estate deals; now he wanted a project of his own. The basic conversion formula had already been set—retail activity on the ground level with residential use above. Like other developers before them, Rich and Terry couldn't get financing because the local banks wouldn't lend on a mixed-use project. Instead, the developers self-financed the project using personal credit cards.

Their intention was to sell off the condos but retain the ground-floor retail as an asset. It didn't happen that way. To complete the conversion, they had to put in all the equity upfront. They had buyers making reservations and putting down substantial down payments. The buyers were buying their units on the basis that the developers would bring the building conversion to a point where the buyers could secure individual financing to buy their unit. The developers had to presell 70 percent of the units to get Federal Housing Administration (FHA) approval for buyers who personally had to finance their own units.

Terry remembered, "It was quite a stressful time for us. We felt personally obligated to make this deal happen. Our strategy was to do a build-out for a buyer for a bathroom and a kitchen so the buyers could get financing for a loan."

The developers were selling a shell with limited improvements. They had constructed a model demonstration unit. However, most buyers decided to take an allowance and make their own improvements. These buyers wanted custom-designed units. Many of the buyers made million-dollar improvements. One unit was designed with secondary interior walls to create an air space for additional sound insulation. The owner wanted to be able to crank up his stereo sound system. Many of the original buyers were attorneys who thought of the project as an investment.

The project had post-construction issues—there were sound attenuation problems and a leaky roof. Rich and Terry had decided for aesthetic reasons not to install drywall on the underside of the existing joists and flooring. By not providing a finished ceiling with insulation material, sound transmissions between units became an issue. They came to regret this decision. Furthermore, a leaky roof resulted in a lawsuit, although the suit was settled in arbitration. The developer and contractor split the pain and suffering.

The City Lofts project was not a moneymaker for the developers. Terry had a serious regret: "We sold the units too cheaply; we didn't know what the market was. And we got out with our skin and teeth intact—just!" In 2020, one of the units was for sale at $1,850,000.

In the early '90s, John Carroll returned to Portland after his travels. Now he had to decide what to do about his partnership with Pat Prendergast.

26

BACK IN THE GAME

JOHN CARROLL WANTED BACK IN the real estate development game. He had left Portland to travel and do some research. In 1994, he returned home. Previously, he had spoken with Homer Williams about selling his interests in Hoyt Street Yards. Now he sold that interest before Pat Prendergast sold his interest.

Afterward, John established John Carroll Investments. Two years later he purchased the Chown Pella building from John Gray. He next acquired several nearby properties, assembling ownership of a whole block adjacent to NW 13th Avenue.

People began to question what he was doing, but he had a plan. He was perceptive enough to see the growing interest in loft living, and so he converted the Chown Pella building into loft residences. It sold out fast. John went on to build several new residential buildings, including the Gregory Condos and the MacKenzie Lofts in 1997–98. He built the Edge Lofts, an eleven-story building with an REI store at ground level, at NW 14th Avenue and Johnson Street in 2004 and the Elizabeth, a sixteen-story tower, in 2005.

Like many of the other developers who did business in the Pearl, John worked closely with the neighborhood association to avoid difficulties. His decision was intuitive; he believed, "Once you are attacked, you can never go back."

Before John decided to build the MacKenzie Lofts, his intention was to renovate the existing building. This was a storied structure. Previously it was called the Palace or the Band Building because the tenants were typically musicians and bands who rented a place to practice. Socially, that was a bonus—the best parties happened at the Palace.

John would have rehabilitated the structure, except for a serious structural problem. Keenly aware of the neighborhood association's desire to preserve existing warehouses, John organized a tour of the building for a few representatives. He showed them a corner of the building that slumped several feet below grade. This situation had compromised the building's structural integrity. He had no choice but to tear the building down and build anew.

When John decided to build the Elizabeth Lofts, it was a direct reference to Charles Rennie Mackintosh. John had gone to Glasgow and toured the 1903 Willow Tea Rooms—one of the few remaining buildings Mackintosh built that were still being used for their original purpose. The ornamentation on the Elizabeth mimicked aspects of Mackintosh's architectural style. The Gregory, by contrast, was definitely an Art Deco building.

John viewed the Pearl District as a kind of "urban laboratory" that allowed developers, architects, city planners, and others an opportunity to try out new ideas. Ideas involved different types of building designs, traditional floor layouts versus open plan arrangements, and marketing strategies that all culminated in new living choices for people who wanted change.

While interviewing John a few years later, I asked him about a local auto body shop that might be demolished to make way for a new apartment building. "Have you heard anything about that?" I asked him. Others I had spoken with had expressed concern about the potential loss of older, contemporary, low-rise buildings that gave the district its distinctive character.

John didn't say anything at first. He stood up and excused himself, saying he'd be back in a minute. He returned, carrying a very thick three-ring binder that he handed to me. "Here's the design book and specifications for the proposed building I want to build when we demolish the auto body shop."

He had purchased Jim Stevens Auto Body at the corner of NW 11th Avenue and Hoyt Street several years earlier, had hired an architect, and was currently in design review with the City. When I asked John what he thought might happen to many of the other contemporary service-oriented buildings in the area, he expressed the opinion that the entrepreneurial community would determine to a large extent what old buildings would remain and which ones would become teardowns.

John was concerned about real estate management during his early career. Managing Chown Pella taught him a valuable lesson. Building maintenance was important if you decided to keep a building for the long term. In 1995, John had formed a building integrity management (BIM) company to deal with window-fogging problems at the MacKenzie. The legal bill for that problem came to $950,000. The BIM group went to the MacKenzie homeowners' association to change the wording of the bylaws to reflect the requirement that the association needed to update their maintenance plan. The association needed to reconcile their budget regarding ongoing building maintenance, and all maintenance needed to be performed on a regular basis in the future.

Bob Ball was among the developers who found success as the Pearl District evolved in the early 2000s. When Bob took on the renovation of the Marshall Wells building next to the I-405 freeway, he also took a trip to San Francisco to check out the Clock Tower building. He needed to know how to make perspective buyers comfortable about living next to an elevated urban freeway.

27

NEW KID ON THE BLOCK

ROBERT BALL BECAME A REAL estate developer when he was a college student in Eugene, Oregon. He purchased several houses near the university and turned them into student rentals.

A native Oregonian, Bob was born on the North Coast near Astoria. He had earned an Elks Scholarship, which enabled him to go to the University of Oregon. During his freshman year, needing extra money, he took a job with a small start-up computer software company that serviced real estate offices. This was his introduction into real estate. The experience put Bob on a career path.

BECOMING A DEVELOPER

While in college, Bob read an article about a New York City billionaire who had been successful buying and renovating old apartment buildings. He found the story intriguing. So, he decided to buy a house in Eugene. He pestered a local real estate agent who found a property for him. Bob proceeded to buy the house, putting 10 percent down on a $20,000 private property sale using savings he had earned busing tables, working at golf courses, and working at the software company.

Once he took possession of the house, Bob painted and fixed the place up. The property was close to campus, so he rented out rooms to students. He lived in the basement. Bob then lease-optioned a couple of other properties to buy, although he didn't understand what that really meant. He was just figuring things out as he went along. It was hands-on learning.

A real estate-oriented investment company took notice of what he had done with his first house. Bob had the vision and energy, and the Connors had the financing, so the family bankrolled him, which allowed Bob to buy more houses.

While working for the software company, Bob had traveled around the United States. During these travels, he had observed different forms of urban redevelopment, like what had happened on Union Street in San Francisco and on Capitol Hill and Broadway in Seattle. He absorbed these experiences. They would become useful to him after he finished college.

THE NORTHWEST NEIGHBORHOOD

By 1993, he was living in Portland. Almost immediately Bob noted that NW 23rd Avenue had become a trendy shopping street similar to what he had seen elsewhere on his travels. Bob was attracted to the vibrancy and cosmopolitan ambiance that had blossomed in the Northwest Neighborhood. He had found his next real estate playground.

He sold his properties in Eugene and bought a sixteen-unit walkup apartment building along NW 21st Avenue. He renamed the building the Sara Ann Apartments and turned it into a class A apartment building. He did it again when he bought the Robert Daniel Apartments in the same neighborhood. After closing the deal, he decided to self-manage his properties. Bob then started his own property management company. His next purchase was the American, another apartment building. Now it was time to change his business model. Bob converted the building to condominiums.

A BIGGER SANDBOX TO PLAY IN

Bob next turned his attention to the Pearl District. In 2002, he upped his game and took a big-time risk by purchasing the seven-story Marshall Wells building. Bob was aware that several of the seasoned local developers had looked at the Marshall Wells building and rejected buying and renovating it. None of them had been able to come up with a workable adaptive reuse plan. Bob loved a challenge. He bought the building. According to him, he wanted to "exercise his creativity and save history."

Why did he succeed in this last venture? First, he thought an atrium was a good idea for such a big building because long units could extend from the exterior wall back into a light well, instead of the dark bowels of the structure. He rotated the square-shaped atrium in the center of the building because he had observed that Daniel Burnham—the famous architect from Chicago who had designed the structure—had framed the building with a diagonal structural system. Bob realized that cutting a light well that followed the architectural framing pattern wouldn't compromise the structural system and create extra construction costs.

Bob was initially concerned about the building's location, specifically its proximity to the elevated I-405 freeway. He didn't know if people would live next to a noisy urban freeway. To convince himself, Bob searched online and found that the Clock Tower building in San Francisco was next to a freeway. Interestingly, the building also had an atrium.

Bob immediately booked a flight, got on a plane, and flew to San Francisco. He hadn't scheduled any meetings with anyone. After landing, Bob rented a car, drove directly to the Clock Tower, and started buzzing units until someone answered. Bob explained he was a developer from Portland and wanted to know what it was like living next to a freeway.

The individual at the other end of the line said, "Oh yeah, sure, come on in," and he buzzed Bob into the building. Luckily, the guy's unit was on the freeway side of the building. Bob asked him: "Has the freeway been a problem?" The freeway noise was not a problem because the 164 units in the building had triple-pane windows. Because the sounds from the freeway got louder the higher you went in the building, condominium owners on the upper floors had quadruple panes that wrapped around to the north and south.

Bob remembered seeing a picture that showed him standing in the mud up to his ankles by the Marshall Wells building. "Everyone thought I would fail," he said. He also remembered looking at the building during construction and thinking: "Oh my god, what have I done! What have I gotten myself into?"

Why did Bob take on this building? He bought it simply because it was an opportunity to use his creativity and artistic sensibilities to make loft living spaces out of something that was at the end of its industrial lifecycle.

◇ ◇ ◇

In 2003, based on the success of the Marshall Wells Lofts project, Bob continued with another condominium conversion project in the Pearl, the Avenue Lofts. However, Bob wasn't the first person to attempt a conversion of what had been the 1923 Meier & Frank Warehouse.

Initially, a developer had bought the building for $14 million to create a telecommunications hotel—an internet datacenter housing hundreds or thousands of web servers. The contractor had begun construction and had cut holes in the floor plate to get a large generator into the structure. The owners had also upgraded the building's structural system to meet Portland's new earthquake code standards. These preliminary improvements had cost the owner another $8 million. When the tech market crashed in the 1980s, the developer went bankrupt.

Lehman Brothers had financed the building purchase, and they ended up with a dead project. Lehman approached Bob. They wanted to partner with his company Astor Pacific LLC and do a residential project. Bob looked at the building, did a walkthrough inspection, and decided that by putting an atrium in the structure a residential conversion was possible.

Right in the middle of those early discussions, competing divisions at Lehman got into an argument about how to solicit bids for the project. One internal group had lost money on the previous deal, and they thought they might be able to recover a few more dollars with someone other than Bob. They opened the process for bids, and several firms in Portland responded. Another division was so mad they passed some information to Bob—basically they told him what the other group would be looking for.

The warehouse was on the historic register at the time, and Bob had just completed a historic building project two blocks away from this site. Bob liked the building, liked the fact the earlier improvements were free, so he bought the building and hired SERA, a local firm, as his architects. Construction began, and in eleven and three-quarters months, all the condominiums were sold because Bob and his team leveraged the historic designation and the associated property tax freeze that made the sale of the individual condominium units more affordable and marketable.

Bob's previous work with the State Historic Preservation Office (SHPO) had given him a good working relationship with the agency. Knowing that noise control was a critical issue in this building, and knowing the structure was a historic building, gave him pause—but only for a half a minute.

An inspection of the building's industrial window sash system indicated there was a lot of rot associated with the existing windows. Both Bob and SHPO wanted to preserve the industrial window character. The existing repetitive, gridded windowpanes system was a prominent architectural feature of the structure. Therefore, obtaining a historic designation required maintaining this feature. But to solve the noise situation due to the building's proximity to an elevated freeway, Bob, through sample testing, convinced SHPO that all the windows needed to be replaced.

He proposed and negotiated a replacement package; it did not match the original windowpane design, but the new design did maintain the industrial look of the building. The package also included some alterations to the windows to provide better light and views for the new residential units. To satisfy SHIPO's concern about this alteration, one window was left unaltered in one of the building's facades to illustrate the original window configuration for historical purposes.

The seven-story building conversion created 170 residential "loft" condominiums with parking. The Meier & Frank property consisted of a block and a half of land. Bob donated a portion of the property for a public easement and created a "street park" as a forecourt to the building entrance. The remaining half-block was sold, and later a new building was erected there.

The Wyatt building was Bob's next project. It was designed as a 245-unit condominium building. But the market for condominiums was beginning to falter. Bob hired his own broker and sales agents, unlike some developers. He had started seeing reports from his agents and had himself observed that buyers were now asking more in-depth questions about ongoing condo projects. In response to this information, Bob shifted gears. He continued to monitor potential buyer interest in condominium purchases and renter absorption rates in the River District. What he saw was disturbing. There was a definite downward trend. In mid-2007, Bob received an unsolicited offer from an out-of-town buyer who wanted to use the structure as an apartment building. Bob returned the deposit money with interest to those buyers who had reserved a future condo in his project. Bob and his investors considered the offer and decided to sell the Wyatt. The deal closed in 2008 to a California buyer for $111.5 million. Bob then decided to sit on the sidelines and wait until a looming recessionary marketplace turned around.

He waited until 2011. The Parker, Bob's next project, was a $35 million apartment building. When questioned by a reporter, Bob commented, "I'd been sitting back until I felt the time was right to get back into the marketplace." He decided the demand for apartments was rising, and bidding for new construction was very competitive.

The Parker got built. Initially, Bob was going to retain ownership, although he doesn't consider himself a merchant builder. However, in 2015, he received a call asking if he had any interest in selling his company and the Parker. Bob quietly sold his parent real estate development company, Aster APEP, and the building to a national institutional investor—INVESCO, based in Atlanta—for $63.5 million. Bob's real estate company, Astor Pacific, was not involved in the INVESCO deal. At this point in his career, this was his best real estate deal.

After selling the Parker, Bob decided he wanted to build another apartment building reminiscent of the older-style residential structures found in the Northwest Neighborhood. Bob switched districts and bought the Chinese restaurant at the corner of NW 21st Avenue and Kearney Street. He called the project 21 Astor. It consisted of twenty-seven rental units in a four-story boutique residential building. The units were targeted to high-end renters who want to live in the center of Nob Hill instead of the Pearl District.

In late 2016, I sat with Bob in his new offices at NW 23rd Avenue and Glisan Street. Bob looked relaxed. He had the air of someone who knew he was totally comfortable with what he'd done in the past and was financially secure. As Bob was in good spirits, I couldn't resist asking him a question that had been on my mind from the first time I spoke with him: "Did you feel like an outlier when you decided to do projects in the Pearl District?"

"Absolutely," he replied. Bob had been the "new kid on the block," and others had referred to him, he said, as the "Peter Pan of the Pearl." But when he finished the Marshall Wells project, he thought he was on the inside of the local game.

He remembered when he first met Homer Williams and Clay Fowler. Bob had seen Homer at numerous public meetings, but at the time, Bob didn't know who Clay was. Homer and Clay had stopped by Bob's office after Bob had successfully completed a couple of projects in the Pearl, and Clay said, "You know, we really wanted to meet you. In all honesty, we really thought you would fail." After that, Bob felt validated.

Bob and I talked about how the development game in the Pearl began as a homegrown story. Later, things shifted when institutional money found its way into the game. He told me he'd been a little blind back then. But he'd sorted things out, and he could see the impact of all the institutional money that's come into the game. This financing has raised the prices for buildings. The developers with institutional backing have so much money they can come in and buy a property where a developer like Bob has to have a spread in the deal to make it work. The new guys are more sophisticated. They have in-house resources and expertise that allow them to build the project and still make money on a 4 or 5 percent return.

What Bob had to sort out was what had happened in the Portland market cycle in response to all the apartment construction that began as the local economy came out of recession. To accomplish this goal, he consolidated all his businesses under one umbrella, Robert Ball Companies. This gave him a multipronged platform to continue development, management, and investment to a selective clientele in the long-term. He now works out of a new modern office built atop a branch bank and FedEx storefront—a perch from which to ponder new projects. He's still young, has the capital, is definitely not risk-averse, and has the smarts to consider projects outside the box.

Up until now, the Hoyt Street Yards had been developed without the benefit of a master plan. The Lovejoy Viaduct was standing and considered to be a major physical barrier to the long-term development of the rail yards property. And there were other issues the private and public sectors would have to deal with that included higher housing density requirements, the provision of affordable housing, and the implementation of needed open-space facilities for future residents. Who would pay for what? When would improvements be made and by whom? What was needed was a document that answered these questions and guided long-term development of the Hoyt Street Yards.

28

HOYT STREET PROPERTIES

HOMER WILLIAMS TOOK HIS STEPDAUGHTER
Tiffany Sweitzer out to the Burlington Northern rail yards one
day in 1993. It was a bleak wasteland. No one imagined this
landscape was a seedbed from which a vibrant urban community
would emerge in the coming decades.

TIFFANY GOES TO WORK

When Homer asked her what she thought about the property,
Tiffany didn't say anything. But she thought: *What the heck are
you* thinking? After more consideration, she decided all that open
space was kind of cool, and she recognized the benefit of land being
close to downtown. Tiffany was aware of the fact housing could
be built there, although not many people lived downtown then.

When we talked about this episode in her life, she remembered
what it felt like to realize she just might want to take on this
property as a project. Tiffany also remembered that no one else
back then had any grandiose ideas about what to do with the
land. It was like a book with blank pages waiting for someone to
fill in the narrative.

A year later, Homer was Pat Prendergast's new partner, and
Tiffany went to work for them as an intern. When she arrived at

Homer's downtown office, he told her he didn't have room for her. He told her to go over to Pat's office. She didn't know Pat, but she packed up her stuff and went over to his office. There, Tiffany became a gofer, doing whatever needed to be done.

Tiffany credits Pat with giving her first valuable lessons as a future developer. You need to go down to the land every day. You need to go down to the dirt. Go down to the project site and see what is going on. Don't just sit behind a desk.

One of the tasks Pat gave her was to collect rent. Tiffany would drive over to Hoyt Street Yards where several emerging artists had rented spaces in the old Burlington Northern wooden sheds. Later, she did building turnovers. That's the process of orienting new renters or buyers to a unit. She also had to deal with problems and management issues. She learned how to be a developer's representative, and she worked with the sale force. Tiffany was learning about real estate development from the ground floor up. What she didn't realize was that she had just signed up for the adventure of her life.

HOMER HAS THE HELM

In 1998, Homer together with Clay Fowler and Roy Disney, his new partners, reorganized the company and renamed it Hoyt Street Properties. The new owners began developing what remained of the old rail yards beginning with the Riverstone, a mixed-use, mid-rise building housing 121 luxury condominiums designed by the architecture firm of Ankrom Moisan.

The building was a very traditional six-story structure adjacent to one of the new city blocks designated for use as a public park. To market the project, the developers took an old railroad car, laid sod for a small green area, and provided a parking area—this was their first sales office. They used several of Greg Baldwin's fantasy drawings to illustrate their design intentions.

The next year Hoyt Street Properties built the Johnson Street Townhomes. This low-rise—thirteen condominium units ranging in size from 1,800 to 2,700 square feet—was a throwback to Pat's early projects. Two decades later, they are some of the most desirable residences in the Pearl. With their flat-roof design, bold metal windows, and contemporary bay window–like protrusions set against red brick walls, they stand out within the surrounding mid-rise buildings that came later. The larger units have attached garages with secure parking, private gardens, gourmet kitchens, hardwood floors, gas fireplaces, whirlpool tubs, and private rooftop patios. The project has been a huge success.

People who believed in, understood, and trusted the notion of contingent relationships could do amazing things. But defining the conditions and responsibilities, getting them down on paper, and getting all parties to sign a development agreement became essential when it came to actually building the River District.

29

CONTINGENT RELATIONSHIPS

HOMER WILLIAMS WAS, FIRST AND foremost, a super showman. He had begun his career as a land developer and deal-maker with Forest Heights, a suburban subdivision in Portland's West Hills. From that point forward he only got better at putting together investor groups, negotiating deals, and dealing with the politics of development.

RIVER DISTRICT POLITICS

The political relationship Homer had with Mayor Vera Katz was extremely helpful in structuring a development framework for the build out of the River District. The mayor was a champion of Homer, and she supported the idea of high-density urban housing in downtown. She has reportedly said of him, "Homer's got a holistic view of the universe. Our conversations are usually about bigger issues, demographics, and how the city is changing."

Homer believed political relationships were an essential ingredient to achieving a successful project. He has said, "You can only do the stuff we do with political willpower, and that takes strong leadership." Because of this belief, Homer was a strong advocate of private-public partnerships. But to come to an agreement with the City, Homer knew he needed to get their requirements out on the table and get an understanding about how to accomplish the removal of Lovejoy Viaduct. This elevated road bisected the rail yards property and was a physical barrier to the goal of creating a new neighborhood.

As Homer and his partners contemplated their approach to building on the remaining open land, he knew City Hall wanted to see some new open space—a few new park blocks—in the River District. Additionally, city officials wanted a significant percentage of affordable units in the evolving housing mix as the district evolved over time. City Hall was also interested in extending the North Park Blocks into the new district.

◇ ◇ ◇

Homer and Greg Baldwin had worked together on a plan for the district. During these sessions, Greg had taught him about contingent relationships. Most developers start a project with the general idea they want to spend a budgeted amount of money to achieve a specific goal. In contrast, Greg believed a developer could begin a public-private project by asking the other party, like the City, "What do you want to see?" It's about respect and the acknowledgment that enlightened individuals can lead and direct the activities of city bureaus. Portland was lucky because in the 1990s and early 2000s, a lot of quality people worked in public service. They cared about the city and wanted to see the River District succeed.

Homer also knew he had to work with the Pearl District Neighborhood Association. He was keenly aware that most associations are focused on self-interest. In the case of the River District, all parties had to compromise to achieve a workable plan. What came out of this situation was the sense that any plan had to have multiple owners. There needed to be a strong sense that everyone had contributed to the underlying process and had an ownership stake. Hopefully, as the plan moved forward, there wouldn't be a surprising right or left turn—a misstep—that might derail the project.

◇ ◇ ◇

Glacier Park's master plan had proved to be irrelevant. The plan had envisaged low-rise buildings for business incubators. What was going to be needed was a substantial increase in building heights and densities—a clear departure from the findings of the 1983 R/UDAT study.

Prendergast & Associates had tried to improve on this old plan, but neither Homer nor the city was satisfied with the situation concerning a district master plan. Both parties sensed that a new deal or agreement was needed. The need was for a more explicit pathway for macro-scale planning and development of the remaining thirty-four acres of land Hoyt Street Properties was eager to build out. With that goal in mind, Bruce Allen—a Portland Development Commission (PDC) staffer, began negotiating with Homer.

THE MASTER DEVELOPMENT AGREEMENT

As the negotiations continued, both parties were aware that the City had to be involved in providing the urban infrastructure—primarily streets and utility improvements—that might be part of an agreement. However, it was obvious to both parties that there weren't any public funds or sources readily available to underwrite a public-private partnership. However, Portland had a different kind of currency available: an urban renewal program. Maybe they could create an urban renewal district with side benefits.

The negotiations ended with the identification of six key topics, among them affordable housing, the viaduct, new parks, and a streetcar. A draft agreement based on a series of contingent relationships laid out and specified the responsibilities for each party. It was signed in 1997. The parties basically agreed, "If you do this, we do that." The final agreement was presented to the Portland City Council for approval with enough fanfare to bring all the city bureaus on board to support the council's actions. This way, the council couldn't be singularly responsible if the project failed. Miraculously, everything fell into place. Hoyt Street

Properties, LLC, and the City of Portland signed an amended agreement in 1999.

That contractual agreement became a workable document for several reasons. First, the project was attractive to the politicians. Unlike many urban renewal projects, displacement of people and business was not an issue. Instead, the project created jobs and homes. Furthermore, the River District Steering Committee had made sure all the key decision-makers were at the table as critical decisions were made as the River District Development Plan was prepared and approved. This ensured that agencies and other public officials couldn't say they weren't informed or hadn't been involved. No one could renege on the deal, and no one wanted to be responsible for its failure. Moreover, it was a homegrown planning effort, owing to the scale of the community that fostered and reinforced the notion of community leaders working together for the public good with the promise of a billion-dollar investment in Portland.

After the final development agreement was signed, the City began discussions about how to demolish the Lovejoy Viaduct. Besides physically removing the structure, the City would have to reconnect Lovejoy Street to the west end of the Broadway Bridge.

30

LOVEJOY VIADUCT

DEMOLISHMENT OF THE VIADUCT, FROM the perspective of the developer, was a crucial step in the implementation of a master plan for the Hoyt Street Yards property. City officials agreed, but they also had another view. A private developer was now prepared to take the market risk and build housing at a density of 125 units per acre. This was a huge leap in density. Vic Rhodes, as director of the Bureau of Transportation, thought that if a new neighborhood with ten thousand residents was created in the old rail yards, this meant the City wouldn't have to add a couple of freeway lanes in the suburbs.

Tearing down the viaduct had a cost. So, the City went after tax increment financing money at Metro. According to Vic, putting the funding together was a real "mess-mash." To accomplish this, Vic told me the City and Metro put their infrastructure project funding dollars into one pot. The first real money had been the $500,000 federal legislative earmark Senator Mark Hatfield had obtained for Oregon.

On the morning of August 1, 1999, the Portland City Council approved closure to traffic on the viaduct. A few months later, the long, elevated ramp that had connected NW 14th Avenue to the Broadway Bridge was torn down. Afterward, a shorter ramp was built along Lovejoy Street between from NW 9th Avenue to the western Broadway bridgehead. All together, the City spent $13 million to resolve the viaduct as a constraint to implementation of the River District Vision.

◇ ◇ ◇

Removal of the viaduct created an uproar and concern over what many considered a local art treasure. Greek immigrant Tom Stefopoulos, a railroad switchman who had worked in the rail yards in the late 1940s, had drawn images from Greek mythology, Americana, and the Bible on several of the viaduct columns. His murals even appeared in several films, notably *Drugstore Cowboy*. This was not your usual gallery art. The murals, surrounded by empty space and the roar of vehicles overhead, seemed to emanate from the soul of the Old World. In response to citizens' concerns, the Portland Bureau of Transportation allocated funds in the demolition phase of the project to safely remove and protect ten of the art columns. An ad hoc citizen committee, Friends of the Columns, was formed to raise funds to store and restore the columns, install them in a public, sheltered place, and ensure their preservation. The total cost of the storage, restoration, installation, and conservation was estimated at $460,000.

Commissioner Charlie Hales said of this effort: "Saving the Lovejoy columns and the artwork provides a real bridge between the rich history of this industrial area and its future as a residential neighborhood." He went on, "I am pleased that we are able to save these columns and look forward to them being placed on some of the park spaces in the River District."

There have been numerous attempts to safeguard and place some of these art columns in the public realm. Developer John Carroll became interested in the future of these artworks. He had seen *Lovejoy Lost*—a video installation—at the PDX Window Project in Portland about the viaduct. Unhappy about the removal of these artworks from public view, John acquired two of the ten columns and, in 2005, had them installed as totem-like features in the sidewalk-oriented open courtyard of the Elizabeth building. The remaining columns are still in storage.

31

A LEGAL TIME BOMB

FOR OVER A HUNDRED YEARS, petroleum hydrocarbons had contaminated the ground at the rail yards at Union Station. Toxic materials—leaked or spilled fuels and lead from battery maintenance services—had leached into and polluted the underlying soil and water table. The property Hoyt Street Properties, LLC was going to build condominiums on was a brownfield.

The railroad companies had known about this contamination before the property sale. They had even begun cleanup efforts on the south-oriented portion of the site. That was part of the reason Pat Prendergast had started building along Hoyt Street back in the '90s. However, Hoyt Street Properties now decided to seek compensation for the existence of the problem on the property north of Lovejoy.

Legally, every entity, past and present, in the property-ownership chain had some level of responsibility. The degree of liability was the issue. So, after a couple of years of talks with the railroad, Hoyt Street Properties sued to get the railroads to pay for the soil contamination they had caused. In 1998, the developers retained Steve Janik, a Portland attorney. To prepare for the federal court trial, they held a mock trial that cost $50,000.

Hoyt Street Properties first sought $26.4 million from Burlington Northern and the Santa Fe Railway Co. The railroads contended they were only liable for $5.6 million in cleanup costs, as estimated by Oregon's Department of Environmental Quality. At trial, Hoyt Street Properties' suit asked for compensatory damages of $30 million.

According to Tiffany Sweitzer, they were buoyed because their mock trial had led them to conclude they would win the suit. The night the jury began their deliberations; Tiffany and Homer Williams went to the Heathman Hotel for a drink. The attorneys for the other side were also there. Tiffany and Homer were so sure of their win that they sent the other attorneys some champagne. The next day, they went to court to hear the judgment. The developers won, but the award was for $1.5 million, a far cry from what they'd sued for. At one point during private negotiations before the suit, the railroad had offered $16 million to settle out of court. Hoyt Street Properties had said no!

After the jury's verdict was announced, the jurors clarified their reasoning. The railroads had operated on the disputed land for a hundred years. The developers had made a choice to build there. Now, in the jury's view, they had to deal with the contaminated groundwater.

After the verdict, an interesting thing happened. One of the representatives from Burlington Northern approached Hoyt Street Properties and requested a meeting. Tiffany has a vivid memory of this guy as the "change guy." He constantly played with the coins in his pocket. Tiffany could always hear the jingling. She even heard it in court.

She and others sat down with him and renegotiated a new settlement figure close to $8 million. The railroad hadn't wanted an appeal, so the increased settlement payment was a sweetener to ensure the complaint was put to rest. The money was put into escrow, and as individual blocks were developed, Hoyt Street

Properties received dollars to defray some of their costs. Roughly speaking, each of their development blocks got about $130,000.

◇ ◇ ◇

The jury's verdict had been a surprise to Tiffany. Two other Portland developers also received a surprise when they purchased an unoccupied warehouse nicknamed the Ice Block.

32

UNFREEZING THE FREEZER

THE W. P. FULLER PAINT Building has a storied history. This four-story structure, which covers a full city block, was constructed in 1908. Many businesses, not just the paint company, occupied the warehouse over the past century, and the building was even vacant for several years in the 1930s. By 2000, the warehouse's interior would be gutted, renovated, and transformed into the headquarters for one of the largest independently owned advertising agencies in the world.

WORLD WAR II AND POSTWAR USE

During World War II, the War Food Administration bought the building to ease the critical storage need for rationed food in the Northwest. The storage of foodstuffs was necessary because the government had to make provision for supplying food to the civilian population and troops. The War Production Board purchased and converted the building at a cost of $700,000 to a cold-storage plant for twenty thousand tons of food. To accomplish this, all the metal windows were removed and bricked up. Then six inches of cork was added to some of the interior walls as well as twelve inches of redwood bark dust that was placed in the exterior walls and ceiling spaces.

Initially, the federal government had arranged for Henningsen Cold Storage Co., a Portland company, to operate the cold-storage facility by lease arrangement. In 1949 or 1950, Henningsen bought the building and continued to operate it as Northwestern Ice & Cold Storage. In 1963, the cold-storage plant was sold to Southeast Public Services, a Florida company. During the next two decades, the building was used to store fruit harvested in and around the Portland Metropolitan Area as well as fish and other perishables. The plant also stored ice because early freight train refrigeration required an ice bunker in every boxcar. There's also a story about how Oregon Fish and Wildlife rented space in the facility to store the carcasses of poached deer for evidence. By the 1990s, the building appeared neglected and disused, its future unknown.

A REAL ESTATE GAMBLE

The brothers from a local family—Unkeles—had brought a small, quaint brick building across the street from the Maddox building back in 1964. There they established a business selling cardboard boxes. By the early 1980s, Ken Unkeles had joined his father and uncle in the operation of the business after his brief career as a real estate agent.

As time passed, the family acquired several other buildings in the neighborhood, which Ken managed. When there was a vacancy, Ken jumped down from the building's loading dock and headed over to Rusty's. There he'd nurse a cup of coffee until a prospective tenant crossed the threshold. Ken has said, "More than once, I'd tell my dad I was going over to the café to rent a little space." And he did.

Over time, Ken personally acquired several buildings outside the Northwest Triangle District. Typically. Ken renovated and subdivided each structure into several individual workspaces, which were then rented as studios to local artists. Ken seemed to have a Midas touch for making sound real estate purchases. He made sure his deals penciled out, but the real estate deal wasn't always about maximizing his profit. He wanted to bring artists together in a physical and social setting, thereby creating informal art centers where public events could take place. He was an opportunist with a heart.

◇ ◇ ◇

Ken was always on the lookout for a good real estate deal. When the vacant Fuller Paint building became available in 1996, Ken partnered up with Art DeMuro. Art was a recent transplant from Phoenix. He'd majored in history in college and had taught the subject for a short while. Art was a passionate advocate for preserving and renovating historic structures. Together they bought the building as a speculative venture.

Both partners thought the deal was a solid purchase due to the building's location along NW 13th Avenue. They did have questions about the structural integrity of the building. To obtain an answer, Ken sought the advice of a structural engineer. He knew an old-timer—a seasoned engineer, not one of those forty-year-old kids. The engineer looked at the building and said something to the effect of: "It's been here nearly a hundred years, and it's still standing." So, Ken and Art figured they were OK.

Ken called the structure the Ice Block because he knew it had been used as a freezer of sorts. Now they had to unfreeze it. First, they organized a cleanup of the building's interior. Next, they removed the plywood sheets that covered the interior walls. Ken thought of this as "pulling the plug" so the structure could "breathe." And that was when—surprise—the time bomb went off. The building dripped water for two months. The interior walls, the ones filled with bark dust, had retained moisture for decades.

As the cleanup progressed, Ken began to wonder what they were going to do with this building. He and Art thought about it and had decided to convert the building into studio spaces for artists. That didn't happen.

A WELCOMED SALE

Shortly after buying the building, Ken and Art were having lunch when Brad Cloepfil, a local architect, approached them and struck up a conversation. The partners were unaware that Brad had been in contact with Dan Wieden, the owner of a local advertising agency.

A native Portlander, Brad had founded Allied Works Architecture in 1994. Commissions were scarce, but one of the firm's early works, Saucebox—Bruce Carey's restaurant and bar on SW Broadway—proved to be a huge success when it opened in 1995. It opened a gateway for bigger projects to follow, many of which were out-of-town commissions.

Wieden-Kennedy or W+K, had grown by leaps and bounds, and the firm's employees were scattered around the city in eight different buildings. Dan was frustrated. It seemed to him that the cohesiveness of the company was being lost. He wanted all his employees in one place so everyone could have a shared sense of what the company's culture was all about.

Dan's executive creative director had happened to be at the Saucebox one day drinking with friends. She liked what she saw. Before leaving, she asked the bartender who had done the restaurant's interior design. She then called Brad and told him W+K wanted to meet with him. Dan ended up hiring Brad.

After they'd cleaned up the Fuller Paint building, Ken and Art received a few offers from interested buyers. One offer had been from an advertising agency, but nothing ever happened. So, when W+K, a local advertising agency, made an offer the partners rejected it out of hand. Some time passed, and then a local developer, Bob Gerding made an offer. He was acting as a straw buyer for W+K. Sometimes this business tactic can work against a deal, given that it can generate a strong sense of misperceived demand. Ken and Art mulled over the offer, but they decided could make more money if they waited.

Eventually a deal was struck. The partners had been right; they made a better deal. Gerding Edlen Development (GED), acting on behalf of Wieden+Kennedy, purchased the old, dilapidated warehouse in 1997. Once the deal closed, Dan and Brad, together with several employees from GED, toured the building. The building was a "big mess." Any sane person would have torn it down. No, Dan wanted to save it. He liked the building's exterior character and wanted to preserve the historical appeal of the structure. However, the interior needed a very expensive makeover.

A STRUCTURAL QUANDARY

This project was GED's first foray into the Pearl District. As they became enmeshed in the project, they found there was also rot in the interior timber frame structure. The building had developed leaks in the corners of the insulated structure, and where the cold air met the hot air, the rot had settled in for years. At this point, Bob knew they were going to need someone special to oversee a replacement structural system. And that someone was standing in the wings, waiting for just this opportunity.

Dennis Wilde had worked for Baugh Construction in 1997. What he really wanted to do was work for GED and become their go-to general contractor. He interviewed with them and was hired. When Dennis went into the old paint warehouse, he found that the building was racked (tilted out of square) on the top half. It was a cruciform-shaped building—cross-shaped in plan. The structure's brick bearing walls intersected in the middle of the structure, and there were four stairwells, each in a corner of that intersection.

One day Dennis and a few other individuals toured the building with a structural engineer. As they stepped out onto the third floor, one of the walls right behind the group fell. Dennis asked the engineer, "How is this building still standing?" "Habit" was his answer.

ANOTHER PIVOTAL EVENT

The W+K project propelled GED toward the Brewery Blocks project. When the W+K renovation was about three-quarters finished, Brad, Bob, Mark, and Dennis walked up to the top-floor balcony. Looking west over the rooftops, Bob asked Brad what he thought about the old brewery buildings visible in the near distance as a redevelopment project. "It would be amazing if you could do it; it would be unbelievable."

Dennis distinctly remembered hearing Bob say while on the rooftop of the W+K building as the group looked at the brewery complex, "We need to buy that. We'll build Stroh a new brewery over here in the Guilds Lake area."

To succeed with the W+K building, the developer had to work closely with Mayor Vera Katz and her team at City Hall. The building didn't fit with the City's building codes because of its wooden structural system. To expedite code compliance issues, the City formed a special team to assist the developer. This relationship paid extra dividends when Bob and Mark took on the redevelopment of the Brewery Blocks.

The completion of the W+K building was a pivotal event—it changed people's perception of what the district could become and the importance of expanding the district's boundaries to West Burnside. Instead of paint cans and frozen food, the building was now full of people. They brought youthful energy and life to the neighborhood. More major companies would soon follow and relocate to the Pearl District.

In the end, Dan and Allied Works Architecture rescued, gutted, restored an old warehouse and turned it into a nationally recognized work of architecture. The renovated interior focuses on a centralized open-air amphitheater that seats four hundred people. This airy, light-filled space engenders a sense of civic identity for the building's occupants.

The industrial character of the building's exterior was preserved, with new windows were inserted into the original bricked-over openings. Careful attention to the restoration of the building's exterior allowed the nomination, approval, and placement of the building on the National Register of Historic Places. Consistent with the City's historic district guidelines for NW 13th Avenue, the loading dock was preserved and a metal handrail added since the raised dock now served as a pedestrian sidewalk and an outdoor dining patio for the Bluehour restaurant.

Construction began in 1998, and it would take two years before a state-of-the-art headquarters was ready for occupancy, at a cost of $36 million.

According to John Tess, a local historic preservation consultant, this renovated warehouse with its historic designation was viewed as a welcome addition because it anchored the south end of the historic district. The building also conveyed a sense of gravitas to the district. Nothing like it had been done before, and it's one of the best pieces of contemporary architecture in the Pearl today.

The founder of Ecotrust would also decide to establish his company's headquarters in the River District and restore another distressed warehouse. Both the W+K and the Ecotrust projects underscored the local banking and development communities' belief that this district was worthy of further investment. Together, the two projects served as a stamp of validation.

33

A PHILOSOPHICAL RENOVATION

THE JEAN VOLLUM NATIONAL CAPITAL Center located in the Ecotrust building opened for business in 2001. If a building can be the personification of an individual, the center embodied Spencer Beebe. Spencer, a fourth-generation Oregonian, founded Ecotrust in the early '90s. The building became home for Spencer and the Ecotrust organization in their community-building mission exploring "the marriage of ecology and economics in ways that are tangible, practical, investment-worthy, and replicable."

ESTABLISHING A HOME BASE

Ecotrust found a permanent home in 1998. Lindley Morton, an architect-contractor friend, told Spencer about the McCracken building. This was a two-story classical Richardsonian Romanesque commercial-style building that was built in 1890. For many years it had been a freight center, known as the Central Truck Terminal, for trucking and rail distribution operations, and in the 1930s, it was the largest storage terminal in the Northwest. The building had been in continuous use by Rapid Transfer & Storage up until 1997. This historic structure occupied a full city block immediately adjacent to Portland's main post office. The structure was rundown and had been listed for sale at $2.5 million.

Local developers—Al Solheim and others—had walked through the structure and kept walking. To them, the cost to fix it up was too much. Spencer walked through the building and then decided to buy it.

At first there was a lot of resistance from his business colleagues and board about buying the building. Everybody thought he was nuts. Everyone was asking, "Why do you want to buy it?" Even Spencer thought the building "a nightmare."

But he also thought it was much more than that. "It was authentic, it was real, it was part of the history of this neighborhood, it had perfect timber, it had all this old-growth spotted owl habitat in it, it was part of developing Portland, and there was talk about daylighting Tanner Creek, which, of course, was not going to happen. It just felt right."

To buy the building, Spencer convinced Jean Vollum, a past Ecotrust supporter, to make a major contribution. The solicited donation was to support a vision to "repurpose a warehouse designed to distribute goods and services for an industrial economy into a marketplace for the ideas, goods, and services of a conservation economy."

The words were somewhat poetic. But what did they mean? This was going to be a place about creating a functioning, organic ecosystem that had some structure but was characterized with courage, spontaneous interaction, and connections between different kinds of people and expertise and shared values. Ecotrust was going to have to find potential tenants in social finance, outdoors, forestry, fisheries, and farming industries. The mix of was going to be unusual, and not the way you typically filled a building with tenants.

What Spencer was after in the building design was a variety of social habitats—small, medium, and large niches where people could sit down and connect. He had envisioned a natural ecosystem translated into a human ecosystem that could become an eco-center for doing business in a nonconventional manner. This notion that the building was to be seen as a counterpart to a natural ecosystem was a critical design requirement. The Ecotrust leadership took two years to figure out what their "organizing statement" meant. When they understood it, they had a design program to give to their architects—John Holmes and Jeff Stuhr of Holst Architecture.

The Ecotrust building is a container. A container that was and continues to be the physical manifestation of Spencer's philosophy and goal of creating social, economic, and environmental benefits in a myriad of cultural expressions and applications throughout daily life.

DESIGNING THE BUILDING

In 2001, Holst Architecture began refurbishing the container to meet the organization's operational needs and image. It wasn't an easy task. The initial pro forma for the project kept coming back indicating the project was going to lose money. Not good. It had to work financially, as Spencer wanted to build up an asset as part of Ecotrust's national capital fund. So, Spencer hired Bob Naito as the developer and told him, "This thing's got to make money; it's got to pencil.'"

At a critical juncture, Ecotrust held a design charrette. Stewart Brand, an old friend and Ecotrust board member, was invited. Stewart reduced their alternative design approaches to two very different choices: a demonstration or a laboratory project—each totally different and mutually exclusive. The building renovation could demonstrate all the latest green and sustainability applications available. However, Stewart advised that in a few short years, everything would be outdated, and this approach required expensive hardware.

Envisioning the building as a laboratory implied experimentation and evolution. This appealed to Spencer since it reflected principles inherent in nature. In the end, Ecotrust embraced the notion of a living, changing environment for a building concept, and they coupled the ideas of diversity and connectedness to this concept. Spencer has written in *Cache*, a book about the Ecotrust concept and philosophy: "I was looking for a social system designed on a natural model. Laboratory meant a place that was always experimenting, an evolving mix of tenants, where people would interact spontaneously and test new ideas. It sounded much more like the 'dynamic marketplace' idea we said we were trying to create."

As a principal at Holst, Jeff worked closely with Spencer on the design of the building. Spencer allowed the architects to go down a lot of different pathways, including, of course, stuff like "green building" because this was a mainstream trend in building design and construction at the time.

Many people might have considered Spencer as way out there. He has always seemed to want to wrap his arms around everything. He has high goals and high aspirations. However, existing conditions at the McCracken building and available funding limited what the architects could do. Jeff and his staff had to deal with physical realities: building and zones codes, structural and earthquake concerns. Ultimately, the architects were charged with ensuring that the pro forma penciled out and, more importantly, delivering a project that created an income stream for the client.

The interior layout of the building resembles a kind of indoor street that leads into a large open space. Speaking with Jeff, he told me the ground-floor design "came from trying to simplify the circulation and turn it into more of a 'stage' where people could come together and gather, allowing communication both upstairs and downstairs" The architects decided to remove some of the second floor, so people on the ground floor could see, hear, and reflect on what was going on upstairs. Since the architects didn't want to alter the exterior of the building, they incorporated a skylight over an atrium space to let natural light in.

Having an atrium was part of the organizing principle on how to take people upstairs. This tied in with the architect's response to the seismic upgrades that were required by the city. They were trying to leave the building as untouched as possible inside so they could preserve and emphasize the original exposed brick walls and heavy timber structural members. They didn't want to have to gunite the interior walls or use seismic bracing inside the building.

Instead, the architects decided to externalize the required seismic improvements by providing external bracing while also responding to and respecting the old industrial character of the neighborhood. To accomplish this, they had to introduce a new architectural language—metal bracing—in association with an old building. This was reflected in the placement of two steel towers on the western facade that basically hold the building up. The towers also serve as exterior stairwells providing access to and from the upper floors, fire exits, and access to a rooftop terrace.

The renovated McCracken warehouse doesn't feel like a typical corporate headquarters. Ecotrust is on the second floor. The office is an open plan with semiprivate spaces tucked in here and there for individuals or breakout groups. Large meetings, private and public conferences, and special events requiring screen time happen on the first floor in the conference center. The public is invited into the building, and you can wander throughout most of the building, even the exterior open-air deck areas. That's the idea behind the building's published brochure that is similar to a trail map in the wild. It's a guide to the building—a map that orients visitors if they wish to explore the building from the bottom to the top.

A small mezzanine—a lofty aerie—serves as Spencer's office. The space is nestled directly under the dimensional timbers that form the original trusses supporting the roof of the warehouse—a forested canopy. This aerie provides Spencer with a retreat to think and work undisturbed.

As I left after interviewing Spencer in his aerie, I glanced back and saw him back to work at his computer. I couldn't help thinking: those Ecotrust concepts like bioregional economics and other transformative ideas will make the world a better and fairer place for all.

HOUSING...MAYBE LATER

When construction began for Ecotrust, there had been a smaller, two-story building on the northwest quarter of the block. The structure was demolished to allow construction of an efficient surface parking facility, and a freestanding wall was left as a remnant artifact along NW 9th Avenue.

A decision had been made to not build any housing on the site. The parking facility was viewed as a placeholder. While limited funds for capital development affected the decision to only renovate the McCracken warehouse, it was a thoughtful, wise decision. A maximum build-out of the block would have triggered a requirement to include residential use in the project. With this came more risk, primarily financial. A limited development approach appears to have been the more prudent course of action. It also allowed the surface parking area to be used for on-site stormwater management and disposal. Since then, the City has increased the building height limits that apply to this site. However, the floor area ratio was also increased for the site. Therefore, future redevelopment of this half-block is possible and may result in significant dividends.

Spencer remembered being told as the building design program was refined, "Don't do everything." This statement also applied to Ecotrust's consideration to place the building on the National Register of Historic Places. They didn't.

A nomination was prepared, but in 2001, Ecotrust withdrew the nomination. Spencer didn't want to be driven by somebody else's checklist. He was more concerned, as an example, about recycling materials from the existing building, notably timber beams, as a way of honoring and respecting the historic nature of the structure.

Once the numbers for the project penciled out, Ecotrust had to secure project funding. A combination of private contributions, loans, grants, and tax credits was assembled to fund a project the required financing totaling almost $13 million.

◇ ◇ ◇

Both the Ecotrust and the W+K project were building conversions that incorporated green building and sustainable architectural design coupled with historic preservation. Both established a high-quality design standard for other proposed building rehabilitation projects to emulate in the neighborhood. The conversion of the McCracken warehouse was the first Leadership in Energy and Environmental Design (LEED) building to achieve Gold-level status in Oregon, and the first Gold-rated historic restoration in the United States.

◇ ◇ ◇

Meanwhile, another pivotal event in the history of the district was on the horizon. As a steppingstone, this project would further expand and anchor the southern boundary as the old warehouse district blossomed into the Pearl District.

To understand how the Pearl District evolved, one has to recognize that the River District was really a subset of the Pearl District. The River District's western edge was NW 12th Avenue, and the southern edge was Hoyt Street. It encompassed the surplus rail yards, Union Station and the immediate surrounding blocks including the railroad tracks between the railway station and Naito Parkway and portions of the riverfront.

In comparison, the Pearl District was much larger in area and was bounded by Burnside Street, the I-405 freeway, and the centerline of Broadway Street. However, on a practical basis, the Pearl was a marketing brand and reflected the triangular shape of the earlier Northwest Triangle District. The Pearl over time became a de facto cultural district.

The district was going to undergo further change. Residents, who now lived in more compact dwelling arrangements, some with balconies and others without, needed access to urban parkland. A theatrical company would find a new home in the district, and long-established services and business like a popular jazz club would disappear under the wrecking ball.

The district was now poised to experience another injection of mixed-use hustle and bustle. A five-block complex was beginning to percolate and take shape in an ex-biochemist's mind. He was imagining the magnetic attraction of Powell's Books and how the daily and weekend swarm of residents and tourists might respond to the availability of storefront boutiques lining nearby streets, the availability of off-street parking, and the chance to participate in a concentrated expression of urbanity.

PART FOUR

The Pearl District

An Expanding Mixed-Use Community

2001-2020

The Pearl District Timeline

An Expanding Mixed-Use Community

2001	Peter Walker Partners submits the Portland River District Park System Urban Design Study
2005	Hoyt Street Properties initiates master planning for land holdings north of Lovejoy Street
2006	The Brewery Blocks opens to the public
2007	The Metropolitan Tower is completed. An economic recession dampens new construction
2008	The City approves the North Pearl District Plan
2009	The City commits to the Burnside-Couch Couplet Improvement Plan
2009	The recession ends
2011	Mayor Sam Adams rejects the Burnside-Couch Couplet
2016	The City purchases the US Postal Service property
2016	Hoyt Street Properties' Cosmopolitan condo tower is completed

34

AN URBAN VILLAGE

GERDING EDLEN DEVELOPMENT BEGAN AS simple partnership and grew into a powerhouse company. By 2000, the Portland-based company had a national reputation for property investment, development, and asset management. The W+K project had been a single-block development. The company was now poised to tackle multiple blocks for redevelopment.

Bob Gerding was a native Oregonian who had begun his professional life as a biochemist and teacher. While working at Good Samaritan Hospital, he oversaw the build-out of the hospital labs, his introduction to project development. Mark Edlen's family had moved to Portland when he was a youngster. As a graduate of the University of Oregon's MBA program, he went to work as a real estate broker with Cushman Wakefield. Mark and Bob met, became friends, and found they had similar work dreams.

After a while Bob became less interested in running labs than in planning and building them. Mark found that working on a stack of papers at the end of the real estate process wasn't as rewarding as building a product people could work or live in. In 1994 they founded their partnership and began doing projects. Two years later, they incorporated the company as GED.

Mark has said of Bob, "He was the best big thinker I ever met and always sought out positive outcomes for all involved." That is a good trait to have when your company is about to tackle a big, complex project. And at the time of this story, GED was about to do just that. Ever since that day on the roof of the W+K building, they had been contemplating buying the brewery.

ACQUIRING THE BREWERY BLOCKS

GED had approached the current owner, the Stroh Brewing Company, with an offer. Stroh had bought the brewery in 1996 from the Pabst Brewing Company. Stroh declined GED's offer, saying, "We're not interested. We're going to brew beer forever."

Forever lasted until 1999, the year Stroh sold its beer labels, including the Henry Weinhard brand, to the Miller Brewing Company. The brewery complex ceased production, and Stroh closed the brewery operations. Stroh then contacted GED and informed them of a pending property sale. There was talk that the owner was going to sell off the blocks—bounded by NW 10th and 13th Avenues and NW Davis and Burnside Streets individually. Mayor Vera Katz intervened in the process due to Bob's suggestion that the blocks should be sold as a single parcel. The mayor recognized the wisdom in keeping the parcel intact. This allowed GED to buy the five-block complex known as the Brewery Blocks in 2000.

A huge part of the Brewery Blocks' story was the role Powell's Books played in the overall development. In 2022, the bookstore—Portland's number one tourist attraction—services about 3,000 customers every day, and, perhaps, another 3,000 visitors a day peruse their shelves. This kind of retail activity contributes immensely to the commercial power of this urban village. As a variety of national retail brands rented ground-floor storefront spaces, the area became a shopper's Mecca. Public officials then realized that the new development anchored the Pearl District to

Burnside Street and served as a bridge to future redevelopment in the downtown's west end.

◇ ◇ ◇

After acquiring the property, GED hosted a limited competition to select an architect. They asked two finalists to prepare a preliminary concept plan for the site. GBD Architects was one of the firms, and they were chosen to be the project architects. Phil Beyl, a principal at GBD, has said, "The single most overriding characteristic of this project was how unbelievably fast it came together."

The Brewery Blocks were now officially part of the Pearl. Bob had several big ideas. He could describe in detail the various components needed for the complex: office space, restaurants, shops, parking, a grocery store, and how the store would activate the street environment and, later, a new theater for Portland Center Stage. Bob may not have known precisely where each use would be located on which block, but he knew what the finished product was going to be, the lifestyle aspect, and the quality of the development. As a visionary, he knew that the "village" would be a catalyst in the overall evolution of the Pearl. And Mark could make things happen quickly. Together, they formed a perfect partnership.

MASTER PLANNING CONSIDERATIONS

GED had their architects prepare a master plan. As the architects began to explore several alternative approaches, their first instinct was to preserve a few of the existing structures, including the facade of the old A. B. Smith Chevrolet auto garage. The Art Deco facade was kept, but the guts of the old building were demolished, allowing construction of a new building. While wholesale historic preservation is not always feasible, preserving the building's exterior wall was a way to maintain the historical context of the old building. Since the partners were interested in historic preservation, both the Weinhard Brewhouse and the Portland Armory were viewed as prime candidates for adaptive reuse. Because of their historical importance, both were nominated and placed on the National Register of Historic Places.

The provision of off-street parking was deemed to be critical to the success of the project. When the developers first discussed financing with banking officials, Mark and Bob initially thought about providing surface parking. But at some point, Mark had commented that there nothing more deadly to the pedestrian environment than surface parking. Surface parking sucks the life out of the street environment.

After studying the parking issue, GED and their architects decided underground parking was the only way to satisfy the projected number of parking spaces needed to support the envisioned density of development. They decided to build three levels of parking. In this instance, the developer wanted to extend the parking structure under an existing public street, subject to approval by the City.

The City entertained the proposal, but a conflict arose concerning the depth of earth cover over the parking structure. The architects wanted minimal cover to minimize the depth of excavation to reduce construction costs. Public officials wanted eight feet of cover and the installation of empty conduit pipes for future infrastructure needs. The two parties resolved the issue by agreeing to hang utility pipes and future services underneath the proposed garage ceiling. Putting the parking underground was one of the best decisions the developers made, considering the demand for parking today.

ARCHITECTURAL DESIGN

As the architects turned their attention to building design, they had to decide what stylistic, architectural treatments were appropriate for this multiblock complex. Mark provided them with a clear direction: "We want big-boned buildings."

The architects believed the buildings needed to reflect structures that were "purpose-driven." There would be no-frills or adornment. In architectural terms, the buildings needed to be "heavy" and physical in the way they connected to the site. This implied the use of substantial columns or other elements that could lend a solid presence. The buildings also needed to be reflective of the past. The windows needed to look punched-in and appear to be functional.

What the developers wanted was a quasi-industrial look. They wanted buildings that reflected the general structural and visual character of the old industrial warehouses. They wanted the new buildings to visually fit into the existing architectural fabric. Looking at the replacement buildings, a pedestrian can see the architects followed the cornice lines of adjacent structures and paid attention to window placement to echo the physical characteristics of older warehouses nearby.

Bob and Mark told their architects to design the new buildings also around the way people behave. The architects started with the viewpoint that the elements of their design needed to promote the behavior they wanted to cultivate in the Pearl. By using program elements, including economic and financial analyses, they stitched together a complex set of uses. For example, there were no conventional means or standards on how to program housing over a grocery store.

The planning process associated with the Brewery Blocks produced what the developers and their architects called the Principles of Place: "Build community, create inviting spaces, minimize carbon footprint and energy dependence, connect people and buildings to nature, encourage transportation alternatives, craft the first 30 feet, inspire communities with art, make 20-minute living real, integrate schools and neighborhoods, preserve symbols that matter." The "twenty-minute living real" principle meant you should be able to walk, cycle, take transit, or drive to all everyday services and needs including work within twenty minutes. The notion of building an urban village was an expression of meeting this goal.

Architects are always thinking about design. Designing a multiblock complex allowed GBD Architects to explore a diversity of architectural styles on a block-to-block basis. Every building ended up with a distinctive appearance. Phil told me that the firm avoided a "project look" by using several different internal design teams. The underground garage had its own team, and they didn't know what was going to be built on top of it. Different teams were assigned to different blocks. Sometimes a team had to change their design orientation. For example, the Louisa started out as an office building but ended up as an apartment building. The architects didn't want a complex that looked like it had been designed by a singular hand. The goal was to have a complex that expressed a variety of architectural styles.

As the planning continued, the developer was also trying to respond to market forces. The ground floor on all blocks had to be committed to retail. They tried to do some second-floor retail, but it didn't work out. All the other floors were market-driven in terms of use.

The developers didn't have any specific thoughts when it came to a retail strategy. However, they went after Whole Foods to be the anchor tenant. This project was Whole Foods' first real estate deal in Portland. In those days, this grocery retailer was a young company. Bob had been looking for a home for them in Portland, and they were a perfect fit in the Brewery Blocks. When approached, Whole Foods took a while to commit to the project, but they eventually did.

Sustainability design was integrated into the project's design development phase of work. Dennis Wilde, a partner at GED Architects, was passionate about how sustainability could be incorporated into the development and design processes. Mark was supportive of the idea, and he responded with the statement: "Make this project environmentally responsible as far as you can—we just can't go broke doing it!" Dennis took on this challenge. He carefully selected consultants and contractors who embraced a sustainability approach. The developers never put stuff out to bid. They told their contractors they were going to marry contractor and subcontractor to the firm's architectural staff. As a team, they all worked to make the Brewery Blocks a very efficient and sustainable building project.

As the project ramped up, the developers got serious about the Leadership in Energy and Environmental Design (LEED) program. Back then, the US Green Building Council was just getting started. There was no LEED certification for neighborhoods. The company and Dennis learned as the job progressed, while getting LEED silver certified, then gold certified, and finally LEED platinum certified. As they grew more proficient at this process, it became much easier to incorporate LEED features, notwithstanding the fact they had always been building class A buildings anyway.

FUNDING AND IMPLEMENTATION

As the project moved from preparing a master plan, putting together a design program, developing a design, and conducting all the research those different phases demanded, everyone was conscious of the fact that project implementation required, at its core, financing. One of the reasons GED took on the project was that they had completed several successful mixed-use projects for which they had arranged the financing. One of their first projects was the Portland Development Services project in Portland's South Auditorium Urban Renewal Area. The developer had put together a financial master plan using a variety of financing sources—a subsidy here, a federal program there, a little bit of equity, et cetera. Because of this prior involvement, the Portland Development Commission (PDC) had played a role in financing the Brewery Blocks. They gave the project a low-interest loan to help fund the underground parking structure.

Implementation meant coordination with the City regarding design review, permitting, and construction. Therefore, code compliance was an extremely important aspect. The major projects group of the City's planning department—it was established in 1999—sat in on all the architect's design meetings. Phil told me the GBD staff and the City's staff got linked together for the duration of the project. The City assigned a senior planner to work directly with the developer and the architects to resolute issues as soon as they were identified, thereby expediting the permitting process.

THE POPULARITY OF TOURS

Once the project was completed, there were numerous requests from officials and professionals from as far away as Australia, New Zealand, China, and Japan who wanted to tour the Brewery Blocks. GED arranged with Portland State University's First Stop Portland tour service to handle those requests. Many wanted to know about the private-public partnership aspect of the development. How did it happen? How much public money was spent? Visitors wanted to see, learn, and understand how a multifaceted project like the Brewery Blocks was planned, financed, and built. These visitors also wanted to know why and how the Pearl District was such a successful urban renewal project.

Chinese officials specially wanted to know how the developers determined what buildings went where. They struggled to understand the concept of development that is market-driven. In China, they got incentives but no requirement to do this or that specifically in response to what market demand may or may not exist. The Chinese and others were always amazed at what they saw. They took pictures. But what they really wanted to take home was the recipe for the secret sauce—how do you achieve this kind of project? There appeared to be a fundamental difference in how urban development was accomplished within the USA and China. The secret sauce, whatever its specific recipe, may not be transferable.

◇ ◇ ◇

The partnership within Hoyt Street Properties was about to go through a shakeup. Homer Williams had a wandering eye. He was looking at another project, and he was considering selling his interest and shares in Hoyt Street Properties.

35

FILLING IN THE CHECKERBOARD

TIFFANY SWEITZER STARTED AT THE bottom of the ladder. The year was 1994. Six years later, she reached the ladder's top rung as the president and managing partner of Hoyt Street Properties.

Homer Williams sold his interest and shares in Hoyt Street Properties in 2000 to Joe Weston to settle an old debt. Now Joe and Clay Fowler were the moneyed partners in a partnership arrangement that had been thrown together by a set of cascading circumstances. Tiffany and Keith Vernon—he had been Joe's right-hand man for many decades—were the minor partners. Importantly, Joe's financial firepower would enable Hoyt Street Properties to become the dominant developer in the Pearl.

This foursome was now charged with filling their property checkerboard with new buildings. This was real-time Monopoly. Each block was the future site of a new building except for the designated park blocks. Soon, construction cranes began to dot the Pearl District skyline like exclamation points. Their prominence signaled that the Pearl District's urban form and scale were about to change—new buildings were about to rise to new heights, dwarfing the older warehouses and one-story service and retail shops. The mini era of the Northwest Triangle, characterized by the adaptive reuse of existing structures, was over. Modest vertical construction was the hallmark of the architecture associated with the emerging River District. Hoyt Street Properties was revving up its development engine, and Tiffany found herself sitting in the driver's seat with her hands on the steering wheel.

Tiffany recalled how difficult it was to build sixty condos in those early years. How could they get sixty or more people to live in this distressed area? She realized you had to have a good story to tell prospective lenders and then buyers. As buyers embraced the trendy loft-living lifestyle, the buy-in story became superfluous.

As Hoyt Street Properties moved forward with development, a master development agreement signed in 1999 with the City provided a blueprint the company had to follow. The document was legally binding and served as a series of integrated guidelines that governed what Hoyt Street Properties could and had to do. The Portland City Council also had strong design oversight through the design review process and commission. One of the main requirements in the agreement was that the developer had to provide affordable housing units in all proposed residential projects. The City required 30 percent of the housing units to be affordable based on a specified income level. Every residential project the developer built during a fifteen-year period had to meet this criterion. Sometimes the developer fell short.

By 2001, the Portland City Council had formally approved the *Pearl District Development Plan*. The executive summary in the plan stated:

The Pearl District Development Plan has been drafted by a 26-member steering committee, representing a wide range of viewpoints. The steering committee met over the course of a year to discuss the future of the Pearl District, to re-evaluate current plans and policies, and to focus on the development priorities for the neighborhood. The committee's initial ideas and concepts were reviewed at a public open house before undergoing further refinement through an intensive subcommittee process. The steering committee then created a draft plan that was reviewed at a second public open house before the steering committee made final recommendations. The Portland Development Commission funded this effort. The Development Plan has two elements: a vision statement and an action plan (to guide future development). The vision is a broad statement about the future of the neighborhood. The action plan includes supporting goals and objectives and identifies specific policies, guidelines, strategies, and projects that will be implemented in order to achieve the vision.

THE METROPOLITAN TOWER

Hoyt Street Properties initially worked with the architectural firm Ankrom Moisan. Later, Pat Harrington from BOORA Architects approached Tiffany. BOORA didn't have a lot of experience in the kind of residential buildings the Hoyt Street Properties was building at the time, but Tiffany decided to have a design competition for the planned Metropolitan building. She had the idea of constructing a taller building than the zoning regulations allowed. To exceed the 175-foot height limitation required a zone change. She also wanted a smaller floor plate. BOORA submitted a design proposal and won the competition.

At their first meeting with BOORA, Tiffany was introduced to John Meadows. She liked him immediately because he was seasoned, and he was a listener. So, she took a chance on John—and got lucky. They made a good team. He could translate her ideas into actionable plans. John became a kind of facilitator for Tiffany's interactions with the City. Both worked closely with Graham Clark—a city planner who was creative in solving building design and code issues for them. The Metropolitan is a good example of what can be done when people are willing to seek solutions outside the building codebook.

Design of the Metropolitan—a nineteen-story condominium tower housing 121 units and an additional fifteen attached loft-style townhomes—began in 2005. The tower was completed and opened in 2007. Selecting BOORA to design the Metropolitan was about constructing a quality building. Hoyt Street Properties wanted a more luxurious building, possibly due to criticism they had received from the architectural community on projects built south of Lovejoy Street. While the first array of buildings and streetscape improvements was considered an urban design success, many felt the district was not dense enough yet.

The site for the Metropolitan faced Tanner Springs Park. Graham was keenly interested in protecting the adjacent park from building shadows. The neighborhood association was also concerned about protecting the park, so the developer and architects started working with the association. In looking at the allowed density, they noted the developer could build a lot of floor area next to the park.

This led to an idea Tiffany and Graham shared. Perhaps the building should be set back from the park. Tiffany didn't want another "slab- or bar-type" building. The newly completed in-house master plan of Hoyt Street Properties landholdings by BOORA had proposed a zoning change to allow a 225-foot-high building, if they set the building back one hundred feet from the park block. A shadow study had been conducted. It demonstrated that if the structure was set back one hundred feet from the south and west sides of the park, there would be fewer shadows than if the structure was set at the zero lot line.

The neighborhood became involved in the review and assessment of the tower design because they believed the Brewery Blocks project felt dark and oppressive. In the past, most developers had proposed new structures using zero lot line construction. There were other people who thought pedestrians lost the sense of the sky because the buildings were so close together. The neighborhood association's leadership was intrigued by the idea of setting buildings back from the lot lines. They supported this zone change. In many ways, the Metropolitan became a poster child for an attitude shift about how to design and build in the Pearl.

In the final analysis, the floor plate for the Metropolitan only required a 9,400-to-9,500-square-foot footprint. This was pretty small compared to previously built structures in the neighborhood. Besides reducing shadows on the adjacent park, the new tower didn't block views from the Park Place building to the south.

AN INTERNAL MASTER PLAN

In 2005, BOORA began preparing a master plan for Hoyt Street Properties' land holdings north of Lovejoy Street. The work, accomplished in concert with Spencer & Kupper, the Portland Development Commission (PDC) and the City's Bureau of Planning, focused on providing consultant services in communicating and interacting with the city and neighborhood association. The architects decided to revisit how the 2.5:1 floor area ratio (FAR) regulations affected the remaining vacant blocks of Hoyt Street Properties in the Pearl District.

During the master planning effort, BOORA also started design work for Block 19—the site for the Encore. The neighborhood didn't like the first design for the Encore. It consisted of two bar buildings. However, the master planning effort continued, and a decision was made to give the City more parkland for what became The Fields. The building design then changed to reflect a single, curved footprint instead of the two separate buildings. The architects also had to coordinate the site design with landscape architect Peter Walker's boardwalk master plan and the open-space design. One of the outcomes was that the park got bigger. The final design of the Encore and the master plan happened concurrently. The master plan recommended that all the blocks adjacent to The Fields should allow new buildings up to a height limit of 225 feet.

The Cosmopolitan site was adjacent to The Fields site. This presented a problem. Tiffany wanted to build a high-rise structure taller than the 225-foot limit. She was thinking about constructing a hotel or a residential tower with a private recreation club. Everything else in the neighborhood was had a FAR of 4:1. Farther north, the FAR was 6:1 or 8:1. Hoyt Street Properties wanted to equalize the FAR for all the remaining undeveloped blocks.

The developer's master plan was nonbinding, so Tiffany decided to go to the planning commission and seek a height change. They needed to get the neighborhood association on board with an even taller tower design for the Cosmopolitan. There were lots of negotiations with the association. Tiffany wanted the City to initiate a process that involved the developers, the residents, city planners, Portland's urban design study group, and representatives from city bureaus. She wanted a holistic look at what should and could happen in the future north of NW Lovejoy Street. This was in keeping with planning the Portland Way.

However, before the City got involved, Hoyt Street Properties' consultants looked beyond the land the developer owned. They recognized that NW 13th Avenue was special, and they recommended special treatment at the north end of that street. The architects proposed a terminus feature—something akin to a plaza. They also suggested the surrounding land uses should include destination retail or corporate commercial activity and more residential use. The City then got involved in this private sector- initiated planning study, at the request of Hoyt Street Properties. Tiffany had offered a land gift to entice the City. The City accepted.

During the deliberations, an issue arose over train whistle noise. There had been lots of controversy about train-oriented noise in the past. Some regulations allowed noise reductions contingent upon improved rail crossings. Tiffany insisted that the City partner with them in a study of how to improve the pedestrian crossings to create associated "quiet zones" as part of the land gift deal.

The process supported a pedestrian gateway—a major pedestrian crossing to get to the river—and lent importance to what might happen at the north end of NW 13th Avenue. Unfortunately, BOORA's original vision of what could happen at the very north end of NW 13th Avenue faded away.

Afterward, Hoyt Street Properties sold some land at the north end of NW 13th Avenue to the City, enabling the construction of affordable housing. This real estate deal was compensation since the developers had failed in the past to provide an agreed-upon percentage of affordable housing units.

The master planning effort also looked at the setback exception that was being applied to the proposed Metropolitan building. The neighborhood voiced the notion: "Why are we limiting heights at all? Surprise. Many people, including city planners, were taken aback by this idea. What came out of this was a radical and innovative approach. They set some base heights, which applied to future buildings. However, if someone wanted a smaller floor plate—say a 12,500-square-foot floor plate as compared to previous buildings having 16,000-to-18,000-square-foot floor plates—then future heights were only limited by the designated FAR on a particular site. And the maximum FAR with bonuses was 9:1. You could start at a FAR of 4:1 and then add in a FAR of 2:1 as a housing bonus and, maybe, another bonus. This meant that as the footprint got smaller, the building could get taller, although economics and technology would still be the limiting factors in determining the final height of a tower.

This new approach set the stage for the possible construction of much taller buildings in the Pearl. In a few years, Hoyt Street Properties proposed the construction of a 350-foot-tall building with twenty-eight stories and two stories for mechanical use. The proposed footprint was eight thousand square feet and would be the smallest floor plate in the city. The Pearl had its first point tower proposal—the Cosmopolitan.

Local architects were shocked by this changed mind-set. The City didn't appear to be concerned about future building heights. What had happened reflected how collaborative efforts produced an innovative approach to increasing and fulfilling the City's goal for denser urban residential in the Pearl District. This process that began in 2005 had produced an updated district plan—a plan the City adopted as the North Pearl District Plan in 2008.

Here was a demonstration of how a creative private-public partnership could produce results unimaginable in previous years. Partnerships in Portland are built on lots of different ideas: shared values among participants, density tied to quality design, innovative problem solving, and solutions everyone can be proud of. It's remarkable what happened in the Pearl when you think back to the recommendations for low-rise, walkup housing in the mid-1970s, and later in 1980s, when a railroad company and Glacier Park proposed building an urban business park on what was Hoyt Street Yards.

CONDO SALES

Hoyt Street Properties sold a lot of condominiums before a downturn in the market. They had set up their own sales office—Hoyt Realty Group—and the sales staff had a front row seat when the housing market downturn arrived.

Around 2002, a headhunter sought out Marilyn Anderson. She was a private broker, and she'd been selling real estate for thirty years. Marilyn was seasoned, she was looking for a challenge, and she signed up to manage Hoyt Realty. When she started, some of the streets were in, and the streetcar was running on tracks surrounded by vacant blocks. Appraising the situation, Marilyn had her doubts.

Condo living was a new lifestyle choice in the city. Portlanders had generally lived in detached dwellings and rentals. She wasn't sure about the type of person who might want to live in a condo. These condos were relatively expensive, and she thought: *Is it a privileged lifestyle?* What she learned was that there were all kinds of people—professionals, empty nesters, people tired of living in the suburbs for whatever reason, young people, singles, couples, and speculators—but all wanted to experience city living.

◇ ◇ ◇

Those first condominium units were marketed and sold as urban lofts. People initially expected brick walls. However, with new construction, you usually didn't get that. As time passed, the term *lofts* became a marketing handle. In past years, Lofts, notably those with a classic, open floor plan were products resulting from the renovation of older warehouse buildings. The conversion of existing warehouse buildings along NW 13th Avenue had popularized the term locally. However, many of the lofts created by new construction were akin to compact studio apartments. Economics and early sale pricing had dictated much of what the market offered to buyers. There were larger condominium units, and, of course, there were penthouse units on the top floors of several mid-and high-rise buildings.

The developers also found that open floor plans weren't that popular. Instead, many buyers wanted walled in bedrooms because most prospective buyers were accustomed to four walls and window shades.

The Pearl turned out to be a good place for seniors. A person can walk to one of several grocery stores or the Good Samaritan Medical Center and other nearby medical services in the Northwest Neighborhood. Marilyn still believes, "It's a very good place to age in place."

Did Hoyt Realty have a special sales strategy? Not really. In fact, it was similar to the way detached single-family homes had always been sold. The company advertised using a lot of internet ads. It became common for people to just come into the sales office and see what was happening. The office had a mockup of a typical kitchen layout, brochures, and architectural models that people hovered over. People who had reserved a unit in a new project brought their friends in, and they would point out the location of the unit they wanted on the model. The sales office ended up functioning as an educational service, in a way, to those potential buyers. Eventually, many returned and wrote a check. Word of mouth was a big deal when it came to selling condos in the Pearl.

THE RECESSION

The real estate and condominium boom was at a peak when the Metropolitan was completed in 2007, and all the units sold quickly. Then, quite suddenly, major problems in the financial markets fueled a collapse in the real estate market. The national economy slid into a recession. Without available financing, condo sales in the Pearl took a nosedive. And it would take a long time for prices to go back up. Buyers with cash got good deals. Some units were sold for half the original listed price.

BOORA Architects had started designing for the Encore building, another luxury high-rise building, after the Metropolitan. The Encore was a sixteen-story condominium tower with 177 units and was completed in 2008 just at the start of the recession. Unlike the Metropolitan building that sold all its units in a month, the Encore took more than four years to sell all its units.

The Encore—the curved, arc-shaped building that looks onto a large open space called The Fields—was a good example of how bad things got. Hoyt Realty had forty-three sales contracts during construction. But construction got delayed, and then Fannie Mae changed their loan approval rules when the recession hit.

Previously pending building projects had to have 50 percent pending sales for loans to be processed and approved. That requirement changed to 75 percent. Loan money instantly dried up. At one point, all but one of the forty-three buyers at the Encore backed out. Tiffany told me she'd looked at the Encore one night back then. All the windows were dark except for a couple of illuminated windows in a single unit. Were the heydays gone?

Before, residential loans had been easy to get because people didn't have to verify their income. When the market blew up, people lost their jobs, people couldn't pay their mortgages, banks foreclosed on units, and getting a loan to buy a condominium was next to impossible. This also brought down the prices on existing condominiums.

While Hoyt Street Properties was building condominiums before the recession, the City was actively planning new parks in the Pearl District. The master development agreement required integrated open-space system so new residents would have outdoors place to use—to enjoy a sunny day outside, lie on the grass or sit on a bench, throw a ball or Frisbee, read, and people watch. These pioneering urbanities didn't know it, but in a few years they would be able sit on a park bench in an urban nature park and watch a bird dive-bomb fish in a pond.

36

PARKS FOR THE PEARL

PORTLAND'S HISTORIC NORTH PARK BLOCKS—A gift from Captain John H. Couch to the citizenry in 1865—are arranged in a row that begins at West Burnside and extends north to Glisan Street. Each of the five blocks are half the width of Portland's standard, square, short block. This urban park, with its towering tree canopy of leafy vegetation, sandwiched between NW 8th and Park Avenues, has always been a welcoming green oasis.

For decades, beginning in the 1980s, city planners and urban designers put forth an array of conceptual plans and ideas about extending this linear park to the Willamette River. Open space for the expanding Pearl District was going to be important, and Portland Parks and Recreation staff felt that future parkland needed to be functional, responsive to a variety of user needs. Community discussions had led to the idea of having separate, detached park blocks each with a distinctive theme. In 1998, the Pearl District Development Plan steering committee recommended that the first two public parks in the Pearl District be of "the quality of other downtown parks and open spaces" in Portland.

In 1999, Zari Zantner, the manager in charge of the Planning and Capital Development Division of Portland Parks and Recreation, was responsible for all decisions related to the design and development of the City's proposed open-space system. She realized the bureau had an opportunity to have major curatorial responsibility for all new park designs by establishing qualitative design standards. In a way, it could be a continuation of what Lawrence Halprin began with his nationally acclaimed fountain design in the earlier South Auditorium project.

As planning continued, Zari spent lots of time with Homer Williams. These new urban parks would have to be built on land parcels owned Hoyt Street Properties LLC. Homer had visited New York and had seen city parks that had been designed for a densely populated urban setting. With coaching, he began to realize the value of providing high-quality recreational facilities, and how the arts could play a key role in the evolution of the Pearl.

By 2000, the Tanner Creek Park and Water Feature Steering Committee and the Parks and Recreation Bureau had decided a third park was needed to service the growing resident population. The question of having different themes had been settled. Each of the three blocks would reflect a different theme.

Following those decisions, ZGF Architects refined the River District Vision Plan, which now depicted three disconnected park blocks that were arranged in a row between NW 10th and 11th Avenues from Johnson to Quimby Streets. These new parks were offset three blocks west of the North Park Blocks. Two of the blocks were first referred to as the South Park and the North Park. The third park, an oddly shaped parcel, had been envisioned as a large lawn area and as a gateway providing a connection from the Pearl District to the riverfront.

AN OPEN-SPACE FRAMEWORK PLAN

A deal was soon struck with Homer, and the development company donated land for the first new park block in the Pearl. Portland Parks and Recreation then decided to sponsor an invitational competition for open-space development in the district. Several out-of-town firms and a few local firms were invited to submit proposals in 2001. The winning submission was by the firm of Peter Walker and Partners (PWP) Landscape Architects of Berkeley, California, along with Opsis Architecture, a Portland firm. Zari and the selection committee felt that this joint effort set forth a "quiet, but elegant" scheme using high-quality materials.

Jim Kalvelage, a partner with Jim Meyer in Opsis Architecture, had called Peter about the competition. Peter flew to Portland and met Jim Kalvelage on-site, and they walked the ground. Both felt the site was a wonderful blank canvas next to downtown. The challenge, they realized, was how to tie together three disconnected blocks. This notion of connectivity then became the central principle they adopted for their master plan. The underlying plan concept was to connect all three parks with a boardwalk and then extend a pedestrian walkway over to the Willamette River.

All their interaction was done over one sunny afternoon, as the submission was due almost immediately. After dividing up the tasks, Jim did a drawing of the concept. To sell their submission, PWP first prepared a master plan around the idea of a boardwalk plus a design concept sketch plan for each of the three individual parks. These ideas were packaged into a master plan report dated January 16, 2001, and submitted to the City of Portland.

The master plan focused on the boardwalk as a device to connect the three parkland blocks. A park block encircled by building facades can be thought of a "public green or focus park." The park would be a focal feature for the surrounding buildings—a forecourt or commons. At this type of park, pedestrian movement is limited to the open space within the park. By contrast, linear park spaces encourage "pedestrian movement along or between activities." The landscape architects at PWP were wrestling with the idea of establishing a common framework for the design of each individual park block, while at the same time encouraging pedestrian movement between the three proposed park blocks. PWP was trying to solve this conundrum and connect the open space to the Willamette River Greenway Trail as previous planning efforts had envisioned.

As Peter explained, the open-space master plan for the district had three basic ideas: The first was using a linear boardwalk to connect the three separate parks. Second, the design concept for the park treated Tanner Creek as a metaphor for an aquifer. Years ago, the creek had been redirected into an underground pipe with an outfall at the river near Centennial Mills. The aquifer metaphor was simply about the presence and continuation of water and the fact the designers felt it was important to recognize the historical significance of the creek. Third, a series of outdoor galleries was added along the boardwalk to allow for new outdoor activities in each of the individual park blocks. PWP had recognized that the River District was developing as a mixed-use area with different overlays, including education and the arts, similar to what had happened in SoHo in New York City.

DESIGNING JAMISON SQUARE

Jamison Square—originally referred to as South Park in the framework study—was built first. Owing to a central water feature, this park became a popular multifunctional public space. The design incorporated a low, terraced stonewall constructed of stacked and stepped stones as a central feature of the fountain. Still water spills out between the stones and continues to flow into a paved half-circular area, forming a shallow pool. When the flow is turned off, the water drains away leaving a paved surface that becomes a stage for public events. The fountain also became a magical magnet for kid's water play after it opened in 2002. The stonewall feature divides the park into two slightly unequal halves.

Just beyond the hard paved surface, a lawn invites people to sit or lie, relax, people watch, talk with friends, or read. A few tree plantings now offer shade. Chairs have been added for visitors to stop and linger in the park.

The organizing principle for the square's form was based on a concept of "clipping layers" of activities onto the boardwalk. That's why you get a walk, a gallery, a water fountain, and a meeting place at Jamison Square. The other, smaller half of the park was left as an open public space with a decomposed gravel surface. Five rows of tightly spaced hornbeam trees form a closely spaced grouping of trees. The landscape architects conceived of this as a flexible cultural space suited for special events or an outdoor art gallery. The presence of a brightly colored sculpture in a circular patch of grass attests to this notion.

Peter had admired Lawrence Halprin's Lovejoy Fountain in Portland. He appreciated the dramatic appeal of this outstanding fountain design with its cascading waterfalls and the fact that kids and young adults played in the water. Peter considered who would use the fountain and figured there would be children either living in the neighborhood or visiting their grandparents—he was well aware that seniors would own many of the condos in the district. Peter liked the notion of a fountain as a place for water play. Kids of all ages delighted in the age-old practice of splashing about in a pool of water. This was an excellent instance of conceptual transference.

Peter was prescient. That is exactly what happened. The fountain became a magnet attracting area residents and visitors. On a sunny, hot day, carloads of suburbanites brought their children to play in the water. What hadn't been anticipated was the level of popularity. Some residents were concerned that a suburban gaggle had invaded their domain. This prompted the need for a public restroom, which was installed in a corner of the park.

The design of the shallow pool proved to be problematic. The original water level near the cascading water fountain was too deep for small kids and was deemed a public safety hazard. Nowadays, the water level is controlled to avoid any chance of an accidental drowning.

The boardwalk along NW 10th Avenue was constructed using wood planks to recall an earlier era. The walking surface is twenty feet wide but expands in one place to twenty-eight feet and acts as a porch to the adjacent pedestrian galleries. The design intent was to encourage the presence of vendor carts and maybe even temporary exhibits adjacent to the boardwalk in the future, thereby attracting more pedestrian activity and enlivening the ambiance of Jamison Square.

The pedestrian galleries were proposed in the master plan as a common feature in all three future park blocks. Peter's thought was that "as one walked down the boardwalk, these layered connections to the outdoor gallery spaces would just become apparent to joggers, runners, and people riding the trolley as they passed by the parks blocks." PWP simply wanted to magnify the sense of urban theater in the district.

Apparently, Portland-based arts groups had told PWP they could fill the gallery spaces with art and people every Sunday. The mantra would be "a place for people to put art outdoors." The landscape architects viewed the gallery spaces as something a little more than a flea market or an art fair but less than an outdoor museum exhibition area. It was envisioned as a grassroots project with, perhaps, some local institutional support.

DESIGN CONTROVERSY

The designs for both Jamison Square and later Tanner Springs Park were not without controversy or challenge. Zari had to deal with a controversial issue when a cancer survivors' memorial was proposed for Jamison Square a charity group of breast cancer survivors had petitioned to insert a memorial element in the park design. Both Portland Parks and Recreation and a community neighborhood group rejected this request as inappropriate.

The square was named to honor William Jamison, who had died recently. He had been a local artist, a gallery owner, and leader in the local art scene. The City had had a restriction on naming a park after an individual unless there was at least a three-year period between their death and the designation. Zari persuaded the powers that be that this restriction should be lifted in this instance. Because of Zari's intervention and forceful insistence,

Jamison Square now honors William Jamison's contribution to the arts community and the city.

A BIT OF NATURE IN THE DISTRICT

The North Park had been referred to as the Wetland Park in the earlier open-space-system master plan. When the second park opened in 2005, it was renamed Tanner Springs Park. The park's design strayed from the master plan vision due to the influence of both the advisory committee and Herbert Dreiseitl, the park designer.

During the design process, Paige Powell, a local arts activist, introduced a proposal by Maya Lin, the architect who had designed the Vietnam War Memorial in the nation's capital. Maya Lin was interested in installing a landform sculpture similar to an earlier artwork she had completed called Wave Fields. This artwork featured a grass lawn sculpted in a continuous series of rolling and undulating mounds and depressions in contrast to a flat plane. The Pearl Art Foundation, under Paige's directorship, had pledged to raise $380,000 to cover the installation.

Incorporating Maya's proposed installation raised a couple of issues: First, it would have occupied about one-quarter of the site. Second, the concept was not site-specific. It did not grow out of this location and did not appear to complement the quiet, meditative character that had been recommended by the steering committee. District residents were vocal about the design; they did not want another child-friendly park. Residents felt the "waves" could attract children's playground activity. They felt Jamison Square already filled that need.

Zari, now the director of Portland Parks and Recreation, recognized there was a serious conflict. She had several telephone discussions with Maya, who realized her proposal had become too controversial. Maya, after conversations with Herbert, withdrew her proposal.

◇ ◇ ◇

Once the design for Tanner Springs was completed, it became apparent that Atelier Dreiseitl had embraced a totally different approach than had been suggested in the open-space master plan by PWP. Herbert, a multi-talented landscape architect, urban planner, and artist, had an international reputation for sustainable design using water as a focal point. Dreiseitl's design features a lily pond as the central feature in Tanner Springs park.

Tanner Springs looks inward; it induces stillness and calmness. The design of the park reflects the historical fact the site was a wetland before European settlement. The dominant water feature—a reference to the past presence of Tanner Creek—is a shallow pond filled with islands of water lilies. Construction of the artificial pond and an associated wetland required extensive site excavations and a retaining wall. Herbert designed the retaining wall as an art feature he called an Art Wall; it is an integrated component with the extension of the wooden boardwalk along the east side of the park.

The Art Wall was built using random lengths of recycled steel rails that were donated by Portland Terminal Railroad. The rusted rails were installed in angled upright positions between the pool and the interior edge to the wooden boardwalk, which extends along the east side of this park block. Hundreds of pieces of translucent fused blue glass enhanced with painted images were adhered to the wall's undulating surface.

Stepped, grassy terraces along the north and south sides of the park provide informal seating for park visitors. Visitors can enter and traverse the park's interior using a network of paved paths and a floating pontoon walkway that meanders across the lily pond. A variety of landscape treatments, including an open lawn along the west side of the park, decorative shrubbery, ornamental grasses, and wetland plants, add texture and color—all imparting visual landscape appeal to an unconventional urban park setting.

AN EXPANSE OF OPEN LAWN

The Fields was the third and last of the parks built in the Pearl. Opened to the public in 2013, it is the largest of the three parks—3.5 acres of grassy open space as compared to the other two parks, which each occupy slightly less than an acre of land. PWP's boardwalk design was extended and terminated at The Fields. The wood planking ends abruptly at an oval-shaped lawn known as the Yard.

However, the overall design for The Fields departed radically from what was suggested in PWP's master plan. In response to existing site conditions and budget constraints, the Office of Cheryl Barton (O|CB)—the San Francisco firm that designed the park—changed the design alignment associated with a proposed boardwalk in the PWP master plan.

Prior to design and construction of The Fields park, the community and neighborhood association were adamant the planked walkway should continue as a straight alignment. The abrupt ending now appears to reflect an unfinished condition—less than satisfactory to many. Uncertain as to why the boardwalk ends so unceremoniously, I spoke with Cheryl.

She explained that by the time The Fields design was initiated, seven years had passed since the City had first received the open-space master plan. By then, the neighborhood and its attitude toward the design of this future park had changed dramatically. Families with children and dog owners wanted unobstructed open space.

O|CB inherited several design program elements when they began the project, including a public dog park. Pearl residents also wanted a structured playground with equipment for children. Since sustainable site drainage from paved areas in the park was an important issue, the design had to include rain gardens. More importantly, because the site was a known brownfield, it became necessary to cap the site for health concerns and sculpt the new landform with several feet of clean fill. This raised the grade level a few feet higher than the surrounding topography.

Contaminated soil wasn't the only serious difficulty O|CB had to face. The firm had to deal with the unresolved status of the Centennial Mills riverfront site. Many Portlanders wanted to preserve and redevelop the historic structures; others thought preserving the old buildings was foolish. Time and weather had accelerated rot in the buildings, and there was no official rehabilitation/redevelopment plan approved by the City for Centennial Mills. This meant there was no way to plan and design a termination for a proposed pedestrian bridge over to the riverfront.

PWP's master plan had proposed a boardwalk that would have bisected the park while terminating at a ramped aerial walkway that connected to a future pedestrian and cycle bridge over Naito Parkway and the adjacent railroad tracks. The purpose of the elevated bridge was to provide access to the riverfront and the Willamette Greenway. Since the community at large still supported this "big idea," the park designers had to find a way to provide for a future ramp connection.

Landscape architects at O|CB had found a design solution that allowed for the eventual construction of the pedestrian bridge. The designers decided the northerly portion of the curved pathway could be extended and elevated as a new bridge alignment in the future. Like many people in the Portland community, the designers felt the provision of the bridge was essential to give residents and visitors in the Pearl District access to the riverfront. Conversely, people using the Willamette Greenway would also have access to the district.

Like many projects, funding for this park was tight. The project was initiated at the beginning of the 2008 recession. As both the national and local economic situation worsened, the park's construction budget kept shrinking.

However, according to Cheryl, the most challenging factor had been the rapidly changing demographics of the neighborhood. The design was accomplished during a period of intense urban evolution as several high-rise buildings were built around the park.

Cheryl believes The Fields and the surrounding urban fabric will be a different place in five years, a different place in ten years, and definitely in twenty years, they will be a really different place. The looming question is: what kinds of open space and recreation needs will residents require in the long-term?

For many years, Portland's traffic engineers had wanted to address pedestrian safety concerns associated with segments of West Burnside Street. Now both public agency and community planning efforts for the Pearl District had revealed that an active constituency had formed to promote the idea of converting segments of Burnside on both sides of the Willamette River as part of a couplet street improvement project.

AN UNFINISHED COUPLET

THE BURNSIDE BRIDGE WAS THE key link in a major arterial route that connected the east side of the Willamette River to the city downtown and westward to the Tualatin Valley. Transportation planners had considered converting portions of East and West Burnside as part of a traffic improvement project. The idea meant segments of West Burnside would become a couplet with Couch Street. Residents living on Couch Street in the Henry Condominiums Tower were angry about this idea.

Couch, a low-trafficked neighborhood street, had always provided access and curbside parking for a concentration of boutiques, Powell's, and other retail shops. The tower fronted onto Couch Street, and the bookstore was directly across the street. The surrounding blocks exhibited the ambiance of an urban shopping village. Condo owners and shop proprietors feared disruption to business due to construction activities and increases of traffic volumes and higher vehicular speeds common to one-way traffic flow.

Many thought this was a disastrous idea. Others strongly endorsed the proposal. People like Mike Powell, the owner of Powell's Books, and Vic Rhodes, the executive director of the nonprofit Friends of Burnside-Couch, were major supporters of the project. Businesses had donated at least $100,000 to promote the proposal throughout the city.

Vic, a former city traffic engineer, felt the heavy, arterial, bifurcated traffic currently using West Burnside divided downtown from the developing River District. To Vic, the underlying issue was safety. Pedestrian safety had been, and continues to be, an issue. It is dangerous for pedestrians to cross Burnside, where there are few pedestrian signals. Historically, a dangerous "hot spot" was the un-signalized crossings at NW 8th and 9th Avenues.

Vic also felt that increased traffic flow wasn't a key issue. He believed projected traffic volumes wouldn't be much higher than existing levels. There was also talk about reducing traffic speeds with posted signage.

Mark Edlen, who had directed development of the Brewery Blocks, was strongly opposed to the couplet scheme. In 2006, as the proposed couplet design project was initiated, Mark was critical of the couplet proposal saying, "Our development company deliberately has tried to create a pedestrian-friendly environment. A couplet would be a threat especially now that Portland Center Stage has relocated to the newly renovated Gerding Theater at the Armory."

PREVIOUS IMPROVEMENTS IDEAS

Making several blocks of West Burnside part of a couplet was not a new idea. The street was and continues to be characteristically different from most of the major roadways in downtown Portland. Many Portlanders likened it to an inner-city highway. Historically, traffic flow and congestion had increased on this major aerial street as the city expanded in population. This congestion resulted in frequent fender-benders. In 1966, the City published a report, *West Burnside Improvements Alternate Plans*. Based on statistics, the city traffic engineer had described Burnside between the river and NW 23rd Avenue as "the most dangerous street within the City." The report recommended the implementation of a full-length couplet between NW 2nd Avenue and 24th Place.

By 1999, there was a consensus among Portlanders that Burnside needed major improvements. Besides reducing congestion, improving traffic flow, providing more on-street parking, and making the street safer for pedestrians, transportation planners saw an opportunity to alter the physical character of Burnside from the North Park Blocks westward to where the roadway crosses the I-405 freeway. This was possible because segments of street had rights-of-way with two different widths. From the river to the North Park Blocks, there was a one-hundred-foot right-of-way. To the west, the width was only sixty-six feet. The eastern segment had two traffic lanes and a parking lane on either side of a treed boulevard median strip. The western segment had no curbside parking and no street trees. Turning Burnside into a one-way street with on-street parking and street trees seemed to invite an easy conversion.

The City, with the support of then Transportation Commissioner Sam Adams, went ahead with preliminary engineering studies. By 2006, the City had prepared an analysis for a Burnside-Couch couplet scheme. This study linked the couplet concept with the idea of including a streetcar line that might cross the Burnside transportation corridor. A year later, Lloyd Lindley, a Portland landscape architect, headed a new study that produced a Phase I concept development plan for the Burnside-Couch transportation corridor. Lloyd and his team continued work on a Phase II Catalyst Development Study. By 2009, the City was fully committed to the Burnside-Couch couplet project at an estimated cost, in 2006 dollars, of $80 million.

Congressman Earl Blumenauer was able to secure federal funding for the construction of the eastside portion of the proposed couplet. Unfortunately, Congressman David Wu didn't advocate for or secure any funds for the westside segment. Subsequently, politics and lack of money influenced then Mayor Sam Adams's decision—Sam had been elected mayor in 2008—about the westside portion of the proposed couplet.

Michael Powell had spent twelve years working on the couplet scheme, spearheading an effort to create a limited improvement district of businesses located along the Burnside corridor. He had viewed the project as a hallmark boulevard vision. Before the final decision on the couplet, he said, "I think it would be unfortunate if we lose this opportunity. It's a street that's not working to anyone's satisfaction. It's been a sad area for a long time, there's been a lot of drug dealing [there]." He felt increased traffic on Couch would bring more "eyes on the street" to the Old Town area.

As the planning effort sputtered along, he became frustrated. He was more than sorry to see the couplet idea rejected by the mayor.

Looking back on what happened: A plan was put together. The mayor came on the scene. He held an open town meeting, opposition arose, and the mayor caved. That's an oversimplification, but the perception remains that the mayor bowed to certain business interests. On June 22, 2011, Mayor Adams announced on his website that he wasn't going to push for the controversial $80 million Burnside-Couch couplet project. In effect, he terminated the westside portion of the project. However, the controversy that engulfed the couplet concept did not threaten proposed improvements on the east side of the Willamette River. They were built at the cost of $17.8 million and opened for public use in 2010.

As of 2022, West Burnside continues to be a designated high-crash corridor. The City continues to recognize the inherent traffic and safety hazards associated with vehicular, cyclist, and pedestrian modes of movement within this multi-mode corridor. Site-specific improvements continue to be studied and implemented to reduce hazards. No new corridor-wide vision is on the horizon.

Every city has a development cycle, but Portland, as well as the nation, was going to undergo a major business cyclic downturn—an economic recession. Pearl developers who had condominium buildings under construction now faced a serious problem.

38

BOOM, BUST, AND BOOM

THE PEARL DISTRICT EXPERIENCED A real estate boom from early 2000 to 2008. Real estate statistics from 2005 to 2008 indicate Portland saw the construction of slightly more than 4,600 condominium units. During the following decade, the number of condos built in the city totaled slightly fewer than 900.

Buyers had lined up to reserve or buy a condominium unit under construction. At the height of this boom, many of the buyers were speculators. As a form of real estate gambling, it was a safe bet, for a while.

People made a profit by reserving or buying and later selling the unit in the short-term as demand pushed up prices. This is called "flipping." Some individuals walked away with profits approaching six figures. Later, when the boom went bust, sales bottomed out, and buyers walked away from their reservations and down payments. As the recession lingered, some new condo buyers got great deals and steals—sometimes at fifty cents on the dollar. Condominium owners who had purchased their sky homes at full price were left with a bad taste in their mouth.

Condominium developers fortunate enough to have not started construction shelved their projects. Many who had already started construction decided to convert their projects to apartment buildings.

Hoyt Street Properties LLC completed the Encore project in 2008. Joe Weston had bankrolled this sixteen-story structure with 177 condominium units. Now Joe found himself in a pickle. If the value of the building became lower than the loan debt, the bank would consider the loan underwater or upside-down.

MAKING A BAD LOAN RIGHT

Joe was Hoyt Street Properties' moneyman. He fulfilled the role of the financier. Joe hadn't had partners in the past, and in general, Joe still doesn't like to have partners. Now he was stuck with partners; he had inherited Homer William's. Joe had taken a leap of faith with Tiffany Sweitzer and his partners when he asked the bank for a loan on the Encore building. In response, his banker simply asked Joe how much money he needed, and the bank approved the loan request with no further questions.

This was a signature loan. Joe had been a successful real estate developer for many years, building thousands of apartment units on the eastside. He was known as the "Apartment King of Portland." Joe's bank approved all his loan requests for a simple reason—all his loans were recourse loans. He personally guaranteed them. Joe does recourse loans for a simple reason—he demands a better rate and gets a better loan.

When the recession hit, Joe went to Wells Fargo to speak with his banker about his loan on the Encore. Joe said, "Well, we are in a hell of a mess now, aren't we?" His banker told him, "If you pay it down $20 million, we'll just leave the loan intact" Joe wrote as big check because, to him, it was good business practice.

Most developers use nonrecourse loans, which means they can walk away from a bad deal. However, sometimes, walking away can have severe consequences on property values at and near distressed buildings. Hoyt Street Properties didn't want that to happen to their investments in the district. The company didn't make what they thought they'd make on the Encore project. But by paying down the decreased value of the Encore building, they protected this investment. They also did this to protect the combined value of their existing stock of building in the district and future unit sales. Six or seven years later, this proved to be a smart move.

BUILDING IN THE NORTH PEARL

The Portland City Council had approved the North Pearl District Plan in late 2008. This plan amended an urban design and guideline framework for ongoing development north of Lovejoy Street in what remained of the old industrial area sandwiched between the I-405 freeway and the Willamette River. Besides amending zoning for the three parks in the PWP master plan, the plan created step-down zoning around future buildings to ensure more sunlight reached these parks, confirmed the need for improved connections to the waterfront as well as a commitment to rehabilitate Centennial Mills, and addressed community-building strategies concerning the need to provide more diverse housing opportunities, public amenities, notably incentives to encourage market rate and affordable housing development.

The plan also revised and doubled the existing floor area ratio to allow for increased housing densities. These regulatory changes helped shape the architectural form of a future high-rise project—a point tower with a more compact footprint, the Cosmopolitan.

The recession had put a damper on construction for a short while. But by now, the Pearl District was on the radar of out-of-town developers. Backed by financing from insurance companies and other institutions, many developers were eager to build in the district, notably to take advantage of the increased building heights allowed under new zoning regulations.

A BUILDING TO SELL VIEWS

The company lost no time in deciding to build another project, a condominium tower. This was a year or two before 2014. Joe, however, was reluctant to do another condominium project. To get Joe on board to do the Cosmopolitan, Tiffany told Joe he was the only person in town who could do another condominium project at this point in time. Which was true. But it took a year for that idea to take root. Once Joe agreed to build the Cosmopolitan, he wanted to do it his way. This was hard for Tiffany because usually he'd let her make most of the early architectural decisions.

Joe hired an architect. However, the architect he chose didn't have the right experience. Tiffany had to convince Joe to change architects. She laid out her argument listing how the firm Joe had chosen might get them into trouble. Joe gave in. He told her, "You deal with it; you take care of it."

Tiffany and others had always known the block between Tanner Springs and The Fields was special. They initially thought the building put there should be tall, have a glass facade, and capitalize on the views that were available in all directions. The project was going to be all about "selling views."

They ended up having another limited competition. But in the end, they choose a firm with whom they had a working relationship. BORA got the job. That's not a misspelling. New leadership had replaced BOORA's old leadership, hence, the new name.

Once BORA was on board, the project kicked off with a meeting attended by John Meadows. He was the project architect. Joe was adamant about the design—he wanted a tall tower. In 2007, Joe had developed the Benson Tower in Portland near the South Park Blocks. Joe liked the idea of high-rise towers that had been built and popularized in Vancouver, BC. He wanted a point tower without really knowing what that was except that it was a tall building with a small footprint and square rooms. What he really wanted was a *standout* building.

John and his associates were tasked with taking design and site principles generic to the point towers associated with the Vancouver False Creek Neighborhood and applying them to a site in the North Pearl. Subsequently, the decision was made to build a tower with a small floor plate, less than eight thousand square feet. The zoning in that area had changed to reflect an unlimited building height as long as the design remained below a 12,500-square-foot floor plate. The new zoning changes had pushed developers toward tall buildings.

When I first spoke to John, he gave me some insights as to why Tiffany had decided to be the first developer to return to building condominiums instead of apartment buildings, which was the safe play at the time. Hoyt Street Properties always thought of the Cosmopolitan site as their marquee property. Smart thinking. The partnership was always testing the market, and they had seen that the demand for condominiums was coming back after the recessionary period. They wanted to capitalize on that.

John also told me that the City of Portland had financial, economic, and density goals the proposed tower could satisfy. There were also nature-oriented goals that suggested having point towers with compact bases allowed better views between groups of buildings. Looking west along Pearl District streets, one can see the forested West Hills. A skinny tower would also allow light to penetrate to the adjacent park block and open spaces around the building.

Correct positioning of the Cosmopolitan tower on the site was critical. The architects located the building in the southwest corner of the site to get the best views given the tower's relationships to the other buildings around it. Brad Dempy noted, "It was the best place so all the tall buildings around us could see around us, and our tower could see around them. We also had to do a shadow study to indicate what the shadows would be on the park versus what the building-zoning balloon would allow. We were able to show an improvement over what was allowed."

The Cosmopolitan had to go through a design review with the City's Design Review Commission. The commission approved the design with no confrontation. There was a lot of excitement about building this project after the recession. There was an air of optimism about having condominiums for sale again in the marketplace.

◇ ◇ ◇

Tiffany was convinced, as a developer, that people are most concerned about the interior of a building. How livable is it in terms of its layout, finishes, closet space, et cetera, et cetera? She was also cognizant of the fact people will tell their friends what the building they live in looks like. This meant the tower's exterior design had to exhibit a high degree of architectural flair compared to what they had previously built.

The Cosmopolitan turned out to be an exceptional building—it is the company's signatory building. Cost-wise, the Cosmopolitan, completed in mid-2016, was the most expensive building the company had ever built, and their most profitable venture. That profitability was achieved with penthouse units selling for upward of $3.8 million. Tiffany was most surprised to see that the building sold out in four months.

Another surprise was that the Cosmo—an obvious nickname— was the first building out of the company's previous fourteen buildings where the ground-floor retail leased up at the same time as the residential units sold out. Usually, retail lagged for months and sometimes more than a year.

Condominium prices at the Cosmo were expensive, but that didn't seem to put off buyers. Although, at the time, there hadn't been any new condos available in the marketplace for several years, and Tiffany told me that she had felt there was a level of pent-up demand for ownership since apartments rents had soared in the last years of the recession.

She also mentioned that there was no other product of this type on the market. Many of the unit floor plans had living rooms with floor-to-ceiling glass windows that intersected at the corners. This offered viewers panoramic views with multiple sightlines. The Cosmo had also attracted buyers wanting the "next, latest, greatest thing." Among the buyers, 40 percent of the people who bought units were seniors. What was even more surprising was that half of all sales were cash deals.

◇ ◇ ◇

There were only four units available for sale when I toured the building with Tiffany in March 2017. We took the elevator to the fourth floor and entered a two-bedroom unit. It was a very compact floor plan. Entering the open kitchen/living area, I was amazed by the floor-to-ceiling glass wall that greeted me. I had a wide-angle view of Tanner Springs Park and a collection of buildings and rooftops that faded away to the south. This was a view to hook a buyer. To my right, the glass wall continued around a building corner where the glass planes met at a right angle. Pivoting to my right, I had a grand view of the forested West Hills. Further along, the window ended at a small balcony that had been cut into the exterior skin of the building.

That recessed balcony feature—they were stacked vertically on the building's exterior—became a signature design element the designers called "a zipper." The zippers were the vertical offsets on the building's facades, owing to the presence of the balconies and the distribution of three basic floor plate designs in the building. The top floors contained three units. As one descended toward the ground level, there were five units and then six units per floor. So, the zippers reflected how the pro forma affected the distribution of units while also relieving the monotony of a tall vertical tower with a change of texture and shadow play on the building facades.

Before leaving the building, we stopped in the lobby. Tiffany introduced me to Deb, the concierge. The building is staffed 24/7. Besides the obvious—the tall building, the modern look, clean lines, et cetera, et cetera—the building is a comfortable home for the two hundred or more residents disbursed over 150 units. The resident population is mixed, lots of diversity—seniors, families, and singles. It's a glass tower, but it's not an ivory tower.

THE LAST BLOCKS
By 2016, Tiffany and her partners had considered selling what remained of the undeveloped blocks of land. There were only five blocks left. It would have been an opportune time to sell because

the company had virtually no debt, so the company was able to sell one or more of these blocks. They had looked at their land more closely than they had ever done in the past because they had never wanted to sell any of the blocks before.

Now they were all getting older. Financially, the remaining undeveloped blocks were worth a fortune. So, they'd had discussions. There was a strong feeling they should sell some of the land. Joe disagreed. Joe wanted to do another condo project. So, in 2017, the developers began the Vista project.

Joe felt the Vista could be successful since there was still no interest by others in building condos in the Pearl. During a meeting, he told me, "People who live in the area want to stay in the area. And some of the renters who are paying very high rent want a chance to buy something, so they can get some appreciation." Joe also mentioned that there were a lot of "jumpers" in their buildings. He was talking about people who move from building to building within a developer's portfolio. They make a profit off each jump. Because of this, a soft opening was planned for the Vista to give people who rented in other buildings first chance at a new unit at the Vista. Joe had told me that the Vista was going to be different because the design included extra-long, exterior decks. Joe wanted the decks to run the full length of the unit—up to fifty feet in some instances.

Many, if not most, of the new condominium owners at the Vista will probably enjoy those decks, but I remembered a comment Tiffany made to me about lessons learned after completing the Cosmopolitan project. She said that the company was back to building a functional living space versus concentrating on the exterior of the structure.

Both Homer and Tiffany, each at a different time in the past, had tried to envision what their primary mission was and how to accomplish it. In a conversation with Tiffany in 2018, I asked her what her thoughts were when she became managing partner.

She told me she "couldn't see the future…none of us could. I just wanted to prove myself in a way I didn't realize at the time. Part of it was because I was related to Homer, and I wanted to get away from him."

Tiffany had wanted to prove to herself that she could do something on her own. She had started out working for Pat Prendergast and Homer Williams. She had sat, listened to, and learned from both of them. When she became company president, she realized it would take a lot of work to accomplish the stories Homer and others had been saying about what *could* happen. She also realized she wanted to make money. What she really wanted…was to become a successful developer. She wanted to make something happen.

She has overseen the construction of fourteen multiuse residential buildings. It was and is striking that a woman succeeded in Portland's male-dominated developer's club. She surely had to work double time to get money, recognition, and respect.

When I asked Tiffany in 2019 if she had succeeded in her job, she gave me a mixed answer. Her short answer was: She doesn't feel she's finished yet. She has more work to do. She wants to do something better on the remaining projects. She knows she's not finished, and one of her main thoughts was: *What's missing from the Pearl?* The company had played it safe most of the time. Tiffany had wanted to do a deal with Four Seasons, but she couldn't get her partners to support the idea. Time was running out, and Tiffany was thinking, *Can we still do something great?*

It may not be very easy because her partners are getting older and thinking about selling. Joe is in his early eighties. He had suggested building some storage facilities. Fast money.

By 2019, Hoyt Street Properties' landholdings were down to five properties—Blocks 23, 24, 26, 27, and 29—all near the I-405 Fremont Bridge. All had been built on or committed for specific uses except for one block. A portion of Block 26 had been developed as a multistory affordable housing project called Vibrant. The remaining half-block remnant of Block 26 was still undeveloped. The Abigail Apartments, an affordable residential project sponsored by the City, now occupied Block 27.

Joe had always wanted to build a self-storage facility in the Pearl. He'd built a bunch of them on Portland's Eastside. He and Tiffany had spent a couple of years planning a facility on the triangular-shaped Block 29, the parcel closest to the bridge. Joe was adamant people buying and living in Pearl condo units needed extra storage space. The growing number of renters throughout the inner city also suggested a high demand for storage space away from people's personal living space.

As Tiffany considered the permitting process for this utilitarian type of use—in contrast to what they previously built—she came up with a different approach. Tiffany came up with the idea of providing a mini public plaza as part of this proposal. Since Joe liked roses, Tiffany suggested they include a columnar sculpture depicting a rose in the plaza design. Ivan McLean, a sculpture artist, designed a rose-themed artwork. The project was submitted to the City and approved, allowing for construction sometime within a three-year construction timeframe beginning in 2018.

Joe had another idea. He'd always wanted to build a senior retirement facility in the district. He'd had thoughts of, perhaps, retiring there. Tiffany had researched and talked with some individuals and companies experienced in senior living and retirement facility development. Block 23 was designated as a site for this type of facility.

So, approval of the proposed senior living referred to as the Holden of Pearl depended upon approval by the Design Review Commission and a future land sale to and development by Alliance Realty Partners, the developer. If the deal with Alliance was settled within a year, it was conceivable the facility might be open by 2021. By 2021, the building was in construction. It's anticipated that the facility will open in 2023.

That left Block 24—the Last Block. What was the ideal use for this block in 2018? It was always on Tiffany's mind: "What can we do on this site that would be great!"

◇ ◇ ◇

The richness of the Pearl neighborhood was reflected in the mix of old and new buildings. Walking around the district, especially along portions of NW 13th gave pedestrians a sense of the past. And there were numerous architectural gems, renovated and repurposed buildings from an earlier era, as well as a variety of interesting shops, commercial services and popular places like the Jimmy Maks, a jazz bar and restaurant. However, the land underlying these buildings had radically increased in value. The appearance of wreaking balls was not far off the horizon.

39

TEARDOWNS ON THE HORIZON

RISING LAND VALUES CHANGED THE real estate game in the neighborhood. A warehouse that sat on a quarter of a block in the 1980s typically sold for around $400,000. By 2019, that same property was selling for millions. Nearly four decades later, a full city block in the Pearl was worth $20 million.

By the late 2000s, many contemporary structures, typically single-or two-story buildings used for retail shops or commercial service businesses, were worth less than the underlying land. These low-rise structures were now candidates for the wrecking ball.

Most of these "teardown" sites were located south of Lovejoy Street. This mélange of old and new buildings presented lots of contrast due to a variety of architectural facades, exterior materials and finishes, and textures, which contributed to the neighborhood's visual charm. Out-of-town money had now found the city attractive for investment, most of it institutional. The availability of new financing resources, up zoning, and other regulatory changes north of Lovejoy Street had created incentives for more redevelopment. Construction cranes and crews were busy in the Pearl, along Naito Parkway, and in other parts of the city. The architectural fabric was under economic attack as new replaced old.

In 2015, the Goodman building—the previous location for the Pacific Northwest College of Art—was sold to finance the purchase of the college's new home. The college had also vacated the Stagecraft, or M. Seller, building they had leased from Al Solheim. The college had used the old two-story Stagecraft building for ceramic fabrication labs, woodworking, and metal activities. The two-story structure sat vacant for a short while as Al looked for a new tenant.

REHAB VERSUS TEARDOWN

After discussing their options, Al and Bob Ames decided to repurpose the Stagecraft building instead of tearing it down. Built in 1890, the footprint of the two-story building occupied a bit more than a quarter of a block. There was about twenty-eight thousand square feet of rentable space. Historically the structure had been two separate buildings with a slight offset in ground-floor levels. Al had had the building's interior walls demolished and the remaining space cleared of debris. What remained was an open-plan layout separated only by one interior wall that delineated two empty spaces, one larger than the other.

The larger space was punctuated with high windows on the north and east facades, and a high ceiling with exposed beams and joints imparted a muscular quality to the building's interior. Thinking about future tenants, Al decided to enlarge the windows by extending them closer to the ground-floor level, allowing in more natural light. This also resulted in new windows that were more suitable for retail display. The second floor had attractive square window openings that ran the length of two sides of the building. The additional installation of more skylights—there were a few existing ones—further allowed more natural light to flood the second-floor interior.

Al and his investor group also owned the adjacent low-rise building and the paved parking lot next door to the west. Therefore, they could have demolished the structures on both properties, and the partners could have built a much taller mid-rise structure.

If they had sold the Stagecraft building at a price approaching $4 million, a new owner would have demolished it and built the tallest structure possible under current zoning and building codes. Economics would have dictated demolition and construction of a new structure.

However, what Al told me was enlightening. He and his investor group had purchased this building decades ago for around $300,000. Owning a building that had been fully amortized allowed the owners to pursue adaptive reuse of the building as opposed to tearing the building down. According to Bob, they were going to bring the 1892 building up to code and preserve it. Bob said, "All our investors are reaching the point where their investments are going to go to their kids."

The investors behind AWS Real Estate could have sold the Stagecraft. But with no basis in it now, they would have created a tax problem for themselves. Between the federal taxes and the State of Oregon, which has a very high capital gains tax it would be about 36 or 37 percent of the profit one might realize. And then what? What do you do with the remaining proceeds? Buy T-bills at 1 percent interest or less? All the investors were going to make their kids partners. At age seventy-five, these seniors were not going to be invested forever.

Al's goal in preserving this property was to "keep its historical roots alive." Al believed this building was a classic—one of the last nineteenth-century warehouses suitable for adaptive reuse in the Pearl. His decision was local leadership setting another example.

As the building was cleaned, upgrading, and painted, Al still hadn't lined up any tenants, but he'd courted several potential ones He finally put together a deal with Design Within Reach (DWR). This national upscale furniture company now has a showroom on NW 13th Avenue—it's their largest store in the USA.

Previously, DWR had rented a much smaller space in the Pearl along Glisan. The company moved its showroom from their previous location because their lease ran out, and the premises were not brand appropriate. The DWR brand is designed around the notion that when you are in the store, you are in a person's home. Each room at their new store's location reflects the fact that a home has a living room, a dining room, bedrooms, a study, et cetera, et cetera. DWR needed space with at least ten feet of floor-to-ceiling clearance. They now have eleven feet. That's even better.

Originally DWR was only going to rent the first floor and the larger available space. But when they signed a lease, they decided to take both buildings and the second floor. The smaller building with a lower-floor level eventually became a storefront for Hay Herman Miller, the company that owns both DWR and Hay. Hay sells Danish furniture, textiles, and was a home goods retailer. The storefront was Hay's first foray into the USA retail marketplace.

Having a second floor in the larger building allowed DWR's architects to create an exceptional entry experience with a featured staircase. Project architect Laith Sayigh, has described the grand staircase statement as an "attention grabber!" DWR believes, as do many retailers, that you win or lose a customer in the first ten feet from the entry. DWR wanted to be in the Pearl because of the vitality and foot traffic in the neighborhood. Laith thinks of the area as the heart of the city, much more than the Central Business District.

PRESERVING TOUCHE´

Sam Rodriguez managed the Portland office of Mill Creek Residential (MCR). I sat down with Sam to find out how this development company assembled and acquired the three properties near the intersection of NW 14th Avenue and Glisan—Touché, Hawaiian Time, and Le Bouchon. Sam had told me it was easy since Bob owned all three. MCR also purchased an abutting property, the former home of Premier Press. Premier Press had sold their building to the real estate investment firm Meriwether Partners LLC. Meriwether had plans to add four floors, about seventy-five thousand square feet of office space, to the existing building. The property included a paved parking lot, which in turn, Meriwether sold to Holland Residential. Holland had a land lease and planned to construct a new building on Glisan across the street from Touché, where a mini strip mall had previously occupied the land. Holland Residential had transferred the floor area ratio air rights from the Premier Press property to their project. Subsequently, the parking lot immediately west of Touché ended up as a pocket park designed by Lango Hansen.

MCR, to create a larger development site, acquired the Premier Press building from Meriwether Partners. Initially, MCR planned to demolish Touché, but they changed their plans due to the public controversy over the potential destruction of this historic 1913 fire station. The developer's new plans called for the renovation of the firehouse, including the preservation of the building facade and roof structure. It's probably a good bet a new restaurant will find a home there.

An L-shaped sixteen-story mixed-use structure, the Modera Glisan building will replace the Premier Press structure and the other buildings that used to front onto NW 14th Avenue with apartment units and ground-floor retail or other commercial uses. A property tax exemption approved by the Portland City Council required the developer to include affordable housing units in 20 percent of the overall unit mix. The top floor of the project will have a wraparound viewing terrace with an indoor amenity commons room with floor-to-ceiling glazing. And, of course, there will a rooftop terrace. They appear to be obligatory nowadays.

GOODBYE JIMMY MAKS

Jimmy Mak's once occupied a building mid-block along NW 10th Avenue between Davis and Everett Streets. Modera Davis, an eleven-story apartment building with ground-floor retail, now occupies the eastern half of the block. Jazz lovers used to queue and pay a cover charge to enter this popular jazz club to hear Mel Brown or a cadre of other great jazz musicians play. You could even eat dinner and pretend you were back in the 1930s or '40s, the golden age of supper clubs.

This popular jazz club is gone—a victim of gentrification. Talking with Sam, I wanted to explore the reasons these older, contemporary one-and two-story buildings in the Pearl District have invisible real estate targets affixed to their facades. Besides rising land values, Sam reminded me that there weren't many full-blocks left for development. Assembling and acquiring a half-block in the center of the Pearl meant MCR could construct a twelve-story building with two hundred apartments and retail on the ground floor.

Sam told me the company had to deal with four primary property owners. One owner was a tenant in common that had seven owners. "So, it's not easy to take four owners, synchronize all that so it all happens together…so you can buy it…but if one owner pulls out, you are screwed. So, it took us over a year to acquire all the properties," Sam said. It took fourteen months, to be exact, to get everyone lined up to secure the property. The good news is that given the scarcity of half-or full-blocks for new construction in the future, assembling a large enough parcel may, in the immediate term, preserve the mix of the old and new buildings that characterize the Pearl's urban fabric.

There were and are other factors that affect an owner's incentive to sell a piece of property. If a commercial property owner in the Pearl has sufficient rental income, it's doubtful an owner will sell unless the offer is "off the charts" attractive because of the tax liability. However, if the owner dies, the inheritors may have to sell to settle their tax bill. Or they might sell to avoid managing and paying tax on the property. So, there are circumstances that can work for or against a developer's ability to buy a piece of property in the Pearl.

Today the lack of available land of sufficient size now limits continued new construction in Pearl. This is clearly evidenced by recent speculative development along Front Ave and elsewhere in the city.

The City's new inclusionary housing policy has also had an effect on the residential marketplace. According to Sam, "Right now, I couldn't make any of my deals work. Either rents go up, or land prices go down for new projects to go forward." Sam always feels "that at the end of the day, the [physical] structure of the Pearl will be somewhat preserved. We are lucky to have NW 13th as a historic street."

The word on said street is that Jimmy Maks will be reborn. A group of private investors are considering fixing up the old one-story building that once housed the restaurant Oba. The developers want to create a musical entertainment venue. They are planning to bring back a version of Jimmy Maks. The appearance of the Covid-19 virus put those plans on hold for a while, as well as other plans for new development in the Pearl.

When you get right down to it, this emerging neighborhood had been subjected to a heavy dose of gentrification, which led to the displacement of the pioneering artists. However, in their place, numerous art galleries have enhanced the Pearl District both economically and culturally. Artists, old and new, now hang their artwork on these gallery walls.

The Cultured Pearl

An Enriched Community

1979-2020

The Cultured Pearl Timeline

An Enriched District

1979	Blackfish Gallery opens
1984	Quartersaw Gallery opens
1985	PDXS Artfest is held
1985	Jamison Thomas Gallery opens
1995	William Jamison dies, and his gallery closes
1998	Pacific Northwest College of Art opens an art school in the Goodman building
2003	The City buys the Armory building from Gerding Edlen Development
2004	Elizabeth Leach Gallery opens
2005	Jim Winkler purchases the Daisy Kingdom building to build an art center
2006	The Gerding Center Stage Theater opens in the renovated Amory building
2006	The DeSoto Project—a cooperative art center with multiple art galleries—opens
2015	Pacific Northwest College of Art opens the 511 building on the North Park Blocks

40

AN ARTS DISTRICT

PEOPLE WHO LIVE IN OR visit the Pearl can shop, dine and drink, get a haircut or a pedicure, have their car serviced, and do whatever else their lifestyle dictates as a pedestrian. While walking around the district, they can experience street art and visit neighborhood galleries that exhibit work by local and national artists. The presence of the Pacific Northwest College of Art (PNCA), the Art Institute of Portland, and Willamette University's writing program means there are interesting higher-ed services and programs. For theatergoers, afternoon and evening performances are available in the historic Armory building.

The artists may have discovered the neighborhood first. But today, the art galleries are the fruits of the seeds those artists planted decades ago. The Pearl neighborhood has truly become Portland's Arts District.

THE EARLY LOCAL ART SCENE

Prior to the opening of the Fountain Gallery of Art in 1961, the art scene in Portland consisted primarily of the Portland Art Museum. The Fountain Gallery was the brainchild of Arlene Schnitzer. It was the city's first "serious art gallery." Unfortunately, the gallery burned down in 1977, but Arlene reopened it at a new location in the Northwest Neighborhood on NW 21st Avenue. In 1986, the gallery closed, and Arlene shifted gears to concentrate on philanthropic projects. However, the Fountain's mission and focus continued when the Laura Russo Gallery opened the same year at another location farther north along NW 21st Avenue.

As artists and a few galleries discovered the Northwest Triangle in the late 1970s and early '80s, they established a beachhead for an arts district that emerged over time. The Blackfish Gallery, a cooperative venture owned and operated by working artists, had rented a storefront on NW 9th Avenue by 1979. In 2020, it was still in place—and still run by artists.

Quartersaw Gallery opened in the mid-1980s, and the owners, Victoria Frey and Luis Lopez, organized a renegade arts festival in 1985 called PDXS Artfest. The street in front of the gallery, NW 12th Avenue, was barricaded, and staging was erected without any permits. The first year it was just performances and an art exhibition by invitation. The second year, the festival was formalized because the organizers got the *Downtowner* publication to be their media sponsor. This gave the festival public creditability and citywide recognition. A walking tour was organized, allowing the public to visit artist's studios in the Northwest Triangle. This led to the formation of a local gallery coalition. These events continued for three or four years under Victoria's leadership. After the first two years, the event became known as the Pearl District Arts Festival. Quartersaw Gallery became a fixture in the Pearl for seventeen years until it closed in 2001.

SHOWING OUTSIDER ART

William Jamison and Jeffrey Thomas moved the Jamison/Thomas Gallery from its downtown location to the Pearl in 1985. Over the next decade, their gallery had a bicoastal impact in Portland and on the East Coast in New York City. They became art influencers on local and national stages. Brad Rogers believes William's impact on the art world was tied to his recognition of the value and importance of "outsider art."

William saw that the art world was changing, and he could either follow or lead. He was an advocate for outsider art because he realized that all artists are the same, whether they are big-name artists or folk artists. Some have degrees, and others don't. Artists in high school used to bring William their portfolios, and he told them to just keep on making art. He would tell them that you do not need to go to art school, and that to be an artist, you didn't need to get a degree.

He presented a different side of art to collectors and the public. Outsider art was sometimes referred to as naïve art because the subject matter and painting or construction techniques could be very childlike. Many outsider artists have no formal art training; they are self-taught artists.

As a gallery owner William had a cross vision. He felt that naïve art, or outsider art, should be shown with contemporary art. William wanted to breach that distinction. He showed artwork by local artists like Tom Cramer, Gregory Grenon, and Deb Norby. He also exhibited artwork by out-of-town artists like Stuart Buehler, Robert Gilkerson, and Georgianna Orr. These outsiders had compelling stories. The artwork by outsider artists tends to be intertwined with the story of their lives. Their artwork is very personal. One way to think about outsider art is to compare it to fine art. The latter has an intellectual or conceptual bias overlaid with urban sophistication. Naïve art has an emotional bias.

William didn't start out as a gallery owner. In 1974, he started and ran a restaurant, Victoria's Nephew, with Emlyn Thomas. His first gallery was the William Jamison Folk Craft Gallery, and it opened in 1980 on SW 2nd Avenue. That gallery, housed in a minimal space, resembled a curio shop at times.

Around 1983, William hired Jeffrey. He'd met Jeffrey when he catered Jeffrey and Laura Cooper's wedding. They had a mutual friend, Neil Goren, and Neil had talked William into hiring Jeffrey, who was about to take a job working on the potato account for a Portland ad agency.

Jeffrey decided to work for William because as a high school student, Jeffrey had interned at a New York gallery. He'd grown up in the art world; his father had been a curator at the Metropolitan Museum of Art. While working with William, Jeffrey became aware that William was short of operating funds. Jeffrey had thought about leaving the gallery, but he stayed because there was something so hopeful and encouraging in William's manner that Jeffrey had to see what might happen to the gallery.

To create more open exhibition space, Jeffrey began reorganizing the Folk Craft Gallery. William and he used eclectic folk art inventory to assemble curious monthly shows and artist openings, and Jeffrey grew the mailing list of lively patrons.

According to Jeffrey, William began searching for self-directed artists. William spent lots of time searching for artists who were labeled "outsiders." It took a lot of word of mouth to track them down. Sometimes it took months to work out exhibition deals with these artists, many of whom were reluctant to show their work publicly. It was difficult for William to get these artists to trust him. Fortunately, he had a talent for artist relations and was persistent in his efforts. In the end, William won them over with his charm and ever-present smile.

When the original gallery needed more space to show the growing roster of artists that William and Jeffrey now represented, the gallery moved across SW 2nd Avenue to a new building next to the Gango Gallery. As a result of Jeffrey's efforts in building the gallery business, William made Jeffrey an equal partner. The gallery became the Jamison/Thomas Gallery.

Two years later, the partners moved their gallery to an old warehouse on NW Glisan Street just off NW 13th Avenue. The ground-floor space was perfect for a gallery. It had a high ceiling, exposed heavy timber beams, and wood flooring. All the interior wood had been painted, but William hired workmen who carefully removed all the paint to expose the natural beauty of those structural timber members. Every month new exhibitions of art filled the space with beautiful objects, paintings, collages, and other exciting and provocative artwork.

That same year, William and Brad Rogers were living in a loft-like space in a one-story building on Glisan between NW 11th and 12th Avenues that now houses Blick, an arts supply store, More space was needed to store the larger paintings that artists were now making locally.

Jeffrey had a lot of art world contacts in New York City. On one of his frequent trips to visit his family, Jeffrey presented a portfolio of Jamison/Thomas artists to the senior editor at *House & Garden Magazine*. The magazine then ran a profile of the gallery in the November 1985 issue. In Portland, the phone at the Jamison/Thomas Gallery began to ring off the hook. Jeffrey remembers the callers were asking: "Where can we see the art?" He and William were so naïve thinking that here in Portland, people didn't have time for that. Then they had a shared thought: *If we can't bring collectors to the artwork, then we'd bring the artwork to the collectors.*

By the mid-1980s, the art world was on fire in New York City, centered around dozens of East Village galleries filled with rough-and-tumble street art, spray-painted graffiti, and primitive figuration. The outsider art program at Jamison/Thomas felt right at home with what the art world was showing. This was the time for them to expand their business on the East Coast. Jeffrey had big dreams about opening a gallery in New York City, so he decided to branch out on his own. Jeffrey eventually rented a portion of a storefront in the West Village. That was how the partners ended up with two galleries. They shared the same moniker—Jamison/ Thomas, and many of the same artists—but they were run as separate businesses.

Two years later, with a successful track record of sales in hand, Jeffrey found some New York investors to help fund a new gallery space in a former brassiere factory off lower Broadway. In 1988, he opened a much bigger gallery space in SoHo with an emphasis on the artwork of several artists from the Jamison/Thomas Gallery in Portland. Over time, the New York gallery began showing more art by contemporary New York artists, eliminating the mounting expenses for cross-country shipping.

◇ ◇ ◇

William knew he had AIDS as early as 1986, and he knew he had a disease that could be fatal. But he had a gallery to promote, and he had started borrowing art from more prominent and more successful galleries, so he could be on their radar. Then he and Jeffrey began collaborating and doing art fairs in Chicago, Los Angeles, and New York City. The Jamison/Thomas Gallery was the first gallery in Portland that did art fairs.

As his illness progressed, William began receiving chemo treatments at home and on planes while traveling to art fairs and to see curators, artists, and clients. William had made an educated decision about how he was going to spend the rest of his life.

Jamison/Thomas had a good run in the New York art market until early 1990 when the art world went into a panic when prices for established masterpieces started to tumble. Suddenly, no one was visiting the galleries, and no one was buying anything. The art business just stopped in New York and would not recover for another decade. Most new galleries had no reserves or inventory to carry them through the high rent and staff costs.

By 1991, the Jamison/Thomas Gallery in New York City was in trouble, and Jeffrey was juggling the responsibilities of being a young father with two toddlers. Miraculously, a string of sold-out exhibitions in 1992 bailed out the gallery, and Jeffrey took that opportunity to close the New York gallery and move his family back to Portland.

◇ ◇ ◇

William didn't run the gallery by himself; he hired people at different times. He hired Pam Johnson to help him with sales in the downtown gallery in the early years. As the Jamison/Thomas Gallery evolved over the decade, William would inspire and train other talents as gallery directors, including Mary Josephson, Charles Froelick, and Jane Beebe.

Jane had moved to Portland around 1972–73 with her husband, Spencer. She met William in 1975 when he was her next-door neighbor in the Northwest Neighborhood.

As a kid, she'd spent time in the Albright-Knox Museum in Buffalo, New York, getting an early education about art. In Portland, she started taking studio architecture classes at the Oregon School of Design. Jane was dipping her toes to see if this avocation would interest her. She ran into William somewhere in town, and he asked her if she was going to continue in architecture school. Her husband had just quit his job, and she decided she needed a faster path to employment when William invited her to work in the gallery. This was in early 1987. She worked part-time doing sales and curation. It gave her flexibility, so she could deal with two kids and a husband who was now traveling all the time. Jane ended up working for William for nine years.

◇ ◇ ◇

Jane loved working with William. However, in 1996, she opened her own gallery—PDX Contemporary Art—at 604 NW 12th Avenue. She purchased a space next to Giorgio's Restaurant and had Brad Cloepfil design the interior space. She had evaluated her personality—friendly but not social—so she didn't follow the usual format of openings and a social setting. The question for her became: *Can you sell art without openings?* Yes, she could.

A decade later, she was operating out of a new location on Flanders Street. Together with the Pulliam Deffenbaugh Gallery, she shared a street entry that served both galleries. After the Pulliam Deffenbaugh Gallery closed, Theo Downes-Le Guin bought the space next to her and created a new gallery.

◇ ◇ ◇

In the 1980s, Mary Josephson had a studio in the same building as Brad. Like many emerging artists, she needed a day job to support herself. Brad felt she was smart and knew about art on the ground level, so he thought she'd be an asset to the gallery. He suggested William hire her, and he did.

Before working at the gallery, Mary had been volunteering at several different events and places in Portland—first for Art Aids and then at the Northwest Artists Workshop. She and other artists liked the community-oriented ambiance of the workshop. Mary worked at the gallery for seven years, first as an assistant to the director and then as director of the gallery. Mentored by William, she used his approach to selling artwork: educate potential customers about the spirit, content, and artist's intentions.

◇ ◇ ◇

By 1994, William was seriously ill, and by the spring, he had lost his sight. By the fall, he had dementia. A couple of years earlier, Jane and Charles had taken on the role of co-gallery directors. William had spoken with Mary, Jane, and Charles about the gallery continuing after he was gone. He had offered the gallery to them.

Unfortunately, the gallery was expensive to run, and all three had personal reasons for wanting to pursue different career paths. Mary wanted to be a full-time painter, and Jane felt she didn't have the financial resources to continue with the gallery. They all also realized that as new owners, they would have to confront a big perception problem: what was the gallery without William? At this point, Brad stepped in and closed the gallery. He made that decision knowing it would have been difficult to keep William's legacy going on without William. The gallery had been a manifestation of William.

Sometime during William's last months, the Smithsonian's American Art Archives made a request to the gallery. The Smithsonian wanted to archive gallery's records because of the role the Jamison/Thomas Gallery had played during a decade when the art world had shifted nationally. William was considered to have been at the epicenter of the shift. He had been a beacon for the recognition of the importance of outsider art. Charles took on this request, and he worked with the attorneys to sort out the documents for the archive. When he finished, all the material was put on a pallet and shrink-wrapped. It was picked up and shipped to the Smithsonian.

William died on June 21, 1995. The art world in Portland was stunned. He was irreplaceable. Portland had lost a great promoter for the local arts and artists. Afterward, both Jane and Charles started their own galleries.

ELIZABETH LEACH GALLERY—FORTY YEARS OF ART

Elizabeth Leach was only twenty-four years old when she opened her art gallery in 1981. Like most gallery owners, she rented space. She had graduated from Scripps College, had worked in the Los Angeles art industry, and had been involved in the LA Light and Space Movement before moving to Portland.

Elizabeth had arrived in Portland a year earlier just after giving birth to a daughter. Elizabeth needed a job. While downtown one day, she walked into Pavilion Gallery, a commercial chain-type art gallery—the parent company being Circle Fine Art out of Chicago—thinking about applying there. As soon as she stepped in, she turned around and started to walk out. Before she reached the door, the sole person in the gallery asked her why she had come in. Elizabeth told that person she had thoughts about applying for a job. The next thing Elizabeth knew she was sitting down and explaining that she had a degree in art and architectural history, and she was thinking about selling artwork to corporations part-time.

She was hired to work three days a week. After six months, she was offered the opportunity to become the gallery director at Pavilion. She declined. But because of her influential work at Pavilion, she had met a lot of people in Portland who wanted to meet her artist husband, Richard Gruetter, and visit his studio. This gave her a base to build a career on.

Richard, who had grown up in Portland, had wanted to open a gallery to show and market his artwork ever since he and Elizabeth had moved to town. However, Elizabeth didn't believe the city could support another gallery. Richard—emphatic about having a gallery—insisted Elizabeth open an art gallery. The Elizabeth Leach Gallery opened in downtown Portland off SW 2nd Avenue in 1981.

By the mid-1980s, she was showing artists like Mark Tobey, Hap Tivey, and Richard Diebenkorn at her gallery on SW Pine. Also, she was competing against the Fountain Gallery, which represented and exhibited artworks by many of the prominent local artists. But she has survived while other galleries have come and gone.

In the 1980s, there was a scarcity of major art collectors in Portland. Most collected regional art, and they weren't comfortable with the higher price points associated with art by East Coast and internationally known artists. A work on paper in Portland would sell for $500, in San Francisco twice as much, and in New York for $5,000. Out-of-town art didn't match the soft local market.

By the mid-1990s, everyone wanted to be in the Pearl. However, gallery space was forty dollars a square foot. It didn't pencil out for Elizabeth to move her gallery from downtown to the Pearl. She, like other gallery owners, had mused about owning her own space. By 2004, after renting a space downtown for many years, she bought a building in the Pearl and reopened her gallery on the ground level.

◇ ◇ ◇

Elizabeth and Sarah Miller Meigs bought Ed Caduro's building after he died. Everybody in the local art world knew Ed. He was the major non-institutional art collector in town. Ed had purchased a building on NW 9th Avenue and had turned the second floor into an open loft space primarily to house his art collection. The gallery space was filled with art—lots of contemporary paintings and some sculpture pieces. As a collector, Ed had surrounded himself with extraordinary artwork.

One time, Ed called his friend Tessa Papas to ask her if she would ask Norman Russell, a contractor, to fix a leak at his loft space. Norman went over to Ed's, but he returned to the Papases' studio after only being gone for a very short time. When he arrived, he was white-faced, and he said to Tessa, "Dammit, I went there, and there was this guy was sitting on the sofa, and he doesn't say anything." Tessa had to tell Norman what he saw as a sculpture by Seward Johnson. Years later I asked Norman about this incident. He told me he was just trying "not to be rude by staring" at this quiet person.

And then there's the story about a thief who broke into Ed's loft and looked around for something to steal. There was a sculpture that consisted of two Hoover vacuum cleaners by Jeff Koons, a nationally known artist. The guy took one of the vacuum cleaners. Upset, Ed called up Hoover and told them someone had taken an old vacuum cleaner that had belonged to his grandmother, whom he dearly loved, and did they happen to have another XYZ model of the same year? The manufacturer did, and they replaced the one that had been stolen.

Elizabeth turned the ground floor of Ed's building into her art gallery, and Sarah converted the upper floor where the loft had been into a combined private residence and an art gallery. The gallery, known as the Lumber Room, opened in 2010 and could be visited on Saturdays by appointment only.

Once Elizabeth's new location was open and operating, she began representing many regional artists. Her mission then became "import national and international artists and export regional artists."

By 2000, the number of high-quality galleries had increased significantly in Portland. Elizabeth and other gallery owners, realizing they needed more marketing power, formed the Portland Art Dealers Association that year. Their mission was to promote business for the members, to educate the public about art, and to advocate for a vibrant art community. This go-to-art organization gave local galleries credibility.

As Elizabeth and I talked about the difficulties Portland art galleries have had, she said, "Art galleries need to be more energetic." She went on to explain that an energetic gallery is one that promotes their artists by exporting and displaying their artwork through visits to other cities and art fairs.

Elizabeth and I covered a lot of topics during our conversation. She had plenty of insights: Now we have another generation of artists being shown outside the region. This generation is not isolated in Portland like the previous generation was for many years. When Elizabeth first came to Portland, there was one local curator. Now there are half a dozen at various colleges and institutions. The only reason an artist of consequence can work and make a living in Portland now is that there is an infrastructure in place to support their efforts.

At one point, Elizabeth brought up the importance of place in the community to the working artists. She posed the question: "How does an artist create relevancy here?" She answered her own question, saying, "They have to have an interesting community that supports the arts. You cannot succeed in a vacuum. We now have internationally known artists here." Elizabeth continued:

In New York City, walking down the street, an artist can run into a museum curator who could put you in a show. You can run into a writer who wants to write an article about you. Or run into somebody who can buy your work. It's all about critical mass and critical edge. Place is important, even in the digital world, and now Portland is finding its place in the art world. However, at this point, Portland is still primarily a city of art makers. We need more visitors, more thinkers, and more buyers of art. We need to make sure the local collector base supports the region; we don't want them flying off to buy art somewhere else.

I asked Elizabeth to comment on the contribution by local galleries to the Pearl and to the city at large. She thought about this for a long minute. Then she said:

For the broader community, they give back so much to the civic fabric. Many gatherings and charity events, in particular, are held in the galleries. The artists give art and space for fundraising activities, while the galleries provide jobs, especially for young graduates from art programs. Galleries offer more attractions for visiting tourists. The city needs to have an "arts district." gallery staff provide information to visitors…where to eat, where to do such and such. They give an elevated cultural dimension to the city.

The galleries in the Pearl provide a cultural dimension that the retail shops can't offer. That was intrinsic to the establishment of the Pearl—a cultural expansion of the city. When a few gallery owners bought their gallery spaces, this type of commitment ensured that art would be a constant contribution to the quality of life in the Pearl. Art enriches the city beyond the commercial aspect of showing and selling artwork. That's why the Pearl, besides making an economic contribution to the local economy, can be thought of as a cultural district—the cultured Pearl.

Other galleries opened in the Pearl, and a small group of gallery owners bought their gallery spaces and operated in a cooperative manner.

41

THE DESOTO PROJECT

DESOTO WAS AN AMERICAN AUTOMOBILE manufactured and sold under the big umbrella of the Chrysler Corporation. Chrysler discontinued the car with 1961 model. Jim Winkler brought the name to prominence again when he decided to build and open a cooperative arts venture he called the DeSoto Project.

But first he had to purchase the buildings that had once housed one of Oregon's first automotive dealerships, where DeSoto cars had been displayed and sold. The dealership had been in the Lombard Automotive building, which consisted of two abutting structures. More recently, the Daisy Kingdom retail store had occupied one of those two buildings. After purchasing both buildings, Jim oversaw the renovation work for the new art center that occupied the north half of the city block bounded by NW Broadway and Park Avenues and Couch and Davis Streets. The converted building with four art galleries and a museum opened its doors in 2007 and amplified the local perception of the Pearl neighborhood as an arts district.

Tad Savinar, a local artist, noted that the DeSoto Project was the most important cultural development in the city that he could remember because it provided a link between the commercial district and the thriving do-it-yourself district. Tad believes,

"Any good art scene has Range Rovers on one end and kids on skateboards on the other. The requirements of a good scene are that the two ends meet."

◇ ◇ ◇

Gallery owners had talked about forming a co-op and buying a building together for years. There had been hurdles. This kind of enterprise was costly and required expertise. How do you put together a deal and arrange financing to make it affordable? The task seemed overwhelming—a basketful of hassles. You needed an architect, probably a structural engineer, and countless other people with specialized expertise and legal advice. People who run successful galleries know art and how to sell art. Most aren't experienced developers.

Jim was a developer—a very experienced one. Moreover, he was interested in the arts, and one of his friends happened to be Chris Rauschenberg.

One time in the mid-2000s, Chris was at a Cascades AIDS Project auction. He was seated at a table that included Jim and Bruce Guenther, the curator of Modern and Contemporary Art at the Portland Art Museum. According to Chris, who was seated next to Bruce, Bruce turned to him and said, "You guys need twice as much space, and you need to own that space." This caused Jim to think about what might happen to Blue Sky, since it wasn't a commercial gallery. And maybe a group of gallery owners should consider organizing collectively and purchasing a building together. It would give them security against rent increases. Jim began to think about how to scale this idea into a project. To make this notion work, he'd need a critical mass.

After that casual conversation at the auction, a series of meetings and discussions were held with Blue Sky to assess whether or not this nonprofit gallery could become an anchor in an arts pioneering venture. Jim felt Blue Sky could be a magnet attracting other arts- and culture-oriented activities into a cooperative deal.

Jim had already identified a half a block of real estate located directly across the street from the North Park Blocks that might be suitable for conversion into several separate large commercial art spaces. He wanted to bring together the "best" galleries in Portland under one roof. The project was also about bringing together galleries that were showing nonlocal artwork instead of concentrating on local and regional artists.

Jim next surveyed several local galleries to see who might be interested in being in a co-op. He talked with Laura Russo, but she liked where she was. There was convenient parking just out her back door. Next, he spoke with Bob Koch and Charles Froelick. Both were financially successful gallery owners, and they were interested.

It didn't take Jim long to act. In 2005, he purchased the buildings for $3.4 million. Spurred on by Chris and Bruce, Jim undertook a two-year renovation of the DeSoto Project. The project became an art gallery complex that eventually housed two nonprofits—Blue Sky and the Museum of Contemporary Craft (MoCC)—and three commercial galleries, The Augen Gallery, Charles's Froelick, and Charles A. Hartman Fine Art. To design the cooperative complex, Jim hired LRS Architects.

To finance the project, new market tax credits were used to make the project affordable to the galleries. Fortuitously, the Daisy Kingdom building was in the Old Town census tract. That meant it qualified as an area under economic stress. The tax credits cut the cost to the participants by almost half. However, the individual costs for each participant were still substantial. The craft museum would spend $3.6 million, Blue Sky a million. Where would the money come from?

BLUE SKY WANTED IN

Chris answered the question about the money. Bruce had told Chris that the Portland Art Museum could afford to make another million-dollar purchase if a superlative work of art could be found. Chris contacted his dad and got him to donate one of his sculptures to Blue Sky. Then Blue Sky would sell it to the museum.

Chris had known that Bruce had wanted to fill out the museum's contemporary collection with a work by Robert Rauschenberg. In fact, Bruce had done some research on this earlier. After Chris spoke with his father, Bruce went to New York City and picked out the sculpture he wanted—the *Patrician Barnacle*. Now he needed a million dollars from the museum.

At this point, the intended artwork purchase hit a snag. John Buchanan, the former executive director of the museum, suddenly departed. The museum was in the middle of their capital campaign with a bunch of pledges that hadn't been collected yet. They didn't have a million dollars to complete the transaction. Bruce immediately began looking for donations, but he didn't have any luck securing funds. Chris was in a tight spot. He was worried. He was on a deadline. Bruce was also worried because he had a deal at a million. He realized if the deal didn't happen now, a future deal might cost $5 million.

Carol Hampton was a longtime art patron of the museum and had made substantial donations in the past. Bruce hadn't contacted her because her husband had recently died. But as time passed, Bruce thought the deal would fall apart. With no options left, he approached Carol and reminded her of a past Rauschenberg show. Carol's response was "Do it," and she donated a million dollars to acquire the artwork.

A million dollars was just openers in this game for Blue Sky. They would need another $2.5 million to buy their space. The museum's million as seed money gave Chris the confidence to approach local foundations and art patrons. They stepped up to the plate, and Blue Sky ended up with five donors who each contributed $150,000. Then Blue Sky went to its members and started an in-house capital campaign. Chris was excited now because the normal life expectancy of any art space was tenuous.

Galleries can end up making do on a week-to-week basis. Chris believes "basically that art spaces are born on hospice."

Chris also believes there is power in having several galleries in one building. He thinks it's similar to why people go to the zoo to see the animals. All the animals are in one place. People don't drive out to the suburbs to see a lion and then drive to the town next door to see a giraffe. They all have to be in one place. Having five attractive art-oriented destinations in one building made each one economically stronger.

ANCHORING THE CO-OP VENTURE

MoCC with fifteen thousand square feet of display space was viewed as an anchor for the project. MoCC—the oldest continuously operated West Coast craft institution in the United States—opened on a high note. Full of great expectations and promise after seven decades of operation on SW Corbett Avenue, the museum fell victim to financial problems two years later. Rescued with a sale to the PNCA in 2009, the museum's program was integrated into the school, also providing students with the opportunity to learn about the curation of art collections.

In 2016, the college's Board of Directors sold the museum's premises in the DeSoto building to another museum. PNCA officially closed the museum. Fortunately, MoCC's craft collection was preserved and integrated into the college's new Center for Contemporary Art & Culture.

The museum's demise was a loss to the city's art community. Originally, MoCC had operated under a very different philosophy. Namita Wiggers, the last museum director, emphatically told me, "The museum was not about being a category of objects or crafts; it was about the question of craft as a process." It had been about being a verb, not a noun.

◇ ◇ ◇

A year later, a museum took over the space previously occupied by the old craft museum. Bruce Guenther, now retired from the Portland Art Museum, was hired to curate the Oregon Jewish Museum and Center for Holocaust Education's first season of exhibitions. The facility, besides being a museum, became a cultural center with a historical, educational overlay. Hope had just made a second appearance. New expectations had taken root in the ashes of the previous museum.

The Jewish Museum has had a nomadic history in the city. Founded in 1990, it began with the label "museum without walls." Over the next few decades, it skipped around town from location to location before settling down on a secluded street in Northwest Portland. It was hard to find and harder to find a place to park nearby. Its new home had better public visibility and accessibility, but it was still difficult to find a curbside parking space along the North Park Blocks.

Director Julia Margoles was excited about the promise of exhibitions and other events to come. However, aware of the concern about the rise in anti-Semitism and other forms of discrimination in the nation, she found the presence of poverty, homelessness, and other social issues at the museum's doorstep particularly troubling. The resolution of these issues has seemed almost impossible. It's complex and will continue to affect the public perception of redevelopment in Old Town/Chinatown.

WHO ELSE WANTS IN?

Bob attended the University of Oregon for graduate work in architecture. After graduating, Bob decided not to pursue a career in architecture or teaching. Instead, he flew to New York City, bumped into a couple of print publishers, became their West Coast representative, and by 1976 was on the road selling prints to dealers.

In 1978, he realized roadwork was too hard on his body, so he established the Augen Gallery in downtown Portland the next year.

During the first three years, Bob specialized in prints. Soon after, many artists who weren't on the Fountain Gallery's A- list began to look around at other gallery opportunities. Things started to loosen up a bit. When the Fountain closed, things really loosened up. There was a "diaspora" in the local art world.

By 2004-2005, real estate prices in downtown Portland were going up. Bob felt the DeSoto Project was a good real estate investment opportunity. He also wanted more exhibition space and a space with high ceilings. So, joining Blue Sky, the Augen Gallery's second location opened at 716 NW Davis Street.

Charles, a transplant from Texas, arrived in Portland in 1991. He had worked at a gallery in Houston where he'd studied art in college. After moving to Portland, Charles decided he wanted to work in the art world. He met William, felt a kinship with William's gallery, and in 1992, he went to work at the Jamison/ Thomas Gallery.

Like Mary Josephson, Charles had learned a few lessons about the art world from William. There were three key lessons: "You have to be able to talk thoughtfully about their artwork and the artists, about who they are, and why they are making the work. It's good to dream big and make big goals. Most importantly, you have to follow through with a strong business plan."

After William died, Charles opened the Froelick Adelhart Gallery in 1995. Charles and his partner, Shannon Adelhart, rented and shared space for nine years with the Augen Gallery in downtown Portland.

Charles had always wanted his own space. He was convinced that having several art-oriented businesses housed at one location would have a strong destination appeal in the marketplace. It might even reduce advertising costs.

Since Charles and Bob shared gallery space, Charles became privy to conversations Bob and Jim were having about purchasing and renovating a building. Charles thought it was a good idea, something to seriously consider. One day when Jim was visiting Bob's gallery Charles asked him if they were still thinking about the co-op idea. Jim was, and in 2003 or 2004, several gallery owners attended an official meeting hosted by Jim. Charles signed on to the project.

Charles bought raw space—what was referred to as shell space—with utilities stubbed out to the space. Everyone in the group used the same general contractor to finish out their spaces. Besides the galleries and museum, the center also had two cafés— the Salad Bowl and the museum's café. Charles thinks the cafés added value to the venture. Gallery and museum staff and visitors can take a break or eat a convenient lunch. Staff can then continue their work and lead tours, and visitors can return to the museum or visit the other galleries in the complex.

◇ ◇ ◇

Charles A. Hartman Fine Art also found a home with the DeSoto Project. After having had a long-established gallery outside of Portland, Charles relocated his gallery to the city in 2007. The gallery provides specialized access to fine art for collectors focusing on both regional and international artists.

◇ ◇ ◇

LRS Architects bought and occupied the upper floor in the building, becoming the sixth spoke in the ownership wheel. This architectural firm was responsible for designing the core and shell of the fifty-eight-thousand-square-foot building, upgrading the seismic conditions to current code standards, adding the entry canopies, repainting the exterior brickwork, and creating a rooftop deck. The architects also designed the main lobby, stairways, and corridor areas shared by the first- and second-floor tenants.

Before their involvement in this project, the architectural staff was scattered in three separate buildings in the city. Buying and consolidating everyone into the DeSoto Project proved to be an excellent opportunity and investment.

Extensive sustainable measures, including re-milling and reuse of the heavy timbers, helped the building achieve a modern interior with material references to the past. LRS was instrumental in the building receiving status as a historic landmark. Paul Frank, a principal in the firm, said, "The bones of the building are so good," and, "As much of the existing components as possible were left intact."

The DeSoto Project offered the museum and the galleries a chance to own their own spaces instead of being at the whim of a landlord. Jim said, "We needed to look for an antidote, and the antidote is ownership." Ownership meant financial stability and protection against rising rents and sustainability for gallery owners.

More importantly, the DeSoto Project strengthened the connection between the official boundaries of Pearl District and Old Town/Chinatown. Geographically, the DeSoto Project, together with Elizabeth Leach's gallery, the PDX Gallery, the Blackfish Gallery, and others form a core component attesting to the Pearl's attraction as a bona fide arts district.

Public artwork has enhanced the neighborhood streetscape through both private and public sponsored efforts.

42

DISTRICT STREET ART

PORTLAND'S SOUTH PARK BLOCKS WAS once the venue for Artquake, an annual outdoor art festival. In the summer of 1995, two hundred thousand people showed up. The next year—it would have been the twentieth Artquake—the festival was a no-show. What happened? The general view was that organizers had "done it all wrong." Bob Hicks, a reporter for the *Oregonian*, wrote: "It's never had the money, and rarely the vision, to truly succeed even as a local showcase. Nobody's been willing to put up the money for them to produce a major show."

Art in the Pearl replaced Artquake in 1996. Since then, this annual fine arts and crafts festival has been held on Labor Day Weekend in the North Park Blocks. Dismayed and disenfranchised artists created a nonprofit organization to revive a popular annual arts event. They succeeded in providing a quality setting for local artists to show their artwork and to promote art education, especially to and for children. Each festival event includes an education pavilion with art demonstrations and hands-on art activities and a world music stage on which local musicians perform. Assuming it doesn't rain, it provides the local citizenry and visitors a good excuse to spend a few leisurely hours with family and friends browsing the artist stands and snacking on local food and sampling the beverages, notably the craft beer. While the crowds at this festival may not be as large as they had been at Artquake events, Art in the Pearl has now been around for more than two decades. Its longevity has exceeded its predecessor's.

A PRIVATE FOUNDATION

Homer Williams established a private arts foundation—the Pearl Arts Foundation—in 1998. He believed that the neighborhood could benefit from public art at select locations. At the same time, after he amended the development agreement with the City, Homer said he "supported opening the district to all income levels and providing amenities for rich and poor alike."

He was thinking about how to provide something in the public arena all people could share and enjoy. To that end, he sought out Paige Powell because of her experiences in the New York City art world in the 1980s. He felt her connections with famous artists might result in impressive local public art installations. Paige served as the executive director of the Pearl Arts Foundation from 1998 to 2002.

Homer capitalized the foundation with a contribution by Hoyt Street Properties, LLC of $50,000 per individual block plus private donations to fund two projects: One was the *Tikitotemoniki Totems*, by Kenny Scharf. Thirty-feet high, the four abstract aluminum tiki totems cover the streetcar catenary poles by Jamison Square. The foundation also commissioned a sculpture called *Dog Bowl*, which was designed by dog photographer William Wegman. Dogs in the park were treated to piped-in water on hot days. Installed in 2002 in the North Park Blocks, the cast-bronze bowl sits on an eight-by-ten-foot square checkerboard resembling a linoleum kitchen floor.

DONATED ARTWORKS

A Chinese foundry owner, Huo Bao Zhu, donated an amazing piece of art that was also placed in the North Park Blocks. The intent was to allow children to play on full-sized bronze reproductions of Shang dynasty elephants. The sculpture is known as *Da Tung and Xi'an Bao Bao*.

Just across the north end of the park blocks, Lee Kelly's *Memory 99*—an architecturally stark, rust-colored sculpture—was installed on the paved half-block owned by the city in front of the Pacific Northwest College of Art (PNCA). This four-thousand-pound weathered steel sculpture faces directly onto NW Hoyt Street. The sculpture being twenty-free feet long and eleven feet tall means it is quite visible to pedestrians and drivers alike.

A CREATIVE CORRIDOR

John Jay recognized the importance that art and design had played in the ongoing improvement of Chinatown. While not officially part of the Pearl District, the businesses located there, the presence of outdoor public art, and the classic Lan Su Chinese Garden attest to the fact Chinatown has been perceived as part of the cultured Pearl.

John at one time worked with W+K. He opened their Tokyo office in 1997 and relocated to Portland in 2001, working with W+K till 2013. A creative presence at W+K, he also sought to rejuvenate Chinatown by organizing art shows and design-oriented exhibits with his J Studio office.

Add to the mix John's conceptual idea of a "creative corridor"— an area stretching from the Ace Hotel south to Powell's Books and the Pearl District—and it's obvious the boundaries of this creative corridor and future connections to and from the Pearl are fluid in different people's minds. What was important was the recognition that because Chinatown has been changing, it will play an integral and vital role in the Pearl District.

Expanding on his notion of creative corridors, Jay proposed another corridor connecting the Pearl District to Old Town/Chinatown along Couch Street. This idea was institutionalized in 2013 by the City of Portland as they conducted public planning events associated with the preparation of the West Quadrant Plan. The Portland City Council voted to adopt this plan in 2015.

◇ ◇ ◇

Several other funded or donated public art sculptures are visible in the Pearl and the Old Town/Chinatown neighborhoods. Brian Goldbloom's *Festival Lanterns* were installed in 2006. Brian designed a series of outdoor granite and steel sculptures that were installed between NW 3rd and 4th Avenues at Davis and Flanders Streets. This public art project was an attempt to honor the multicultural Asian presence in Portland. Unfortunately, several were vandalized. Eventually, elements of the installation were removed.

Other public artworks in Old Town/Chinatown include David Kerner's 1990 sculpture *Untitled*, Michihiro Kosuge's 1995 basalt artwork titled *Japanese Maple Tree with Rocks*, and Masayuki Nagase's 2011 *Waves of Breath* that was carved out of granite. The latter is located at Broadway and Irving in the courtyard at Bud Clark Commons.

The Chinatown Gateway is the oldest artwork in the area, on West Burnside. Architect Yu Tang Wang and artist Sun Chau under the sponsorship of the Chinese Consolidated Benevolent Association designed the gate. It was built in Taiwan by Ting Hwa Architects and shipped to Portland.

The design of the gate features two lions—one male and the other female—representing the concepts of yin and yang, the principle of natural and complementary forces in nature and the balance between. The gate was installed in one week, dedicated in 1986, and presented to the city as a "gesture of goodwill from the Chinese community."

ART FOR PEDESTRIANS

Tad Savinar, having married his artistic talents to urban design, was always on the lookout for a way to interact with Portland's urban fabric. In 2008, TriMet had recently completed a light rail transit project in downtown. A review of the construction funds revealed some leftover construction money. These funds had to be spent on neighborhood improvements in downtown, and TriMet hired ZGF Architects to help do that.

ZGF received $400,000 to identify ways to enhance the pedestrian experience in Old Town/Chinatown. Tad—who had a longtime working relationship with ZGF—got a call. He ended up undertaking a project he called Block by Block that focused on new uses for street environments adjacent to the new mall on NW 5th Avenue.

He inventoried several of the adjacent streets and ended up selecting Davis as a street that could provide pedestrian connectivity between the Pearl District and Old Town/Chinatown. Tad then studied and identified several types of enhancements that might be appropriate along this street beginning at NW 2nd Avenue and extending all the way to the Armory.

One of the exciting outcomes of this urban design study was the notion of creating specialty lighting along Davis. The Regional Arts and Cultural Council (RACC) got involved and commissioned a series of light-generating sculptures by Dan Corson, a Seattle-based artist.

Dan designed four seventeen-foot sculptures titled *Nepenthes* that greet pedestrians walking along Davis for a four-block stretch in Chinatown. These beautiful curvilinear sculptures, resembling larger-than-life carnivorous plants, contain photovoltaic devices that light up at night. The glow comes from LED lights powered by photovoltaic units inside the sculptures. Each has a different translucent color pattern expressing a distinctive personality.

When PNCA moved next to the North Park Blocks, this gave rise to the idea of developing an expanded urban college campus around this linear open space.

43

AN ART CAMPUS

CULTURALLY AND ENERGETICALLY, THE PRESENCE of the Pacific Northwest College of Art (PNCA) imparts a sense of the artistic ambiance the pioneering artists brought to the industrial warehouse district back in the 1980s. The college, a century-old institution, began as an extension of the Portland Art Museum in 1909. Formed as the School of the Portland Art Association, it was the first museum art school on the West Coast. In 1981, the name was changed to the Pacific Northwest College of Art. By 1994, PNCA had become an independent institution, and the *Oregonian* described the college as "a sprout moving from the greenhouse into the open air."

In 1998, the "sprout" planted new roots in the Pearl. Staff and students moved into the Goodman building, a ninety-two-thousand-square-foot warehouse on Johnson Street. Almost immediately, they needed design help. Sally Lawrence, the college president, and Kristy Edmunds, a local artist, hatched a competition to support emerging local architectural talent. Holst Architecture won the competition based on their idea of creating a large commons in the center of the building for staff and student use.

After being awarded the job, the architects were told that the project budget was fifteen dollars a square foot. They responded by saying they could probably accomplish the project at thirty dollars a square foot. The project turned out to be a catalyst for both the college and Holst.

◇ ◇ ◇

The school began with an enrollment of 127 students. One hundred ten years later, 549 full-time students attended the school as well as approximately 1,450 part-time students. Most of that growth happened under the leadership of Thomas Manley, who replaced Sally as college president in 2003.

The college's education program changed significantly under Tom's leadership. He had graduated from Claremont College for Asian Studies in 1980. He had stayed at Claremont and had taken a series of administrative jobs that allowed him to explore how college education could become "transformative." He also got into fundraising, which he loved doing.

One day he realized he'd spent twenty-three years at Claremont College. For some time, colleagues had been telling him to consider becoming a college president. Tom learned that an art college in Portland, Oregon, was searching for a president. He applied, was selected, and began with the personal and professional goal of preparing students for lives of creative practice. To accomplish this, Tom changed the structure of the curriculum, instituting platforms versus programs.

The platforms Tom instituted reflected the view that resources can be incredibly scarce and with the associated challenges, how does one foster good design, what is the best design, and how does one best communicate it? He was always looking or searching for the power of metaphor. What Tom brought to PNCA, outside of his experience in higher education, was a way of thinking about how to reflect the world we inhabit now, the world that was changing, and the world to come. The new platforms expanded the curriculum beyond the nineteenth-century model that most traditional art institutions were using at the time.

Tom knew he had a few strikes against him and that there were some serious hurdles to overcome. One, he was an outsider, so Tom had to form a new network. Two, he wasn't an expert in art. Instead, he had a vision about what higher education in a changing world could become. Three, the college had few resources and some debt. Unfortunately, it was undercapitalized because of its separation from the art museum and relocation to Johnson Street.

Furthermore, the school didn't have much credibility; people didn't believe it could survive because it had no endowment to speak of. It had had to rent space for its program in a large warehouse that had been renovated on a low budget. The college was also saddled with a five-year remaining lease in one of the highest-rent areas in the city. What PNCA needed was a vision and a strategic plan. It needed to raise money and take the school to the next level. It was time for a master plan.

A CAMPUS MASTER PLAN

As soon as Tom went to work, he and the PNCA board of governors started to think about having a master plan to guide the physical expansion of the college. This would become a big challenge. During Tom's first year, an administrative staffer put together a lunch meeting with community leaders and interested parties. Architect Brad Cloepfil attended this luncheon during which there was a lot of discussion about sustainability.

At the same time, PNCA was putting together a group to collect information about the city and art. In 2004, a blue ribbon committee that included other architects, artists, developers, and architectural enthusiasts contributed to this effort. The group ran through a series of questions that included: What kind of campus should PNCA aspire to? Should it be an urban campus in downtown or be elsewhere in the city? Should the college become an anchor in its neighborhood? What is the value of being in the urban center? Cost was a big concern. Land was expensive, and rents were high in downtown Portland.

The board decided to stay in the urban core. They felt the college connected to the city's DNA. An urban location formed an essential part of the college's brand. Going to the perimeter of the city would have diffused the brand. In essence, the committee was saying, "We want to be true to our roots." PNCA had always been a downtown institution. They had been in the district before it became the Pearl.

Another question had arisen: Is it possible for to have a multidirectional campus? Tom had called it a "compass campus." The campus would have many parts—some in the Pearl, maybe facilities at Lewis & Clark College, in North Portland, or elsewhere in the city. This was possible given Portland's exceptional public transit system and designated bicycle lanes. It was possible, but the committee also realized the college still needed a kitchen, a living room, a commons, and other specialized rooms. What they really needed was a home base, and one they owned outright.

There was a lot of skepticism about what the best direction was when the college issued a request for master planning services. They got six responses, and it came down to a choice between Thomas Hacker's firm and Brad's firm, Allied Works Architecture.

Thomas Hacker's presentation was superb, and Allied Works' presentation, though seemingly more by-the-seat-of-your-pants, had a heart that appealed to PNCA's leadership. Allied Works' presentation was all about "leaping metaphors." They emphasized paintings, Donald Judd sculptures, and other images that spoke to a "thinking process," and the ideas presented were provocative. Since it was a master plan, it wasn't about architecture and defining spaces; it was about creating a framework that emphasized merging the PNCA brand with the city's brand.

Tom went with philosophy. He liked Brad's thought process. The selection committee liked Brad's approach, but they suggested that it was going to cost PNCA a fortune in fees. Tom went to Brad and told him, "You're going to get paid, but you won't get paid very much, and you're not going to get to build anything."

Allied Works and PNCA worked well together. When it was time to pick an architect to provide design services for the renovation of their new home, PNCA sent out another request for proposals. Afterward, Tom got phone calls from local architects who told him they weren't going to submit a response because they felt he should select Allied Works Architecture. And he did.

BUYING THE 511 BUILDING AND A MUSEUM

After 2004, the board committed the administration to make facility ownership a priority. Based on this commitment, the board initiated a capital fundraising campaign. In 2007, the college received a $15 million donation from Hallie E. Ford. Later, at its tenth annual gala in 2012, PNCA announced the launch of a philanthropic campaign, Creativity Works Here, to support the renovation of a historic federal post office building at 511 NW Broadway. The college received additional donor pledges and gifts that totaled $11.5 million. PNCA was now able to commit to a long-term real estate deal with the Portland Development Commission (PDC) for the future purchase of the 511 building.

In 2008, the Museum of Contemporary Craft (MoCC) approached PNCA regarding a possible sale of the museum. A year later, the college bought the museum and assumed its debts. The board had five years to evaluate the situation.

By 2010, the board had resolved to establish a campus on the North Park Blocks, anchored by the 511 building. In 2013, in collaboration with the Powell family, PNCA opened the ArtHouse—a facility that provided living spaces for art students—on the west side of the North Park Blocks near Couch Street. The board also sold the Goodman building to Seattle-based Security Properties. Security Properties then demolished the old warehouse and built a new high-rise apartment building.

The year 2014 saw renovation work begin on the new college headquarters at the 511 building. In 2015, the $32 million renovation was finished, and the college opened its doors for classes. Tom's dream of building an urban art college campus in Portland was moving toward reality.

However, he wouldn't be able to enjoy working in the college's new quarters for long. He had been offered the presidency of the storied Antioch College, a liberal arts college in Ohio. Tom decided to move on after a dozen years in Portland. He had overseen the establishment of a new curriculum that had resulted in unprecedented growth and expansion of Portland's premier art institution. On December 31, 2015, Tom's PNCA contract ended.

Before he left, Tom and a select committee at the college assessed the overall financial needs of the art college. There was concern about the school's long-term financial stability, and the committee had considered a potential sale of MoCC to stabilize the school's financial future. On February 3, 2016, PNCA announced the closure of MoCC. The college planned to absorb the museum's collection and programs into the arts college's new Center for Contemporary Art & Culture.

◇ ◇ ◇

Donald Tuski was appointed the new college president. MoCC was a co-op owner in the DeSoto. One of Don's first tasks was to oversee the sale of the MoCC premises to the Oregon Jewish Museum.

Don had been hired primarily to increase student enrollment and to expand the school's creative legacy. The college wanted to grow through increased student enrollment and a new fundraising program. The college's pathway to a brighter future had dimmed, given higher operational costs and flat tuition revenues.

Another big question arose in 2018. There was talk about a merger with the Oregon College of Art and Craft. This discussion wasn't a new one—the two institutions had considered it on and off over the past thirty years. This discussion lasted about three months. Finally, just before the year ended, the talks ended. Both institutions said no.

Although PNCA occupied a new showcase building, absent the recently discontinued Master of Arts in Critical Theory and Creative Research degree program, there was another question about the long-term growth of the college. How would the redevelopment of the adjacent US Postal Service property and potential expansion of the North Park Blocks affect the school's image and operation? The City was now engaged in the Broadway Corridor Study to determine the best redevelopment strategy for the fourteen-acre property. The school's property abutted the Broadway Corridor property directly north of the school.

On April 25, 2019, the college announced that Don had resigned as the president. He had decided to accept the position of president of the College for Creative Students in Detroit, Michigan, his hometown. PNCA's board of governors immediately began developing a transition plan that included a search process for a new president. Meanwhile, the school waited to learn the outcome of the ongoing master planning by ZGF Architects for the Broadway Corridor property under the auspices of Prosper Portland, formerly the Portland Development Commission.

Bob Gerding didn't quite know what to do with the Armory building as he and Mark Edlen began the Brewery Blocks project. But one of his passions provided the answer.

44

A NEW THEATRICAL DIRECTION

THE BOARD OF DIRECTORS OF Portland Center Stage needed new leadership. The retirement of Elizabeth Huddle from the directorship had prompted the board to pose a soul-searching question about how the organization was going to survive because the company wasn't financially healthy, and they were growing. At the time, Portland Center Stage was a nine-hundred-seat venue in the Newmark Theater with a $3.2 million budget, and productions weren't filling the theater. The theater was over-sized, ill-suited for small, intimate performances, and undercapitalized. A new director had to have the skills and temperament to "make the company artistically and economically viable." Chris Coleman, a candidate for the directorship, wanted to run a bigger theater. He wanted to give theatergoers an experience that was outside the traditional walls of most contemporary theaters in the nation.

HIRING A NEW DIRECTOR

Julie Vigeland, the chairperson of the search committee, clued me in to why the committee became interested in Chris. A new director would have the opportunity, almost from scratch, to create a special program. Chris, as one of the three finalists, had been throwing crazy ideas at the board, and though he thought, *They'll never be interested in what I'm suggesting,* the group representing the board knew they had to make a big change. They chose Chris. They took a big leap, and Chris took a big leap. He was moving clear across the country from Atlanta, Georgia, to a place he didn't know much about.

When I spoke with Chris, he told me he'd lived most of his life in larger cities. He had a fantasy he could live somewhere where he could walk to work in a place where it was still exciting. At first, he wasn't that interested in Portland, but his interest grew as he spoke with more and more people about the opportunity on the West Coast.

Chris was aware that the theater group was in a mess. But there seemed to be a great opportunity if he could find the resources needed to create a program that could make a big impact on the community. He also realized having a new building was a necessity because he wanted to "reimagine a regional theater that could became a flagship theater that was more responsive and more porous in its relationship to the community."

The questions on his mind when he arrived in Portland were: *How do you define regional theater, and what differentiates it from Broadway and off-Broadway? What makes it relevant?* Chris was also thinking about how he might use the public spaces of the theater for other activities. He believed the premises shouldn't be left unused or inert, used only during rehearsals and performances. They needed to be repurposed to activate the spaces. Inviting the public into the theater for other uses was a way to recruit new audience members.

Chris's last interview was one-on-one with Bob Gerding, and Bob told him, "If you take this job, I'll help you find the resources to make it successful." That was what Chris needed to hear. He took the job and the challenge. He knew he was going to have to change the programming, change the profile in the community, build a new home, and get some real dollars and community leadership.

WHAT DO YOU DO WITH A FORTRESS?

The Armory was a vacant, fortress-like relic from the past. Built in 1891, the Armory Annex, as it was originally called, exhibited a rare architectural style known as castellated. The structure originally housed the First Regiment of Oregon's National Guard. Within its walls built of ashlar stone and brick, militia members had practiced indoor drill maneuvers and fired weapons in an underground target range. This Romanesque revival–style building later became a popular public hall. Much later, it was used as a civic meeting place by local Masonic organizations, the American Legion, the Portland Rose Society, and the Camp Fire Girls, for Olympic wrestling trials and basketball games that featured the Portland Indians of the Pacific Coast Professional Basketball League, and during the Vanport flood of 1948, refugees were housed in the Annex.

When Gerding Edlen Development (GED) bought all five of the Brewery Blocks, they wisely decided to preserve the Armory. Recognizing the historical value of this landmark, GED placed it on the National Register of Historic Places. At the same time, they transferred unused air rights from the Armory site to build the Henry, a condominium tower, next door.

The Armory was scheduled to be the first building for renovation. Instead, the Armory ended up being the last because the developer struggled to find a suitable tenant for the structure. The task proved difficult because the exterior of the structure had limited appeal to retailers. The developer had first discussed a lease with REI, a national outdoor recreation retailer. But REI decided they didn't like the Armory building for three reasons. First, two tiers of narrow, vertical-slotted gun-sight window openings allowed little light into the building's interior. Second, the windows offered no opportunity for retail window display. And third, there was no way to provide off-street parking within the structure.

GED had told REI they were willing to dedicate parking for them in an underground garage they were building for the project. REI backed out of the deal. Instead, the store leased the ground floor in the Edge project built at NW 14th Avenue and Johnson, where they built a climbing wall that was highly visible at the store's entry.

Soon another prospective tenant—LA Fitness, a national chain—appeared. LA Fitness had signed a letter of agreement, but they hadn't signed a lease when Bob suddenly got upset and changed his mind. He had realized having a fitness club in the structure limited the number of people who would be able to appreciate this iconic building. Bob pulled the Armory off the market and asked Chris if he thought the building could work as a theater. Yes was the answer.

In short order, Bob and Chris initiated the architectural design for the new theater. They sat down with Steve Domreis, an architect at GBD Architects, and began formulating a design program for the theater. When the question came up about the number of performance stages, they decided to build two. They also decided to hire a theater design consultant, who recommended constructing two 350-seat theaters side by side while keeping the wall surfaces raw. The final design produced the 599-seat US Bank Main Stage and the 190-seat Ellyn Bye Studio.

WHERE WILL THE FINANCING COME FROM?

Bob now had to figure out how to finance this project. He considered several different strategies, but none seemed viable, so Bob decided to talk to Mayor Vera Katz and the Portland Development Commission (PDC). The mayor liked the idea of a cultural facility in the Pearl. To advance the concept, she directed the PDC to investigate potential funding sources.

From the beginning, it was apparent this was going to be a complicated and expensive renovation. After several meetings, GED worked out a deal with the mayor and Sam Adams, her chief of staff. The city purchased the building in 2003. Then the City arranged a loan package that was somewhat outside of standard business practices. The approach was modeled on a San Francisco project that had used public dollars as a catalyst for a private project. Portland Center Stage would wait until the renovations were completed and then purchase the building from the PDC.

The final cost to renovate the Armory was $36.1 million. The commission had structured a financing package using tax increment financing, River District urban renewal funds, historic and federal new markets tax credits, and a $10.6 million loan from US Bank. This financial cocktail leveraged somewhere between $11 and $15 million dollars of outside capital to obtain a state-of-the-art theater for the city.

To understand the murky waters that swirled around the financing story, I spoke with Colin Rowan, who worked as an advisor in the financial services sector. Colin pointed out that the financing had come together as a convergence of several critical factors, both public and private, both individual and institutional. Tax increment dollars were used to stand behind the debt as a moral obligation and guarantee for funds sourced from US Bank.

This was important for this single-purpose project because there was only going to be a single tenant, Center Stage. Although the company had a reasonable operating track record for a local nonprofit theater, it wasn't straightforward for commercial real estate lenders to underwrite this type of business from a banking perspective. Nonprofit theaters are dependent upon ticket sales and donations for their revenue. Realistically, their sources of revenue are fickle. Their revenue stream was entirely reliant on the popularity of their shows, ticket sales, and the company's net profitability at the end of the theatrical season. Therefore, if a bank was going to lend money on this type of risky business, they needed some entity—in this instance, the City—to backstop the loan in case of default. The City's decision to guarantee the loan was not without controversy among the locals.

Colin's view was that Vera actively supported project because of the historic preservation story attached to the Armory building's renovation. She was also concerned about the disposition of the building if it was left to market forces because the building had very few potential commercial uses. If the structure hadn't been saved and renovated, it would have been likely the building would have been demolished to make way for new development. Furthermore, there was also the general recognition of the resurgence of commitment to regional theater in Portland, and what the theater could become in the future.

As Colin and I talked, it became clear why the City and others had gone along with this unconventional financing deal. Dealing with a nonprofit required more flexibility than a typical commercial business. US Bank supported the idea all the way. It was early in the history of a new federal tax credit program put in place under President Bill Clinton, which had been signed into law under President George Bush. The bank saw an opportunity to be part of a groundbreaking and important project from an environmental, historic preservation, and cultural arts standpoint. The fact that this was going to be a LEED (Leadership in Energy and Environmental Design) project added to the appeal of using the new market tax credits for the project.

Some misinformation and misperception arose about why these public funds were going into this theater project. There had been the misperception you could transfer the capital dollars that had been raised to another project. This was a failure to recognize that the funds had been raised to support a visionary project, not just a project among projects. Furthermore, Goldman Sachs had raised a portion of the funding, and they had specified the Gerding Theater was to be the recipient of the funds.

As the financing deal was being worked out, the Center Stage board of directors had to show good faith by contributing the sum of $2 million toward the project. Chris and Julie had to start a capital campaign immediately. They took people to breakfast and lunches and asked for donations. Typically, they received donations ranging from $1,000 to $50,000. In the end, Julie and Chris came up with the good faith money.

As the architects prepared to start the design process, they quickly realized this was going to be a complicated project. The design specified multiple stages, administrative staff office spaces, extensive back-of-house areas and storage requirements, a rotating stage component, a kitchen, and a sit-down dining area, and they had been told the complex needed to serve as a community-oriented space for public activities. This wasn't a simple interior renovation of the old Armory building.

The architects faced the reality of designing and constructing a new building inside a designated historic structure that had been placed on the National Register of Historic Places. There were going to be strict constraints associated with preserving the integrity of the historic structure.

45

LIKE A SHIP IN A BOTTLE

BESIDES THE DIFFICULTIES ASSOCIATED WITH a hands-off approach to the structure itself, the developers had realized there was a noise issue due to the fact the Armory was sandwiched between two streets each with embedded tracks for the Portland Streetcar. The performance halls would need to be isolated from the rumble of both the streetcar and vehicular traffic on NW 10th and 11th Avenues.

Construction access to the interior of the Armory was limited from the onset. The National Park Service had advised the developers that the roofing materials and structural members including purloins could be removed and replaced. The interior of the existing structure could be and was gutted to allow construction of a new concrete structure that sits inside the existing building shell. But the existing roof trusses could not be removed or damaged in any way. It was like building the proverbial "a ship in a bottle."

In addition, the National Park Service, the Oregon State Historic Preservation Office, and the State Historic Landmarks Commission were all involved in the regulatory aspects of the project. The director and staff of the State Preservation Office understood the principles at hand and didn't get hung up on details. As long as the architects adhered to the intent of and retained the historic character of the structure, the director was OK with the construction activities.

The building's interior consisted of a single, large open space since the roof was held up by a system of wood bowstring trusses. The trusses were unique because they had been constructed from laminated wood and wrought iron bars that had minimized the use of metal thereby reducing structural and roofing costs without compromising the strength and durability of the supporting system of bowstring trusses. Being unique and expressive of the historic era, the trusses were considered a key architectural feature of the building by the historic preservation authorities. By preserving the trusses, the project received $3.2 million in historic tax credits.

The preservation authorities also wanted the public to see these trusses when the renovations were completed, and they wanted them seen in the spatial configuration that defined the volume of the interior space. Therefore, the architects had to create an atrium-like space that, in turn, affected their vaulted ceiling design for the entry lobby with an integrated mezzanine level for dining activities.

The mezzanine needed to seat three hundred people for a dinner event. The design of the space was complicated because the architects had to determine what shape accommodated this number of guests, while also providing a clear view of the trusses and curved ceiling. A rectilinear cutout on the floor didn't work—plus, it wasn't dramatic enough—but an oval-shaped cutout did a better job, and an associated curved staircase provided a gracious architectural statement. The combination of all these curved elements produced a perfect, delightful solution. When the people entered the theater lobby, patrons found it impossible not to look up...especially at the stars.

During evening performances, the lobby ceiling was lit with blue lights to simulate a night sky. An array of small lights representing stars was hung from the ceiling; they created a stunning visual environment. As the last person leaves for the night, the stars go out, only to return the next night. It's a reminder that even though the curtain goes down on an evening performance, the curtain will rise again for another show. As an intimate example of placemaking, the foyer has become a special place in the Pearl.

Bob Gerding had a real concern about the design of the seats for the main stage. He was a big man. He wanted to make sure they were comfortable. Bob also wanted to make sure a big person could walk in front of seated patrons without them having to stand up. The architects made sure there was extra legroom.

Julie Vigeland related a story about a meeting that took place at the architects' office. Seven or eight individuals were in attendance. Several different types of seating had been assembled. Each person sat down in each of the sample seats to assess the degree of comfort. Julie explained to me how some were too small. Others didn't have enough room from the back to the front of the seat. Comments ranged: This will never work; this is too hard; yikes, this is too soft; and before I even finish getting up, the seat is springing closed and hitting me. Eventually, among the available samples, everyone favored the same one. It was reminiscent of "Goldilocks and the Three Bears." Only one of the seats was just right!

Additionally, there was considerable interest in the design of the seat coverings. There was a discussion about occasions when there would be a half-full house. When this occurs, in most theaters, actors look out at lots of obviously empty seats, the backs of which typically have a dark coloration given the low light level. Someone suggested they put some color on the backs of several seats in a random pattern. It was a purposeful way of creating the impression that the house was fuller than it actually was, for the benefit of the actors.

OPEN TO THE PUBLIC

The new theater produced several benefits. Once the company was established in its new quarters, after the initial season of performances, audiences doubled in size, and the number of young people attending increased by 76 percent. The dollar base tripled. As a result, Center Stage's brand in the community got much clearer. The company's identity and what they were trying to do artistically shifted. In the old space, if the company did something edgy, they sometimes got a lot of pushback. In the new Gerding Theater, that attitude seemed to disappear. People just thought, "That's who they are."

Center Stage's mission statement was: "Inspiring our community by bringing stories to life in unexpected ways." It's purposeful that the words *theater* and *play* are not in that statement. The company doesn't always bring productions to the stage people expect to see. Instead, it's about building relationships and creating conversations around events. This approach is similar to Thomas Manley's idea of platforms instead of programs.

Theater management used dynamic pricing. High-ticket demand resulted in higher ticket prices. This advice came from one of the Portland Timbers executives. It is part of the for-profit box office marketing strategy Center Stage management uses. Subscribers have prices that are fixed and not subject to dynamic pricing. This incentivizes season ticket purchases.

The idea of keeping the building open during working hours introduced anxiety into the conversation during the programming stage of the process back in 2003. Some of those involved in the design approach were concerned about what might happen if people started to camp out in the lobby. After the doors to the theater opened to the public, that concern faded away. You can get a cup of coffee there at any time during the day. Administrative staffers view themselves as managers of a community complex, not just people working solely for the theater company.

The architects were impressed with how Bob drove the team forward. He was broadminded, creatively inspiring, and not someone who could be deterred. The idea of going for a platinum LEED designation was an audacious goal. It became a challenge for everyone affiliated with the project. This design objective opened a different conversation with the Portland Center Stage's donor base. Once environmentalism and sustainability were part of the brand, Center Stage was positioned as a progressive, forward-thinking organization.

◇ ◇ ◇

Vera Katz Park—the narrowest park in Portland—honors that mayor's commitment to and support for the roles the Armory and theater play in the city. Originally, a much larger park had been proposed for the block Henry Condominiums now sits on. Instead, this sliver of a park was designed as part of an extra-wide strip of sidewalk along Davis Street between NW 10th and 11th Avenues next to the Armory.

Murase Associates, a local landscape architectural and planning firm, designed a series of runnels and troughs that form a linear, flowing water feature between the sidewalk and the Armory's north wall. The design is pure simplicity. Sculptural in form, the stonework runnel walls rise above the sloping grade line of the sidewalk and terminate in level, horizontal surfaces that function as informal seating for pedestrians.

Hidden is a cistern that stores rainwater used to flush toilets and urinals in the theater. The fountain uses a recirculation system as part of the sustainability philosophy of the overall project.

CENTER STAGE'S CONTRIBUTION

Besides being a cultural performance center, Portland Center Stage became a unique community center. That intent was programmed into the design process from the very beginning. The building opens at 10:00 each morning and remains open late each evening. Unquestionably, the board succeeded at what they set out to do. Center Stage has become a regional theater well known for its excellent productions. The facility is a travel-oriented destination attraction and an asset for the city and the Pearl.

The Armory provides educational opportunities for kids that include inexpensive and sometimes free tickets. There is a huge outreach to local schools—typically five hundred events a year—and some of the events are sponsored by organizations renting space in one of the performance halls. The theater and its stages are all rentable spaces, allowing private parties to program events for their own purposes.

In many of the theaters in New York City, you will see some people dressed to the nines. I like to remember what Julie told me about the Gerding Theater: "One of our concerns about being in the Newmark Theater was that people thought they had to dress up to attend an event. We wanted the new theater to feel like it was a place for everyone. You didn't have to dress up to see a show here. Portland has a different DNA. People here like lumberjack shirts and jeans."

PART SIX

THE POSTPONED PEARL

UNDER THE COVID PANDEMIC

2020-2022

THE POSTPONED PEARL TIMELINE

Under The Covid Pandemic

2008	Portland starts to recover from the most recent economic recession.
2017	Portland State University students publish the RETHINK NW 13th Phased Action Plan
2019	Lynd Opportunity Partners withdraws from the Centennial Mills project
2020	Covid-19 hits the City of Portland.
2021	Initial mandated restrictions to prevent the spread of the virus are lifted
2021	The City approves vehicular traffic restrictions for NW 13th Avenue
2021	Continuum Partners withdraws from the Broadway Corridor project
2021	Prosper Portland sells the Centennial Mills property

THE PEARL DISTRICT STORY EXEMPLIFIES how a successful urban renewal project at the beginning of the twenty-first century in Portland turned an old warehouse district into a renowned downtown mixed-use district. Many cities wanted to emulate this achievement. Working together, both the private and public sectors transformed an old manufacturing-industrial area into a lively urban community with a strong arts cultural overlay. National and international visitors marveled at the dynamic mix of land uses, the presence of modern streetcars, and the active, vibrant pedestrian street life that permeated the district.

On display was an urban lifestyle that suited the desires of both homeowners and renters. The developers had promoted this new lifestyle, and many made a handsome profit. City officials, they were rewarded with an enlarged tax base. And, over time, the district had welcomed an assorted variety of boutiques, restaurants, pubs, and hotels that catered to a youthful market of travelers. This lively sense of urbanity was now a destination playground for those seeking a unique urban getaway experience. The recently opened Hoxton Hotel attested to the Pearl's popularity to attract a new kind of tourist to the city.

The transformation began with the conversion and adaptive reuse of old warehouses and ended with the construction of high-rise point towers. The early years were heady times. It seemed like a new spirit born on NW 13th Avenue had been injected into city life. Few, if any, of the local entrepreneurs responsible for these building conversions, their tenants, and the pioneering individuals that homesteaded the new condominiums and real estate marketplace had any notion of what the Pearl would resemble in 2022.

As the district matured, the word *gentrified* crept into the vocabulary. Artists had flocked to the district for inexpensive studio space. They were displaced as rents increased. Artists now returned to the Pearl to view their artwork that was being exhibited in storefront art galleries. The short-block grid that had been imposed on Hoyt Street Yards had been built out to house a new urban community, and there were plans afoot to redevelop an existing US Postal Service property into a major mixed-use project in the Pearl. The 2008 recession was a thing of the past. By 2019, continued growth and development in and around the Pearl seemed to delineate the path forward.

Then in 2020, things changed. Covid-19 arrived in Portland, as it did most other places, like an uninvited guest to a dinner party. Motivated by fear, uncertainty and governmental mandates people began staying home. If they ventured outside, they wore masks. Retail business, services, and restaurants closed their doors, some eventually switching to takeout sales. In the Pearl, sidewalk tables and chairs sat empty; the district's street and café life disappeared. Before the pandemic, it could be difficult to find an on-street parking space. This was no longer a problem.

By spring 2021, many of the restrictions had been eased. The growing availability and use of coronavirus vaccines diminished the impact of the public health crisis in Portland. As seasonal temperatures rose to warmer levels, T-shirts and shorts appeared as pedestrian traffic—young, old, and a few tourists—returned to the Pearl District. Things were far from perfect, and not every business had survived the squeezed global supply chain and changing local and federal mandates, but the district was once again adapting.

One of the most visible changes in the Pearl was the introduction of outdoor dining facilities; sections NW 13th Avenue were closed to cars to allow big stretches of dining tents and tables. The owners of restaurants and bars in buildings facing NW 13th Avenue had decided they needed to build outdoor dining facilities to replace lost indoor dining capacity due to mandated restrictions. Back in

2017, a planning study and report undertaken by Portland State University (PSU) graduate students supported by the Pearl District Neighborhood Association (PDNA) and the Portland Bureau of Transportation (PBOT) had advanced the idea of converting this special street into a car-free pedestrian-oriented space. Forced into reimagining the street by the pandemic, PBOT approved applications to close portions of the roadway between NW Everett and Irving Streets to allow dining facilities in the public street. This was transformation in action.

PROJECTS IN THE REDEVELOPMENT PIPELINE

The evolution of the Pearl—it's not finished. The big question is how long new development will have to wait as disruption caused by Covid-19 settles out or we continue to adapt to it. Currently, the City has several major development projects in the pipeline they need to get back on track. City officials have approved master plans for the Broadway Corridor and Centennial Mills. Both projects, after implementation, will reshape the Pearl's physical form while increasing its population density and its visual character.

For decades, a fourteen-acre land parcel situated along the eastern edge of the Pearl District served as the city's main post office. In 2016, Prosper Portland paid $88 million for the property. A spokesperson for the city's urban renewal agency publicly stated that this land was a "once-in-a-generation opportunity to add to Portland's economy and vitality and to deliver community benefits" to the wider metropolitan area.

In 2018, Prosper hired Continuum Partners, a Denver-based development company to advise and work with ZGF Architects on a community-based master planning process for the Broadway Corridor project. By September 2020, the city had approved a master plan for the project. Initial construction anticipated 700 new residential units, including a significant number of affordable housing units. The project heralded the arrival of another mixed-use, multi-block urban village composed of mid- and high-rise buildings akin to the Brewery Blocks. A year later, the counter services in the main post office building had been relocated into the ground floor of an adjacent multiple-story parking structure. City officials then began to consider demolition of the old post office building.

However, on September 8, 2021, Prosper Portland announced that Continuum Partners had withdrawn from the project. Kimberley Branam, Prosper's executive director, said, "We're thankful for Continuum's significant expertise and partnership as development advisor throughout the master planning and steering committee process." She also said Continuum would continue to advise the city on project implementation. Mark Falcone, Continuum's CEO, aware of the changed and challenging local real estate market, had decided his firm needed to redirect their focus to other projects. In his statement. Mark also referred to "the complexities of the project" as a factor in his firm's decision to focus on other projects.

So, why did Continuum sign up for the project in the first place, five years earlier? Well, back then things looked rosy. Portland had been a dynamo investment market. Institutional investment money was readily available to finance projects in downtown Portland, and development in the Pearl District had peaked.

What happened and caused Continuum opt out of the project? The Covid-19 public health crisis happened and clouded Continuum's perception of being able to implement the USPS master plan, which was the first phase of the broader Broadway Corridor project.

Furthermore, political discord and more than one hundred consecutive days of social protest, riots, and vandalism added to an unsettled atmosphere that permutated the city. Storefronts in the district and downtown were boarded up. The city's homeless population had erected pockets of tented living quarters on the outer edges of the Pearl District. The quality of city street life, at one point, had virtually vanished. Public service offices and public schools had shut down. Zoom meetings replaced face-to-face meetings. The ambiance of normality had disappeared. People complained about feckless leadership at City Hall. There didn't seem to be any real effort to bring back the city's economic vitality. Locally, people began to speak about a city in chaos.

These were the complexities Continuum had faced even before the public health crisis impacted the city. In addition, segments of the public had begun to lose confidence in Prosper Portland. There were unanswered questions about the leadership role the city would and could play in the future.

Portland has always had a commission government system. Four commissioners and a weak mayor make up the city council. Back in the 1980s and '90s, the city council established policy. The city's planning bureau regulated the policy, and the Portland Development Commission (PDC) implemented the policies. These governance responsibilities had been clearly delineated, and, generally speaking, things worked smoothly. Bureau heads and senior staff operated with an underlying sense of cooperation as exemplified by advocates of the Portland Way.

Unfortunately, this established system of governance has changed. Prosper Portland, a revised version of the PDC, adopted a new role that combined adopting social justice policies and a focus on building an equitable economy for all Portlanders.

Previously, the PDC had been very successful in bringing several complicated urban renewal projects to the local marketplace. The real estate deals and financial strategies had focused on the public sector providing the necessary physical infrastructure, which had incentivized the private sector to act. The City's recent adoption of new social policies for more affordable housing began to complicate the deal making. As an example: Requiring a developer to include a significant percentage of affordable housing units in the market mix had cost implications. Lowering the market price of some units meant someone or something had to subsidize the cost of those units.

By fall 2021, Prosper Portland had established an implementation schedule for the Broadway Corridor project. Demolition of the exiting the U.S. Postal Service building in preparation for street and utility infrastructure necessary to permit construction of the initial phases of site redevelopment was scheduled for summer 2022. The proposed work included demolition of a small electrical transformer structure and remediation of contaminated soil on the property. The existing parking garage would continue to operate as a public facility as part of an interim use plan for the property. The following year, from January to June, the City has plans to begin construction of new streets, starting with the extension of Johnson and Kearney from NW 9th Avenue to NW Station Way and Union Station. Phased development of new office and housing towers would follow over the next fifteen to twenty years. The construction of a new park and the Green Loop bike and pedestrian pathway would also be phased over this timeframe.

However, Prosper Portland has a new challenge. They need to attract a replacement developer for the project. Given all the new realities and complexities, is this schedule realistic? The timing for the planned construction of streets and utility improvements couldn't be better given the recent passage of President Biden's hard-fought $1 trillion infrastructure deal with Congress. Portland will be among many metropolitan areas preparing to request an allocation as those funds are distributed nationwide.

However, as has happened in the past, city officials need to avoid the missteps that have plagued the Centennial Mills waterfront project.

◇ ◇ ◇

Centennial Mills—a highly visible, desirable waterfront site on the Willamette River—has been and remains today a forlorn sight along Naito Parkway. The City purchased the property in 2000 for $7.7 million and later spent another $20 million for cleanup and demolition. It's too early to tell how this tale will end.

Many have advocated for a teardown approach, while historical preservationists have actively supported preserving and rehabilitating the structure. The City has been trying to redevelop this riverfront property for decades. To date, the history of this project has been an example of one failed attempt after another.

After purchasing the property, the City in 2006 produced a framework plan while not detailing or recommending any specific activities. Instead, the plan, inspirational in tone, identified several development opportunities. Using this plan as a point of departure, the City attempted from 2006 to 2013 to prove out the feasibility of development with two different developers, one after the other. Both developers came to similar conclusions: a "combination of market conditions, technical challenges, and resource constraints" made the project infeasible.

After numerous failed attempts to redevelop this waterfront property, the Portland City Council decided on March 22, 2017, to pursue a full-site redevelopment approach. They wanted four hundred thousand square feet of development consisting of 426 units, with a portion of affordable housing; seventeen thousand square feet of commercial space; and twenty thousand square feet of creative office space. Prosper then listed the 4.4-acre property for sale in June 2017. After receiving fourteen offers, Prosper eventually selected a proposal by the Lynd Opportunity Partners, a Texas-based developer with no experience in Portland. Lynd, in concert with SERA, a Portland architectural firm, had been tasked to determine if the remaining historic structures on the site can be rehabilitated and to come up with a final solution for this historic waterfront site.

In 2018, the project was kicked off in a public forum. Prosper introduced the developer's team to a group of interested citizens and interest groups. And then history repeated itself. In mid-June 2019, Lynd notified Prosper that the company was withdrawing from the project. By 2021, Prosper Portland was still seeking a new developer for this valuable riverfront site.

And then, on November 10, 2021, the Portland City Council announced the sale of the Centennial Mills property to the California-based developer Handson Equities LLC, Emma Corp., and MLR Ventures LLC. The commissioners had signed an agreement to sell the riverfront property for $13 million with the expectation the developers would begin construction within a ten-year timeframe.

The prospective developers were given a 180-day inspection period to conduct a due diligence study to determine the viability of the project and another six-month period in which to close on the agreed-upon real estate deal. The agreement will require the developers to build the Willamette Greenway path along the property's riverfront and meet Portland's inclusionary for affordable housing units, if any residential uses are included in the project. City officials have also decided not to require preservation of the historic flourmill structure on the property, as had been the case in previous redevelopment plans for the site. Since the property was and is a confirmed brownfield site, the developer will be responsible for cleanup activities. More than likely, this will require either removal of contaminated soils or a cap-and-cover approach to ensure safe development and public use of the property.

Therefore, after purchasing the property for $7.7 million, the city has invested a total of at least $30 million in public funds during two decades of public ownership. These expenditures include funds to demolish a riverfront wharf, remove unsafe accessory buildings, determine the site contained toxic materials, and spend assorted monies for public safety and security purposes. The new sales agreement may now allow the prospective development team to formulate a practical and economic development program suitable for construction sometime in the next decade.

◇ ◇ ◇

A London-based developer, the Hoxton Group, purchased the old Grove Hotel and renamed it the Hoxton Hotel. This boutique, or house, hotel, located next to the Chinatown Gateway at NW 4th Avenue and West Burnside, with its multiple dining and drinking facilities, had demonstrated there was renewed interest in improving the Chinatown section of Old Town.

Recently, Guardian Real Estate, a Portland developer, obtained approval to build a high-rise complex consisting of two buildings a block away from the hotel. The site, referred to as Block 33, had been a surface parking lot for decades in the middle of Old Town/Chinatown. In approving the project, the City up-zoned the neighborhood allowing significantly higher buildings. If built, the project could spur more urban renewal in this neighborhood that has considered itself as part of the cultural Pearl District.

All three projects have been saddled with uncertainty swirling around public perceptions and responses to the coronavirus public health crisis, Portland's homeless issues, and reduced demand for ground-floor retail space and commercial office development. Local developers appear to be nervous and apprehensive about committing to new projects as evidenced by Continuum Partners pull out from the Broadway Corridor project.

Portlanders, concerned about the lack of leadership at City Hall, have been heard saying the city needs a city manager instead of a mayor and that the commission form of government needs to be replaced by a council/manager form of government. Under this different system, the council would be the policy makers and goal setters for the city and might initiate major projects. A city manager would be responsible for carrying out council policy, appointing bureau directors administering all the functions of government. In this system, the manager and bureau directors are tested daily in terms of their responsiveness to council and community wishes.

Amid this negativity, local citizens continue to embrace a positive view—they see change as an opportunity. It's a chance to correct mistakes, try new ideas and planning concepts, and make structural changes to better serve a wider spectrum of citizens. The Community Benefits Agreements incorporated into the Broadway Corridor project was a good example of how to implement economic and social change at a local project level. But to accomplish that specific goal for the Broadway Corridor and Centennial Mills projects, the city needs to find another qualified, creative developer for each project.

The Pearl District has always been an experiment in city planning and urban design. It will continue to be, but it will also have to embrace this newfound concept of integrating social infrastructure with the creative physical infrastructure inherent in good urban design.

◇ ◇ ◇

The Pearl District has also always been subject to change. That's part of the organic nature of city planning and development, which is subject to economic, social, and technological trends with a bit of politics thrown in to liven up the process. A city's urban form never remains in stasis.

However, the public health crisis has magnified the nature and timeframe for continued redevelopment of the Pearl District neighborhood. The Covid-19 crisis has been and continues to be a transformative event with unknown, longer-term effects. It's anticipated that some people who worked at home will not return to the office. Some people who lost jobs they didn't like are making other employment choices. This has and may continue to reduce the projected demand for commercial office and retail space in the Pearl District and other nearby downtown sites like Centennial Mills. The new face of the Pearl District may not turn out to be what city officials, city planners, urban designers, and others had envisioned.

The story of the Pearl District's earliest physical manifestation was the recognition that NW 13th Avenue was a special street in the North Downtown. Several blocks facing that street were designated as a historic district and placed on the National Register of Historic Places. But even as Portlanders sheltered in place during the public health crises, the Pearl District's heart and soul was still beating on NW 13th Avenue. Hopefully, this historic district will remain a testament to an earlier era as more transformative changes occur in the surrounding neighborhood.

Covid-19 and its variants have and will continue to disrupt planned redevelopment projects in and around the Pearl District. But because the city is an organic creature, the evolution of the Pearl will continue. We just don't know what the schedule or program is anymore due to the uncertainty associated with the pandemic.

Unfortunately, several restaurants in the Pearl have closed, and a few businesses have departed for new locations. Building owners are now looking for new tenants. Meanwhile, on the plus side, development in the Pearl District continues, as evidenced by the construction of the new Hyatt Place hotel.

However, Block 24—Hoyt Street Properties' last remaining block from the original Hoyt Street Yards property—is still vacant, undeveloped land. Tiffany Sweitzer still has time to contemplate doing something great. The Pearl story is still an open book, and there are more chapters to write.

ACKNOWLEDGMENTS

Portland's Basketball Team is aptly named the Trail Blazers. Developers and investors, especially the early birds based in Portland, took remarkable risks in their quest to build a new urban neighborhood. They are trailblazers too. When it came to Portland's redevelopment of the Northwest Industrial District, the city owes a civic debt to these individuals as well as other trailblazers—city planners, architects, engineers, neighborhood activists, city bureaucrats, politicians, and ordinary citizens who all played key roles. Propelled by foresight, visionary energy they participated in the evolution and transformation of the Northwest Industrial District into the Pearl of today—this is their shared legacy.

I owe a debt of gratitude to all those individuals who agreed to an interview with me. Later, many provided me with their critiques, clarifications, corrections, and suggestions to my draft manuscripts. Paddy Tillett gave me two great suggestions—add a graphic timeline of key dates and provide a list of the characters mentioned or quoted in the book.

Throughout my research for this book, I also drew upon interviews Ernie Bonner, a past Portland planning director, conducted and recorded. These are archived and available at Portland State University. The writings of Carl Abbot, Jewel Lansing, and Sy Adler were beneficial in providing me with background material on planning and political activities in the 1960s and '70s.

To all those individuals I interviewed for the book—they are listed in the bibliography, thanks again for your contributions.

BIBLIOGRAPHY

Abbott, Carl. Portland Planning, Politics, and Growth in a Twentieth-Century City. Lincoln: University of Nebraska Press, 1983.

Abbott, Carl. Portland in Three Centuries. Corvallis: Oregon State University Press, 2011.

Adler, Sy. Oregon Plans—The Making of an Unquiet Land-Use Revolution. Corvallis: Oregon State University Press, 2012.

American Institute of Architects. Regional–Urban Design Assistance Team. The Last Place in the Downtown Plan. Portland, OR, 1983.

Baker, Ann. "Neil Goldschmidt, He Wants to Beat 'System.'" Register Guard (Eugene, OR), May 28, 1972: 8A.

Breen, Ann and Rigby, Dick. Intown Living—A Different American Dream. Washington, DC: Island Press, 2004.

Brown, Peter Hendee. How Real Estate Developers Think—Design, Profits, and Community. Philadelphia: University of Pennsylvania Press, 2015.

Comerford, Jane. A History of Northwest Portland from the River to the Hills. Portland, OR: Dragon Fly Press, 2011.

City of Portland, Mayor Office/Portland Office of Transportation/Portland Development Commission. The Emergence of the River District—A New Urban Community. Portland, OR, 2003.

Gifford, Laura Jane. "Planning for a Productive Paradise." OHQ 115, no. 4 (2014.

Gorsek, Christopher S. Portland's Pearl District (Images of America). Mount Pleasant, SC: Arcadia Publishing, 2012.

Lansing, Jewel. Portland People, Politics, and Power 1851–2001. Corvallis: Oregon State University Press, 2002–2005.

North Downtown Consortium/Shiels & Obletz/Zimmer, Gunsul Frasca Partnership. A Vision for Portland's North Downtown. ZGF, 1992.

Northwest Industrial Sanctuary Task Force. Recommendations to the Portland City Council on Changes to the Planning and Zoning Code and Maps, Portland City Council, 1996

Northwest Triangle Business Association, Bureau of Planning, Office of Transportation. Thirteenth Avenue Urban Design Plan. January 1990.

OTAK. River District Development Plan, A Technical Memo #2. Bureau of Transportation Engineering and Development, Portland, 1993.

Ozawa, Connie P. (Ed.). The Portland Edge—Challenges and Successes in Growing Communities. Washington, DC: Island Press, 2004.

Peirce, Neal R. and Guskind, Robert. Breakthrough, Re-Creating the American City. New Brunswick, NJ: Center for Urban Policy Research, Rutgers, 1993.

Portland Bureau of Planning. North of Burnside Land Use Policy. Adopted by the Portland City Council. Portland, Oregon, 1981.

Portland Bureau of Planning. North of Burnside Supplemental Report. Adopted by the Portland City Council. Portland, Oregon, 1981.

Portland Bureau of Planning. Northwest Triangle Study Background Document. Portland, Oregon, 1984.

Portland Bureau of Planning. Northwest Triangle Report. Adopted by the Portland City Council. Portland, Oregon, 1985.

Portland Bureau of Planning. Proposed Central City Plan. Portland, Oregon, 1987.

Portland Bureau of Planning. Recommended Central City Plan. Portland, Oregon, 1988.

Portland Bureau of Planning. North Downtown Development Program. Portland, OR: Portland Development Commission, 1990.

Portland Bureau of Planning and Sustainability. Central City 2035 West Quadrant Plan (Recommended Draft). Portland, Oregon, 2014.

Portland Development Commission. Agreement for Development Between the City of Portland and Hoyt Street Properties, LCC, dated September 8, 1997.

Portland Development Commission. Amended and Restated Agreement for Development Between the City of Portland and Hoyt Street Properties, LCC, dated March 12, 1999.

Portland Parks and Recreation/Peter Walker and Partners Landscape Architects/Opsis Architecture. Portland River District Park System Urban Design Framework Study. Portland, OR: PWP, 2001.

River District Steering Committee. The River District—A Development Plan for Portland's North Downtown (Final Draft). City of Portland, 1994.

Shiels, Obletz Johnsen. Old Town/Chinatown Development Plan. Portland, OR, 1999.

Skidmore, Owings & Merrill. Urban Design Plan and Program Waterfront Renewal Area. City of Portland, 1975.

Skidmore, Owings & Merrill. Union Station Transportation Center— Concept for an Intermodal Transportation Center. City of Portland/Office of Planning and Development/Portland Development Commission/ Portland Bureau of Planning, 1975.

Smith, Christopher and McMorran, Megan. Voices of the Armors—A Chronicle of the Transformation of a 19th Century Icon into a 21st Century Theater. Portland, OR: Friends of the Armory and Portland Family of Funds Holding, Inc., 2006.

SRG Partnership; Papers/Cooper Consultants; Gary/Barton, Rudolph/ Carol Mayer-Reed. North Terminal Planning and Design Analysis. Portland, OR, 1989.

Suutari, Amanda. "USA—Oregon (Portland)—Sustainable City." The Eco Tipping Points Project, Models for Success in a Time of Crisis, June 2006.

The River District Steering Committee, City of Portland, Shiels Obletz Johnson, LLC Zimmer Gunsul Frasca Partnership. The River District Investment Strategy. Portland, OR, circa 1995.

Union Station Task Force. Development Plan and Implementation Program. Portland Development Commission, 1992.

von Hagen, Bettina, Kellogg, Erin, and Frerichs, Eugenie (Eds). "RebuiltGreen." Portland, OR: Ecotrust, 2003.

Zukin, Sharon. Loft Living, Culture and Capital in Urban Change. New Brunswick, NJ: Rutgers University Press, 1989.

Zukin, Sharon. Naked City, The Death and Life of Authentic Urban Places. Oxford, UK: Oxford University Press, 2010.

◇ ◇ ◇

Personal interviews conducted by me were critical in obtaining detailed information from individuals who contributed directly to the comprehensive planning, design, and construction processes that reflect the Pearl District's built environment. Individuals interviewed include:

Al Solheim, Alan Webber, Bill Naito, Bill Will, Bob Ames, Bob Ball, Bob Frasca, Bob Janik, Bob Koch, Bob Naito, Bob Packard, Brad Cloepfil, Brad Dempy, Brad Rogers, Brian Libby, Brian McCarter, Bruce Allen, Bruce Forster, Carl Abbott, Carol Smith-Larson, Carolyn Cook, Charles Froelick, Charles Kelley, Charles Redmon, Cheryl Barton, Chris Coleman, Chris Zahra, Christopher Rauschenberg, Colin Rowan, Curt Gottfried, Dave Mayfield, David August, David Harwood, David Leland, Dan Volker, Debbie Thomas, Dennis Wilde, Don Stastny, Don Magnusen, Don Mazziotti, Don Vallaster, Doug Macy, Elizabeth Leach, Ethan Seltzer, Gary Reddick, Geoffrey Pagen, George "Bing" Shelton, George Crandall, Gordon Davis, Hiroshi Iwaya, Homer Williams, James Pettinari, Jane Beebe, Jeff Joslin, Jeff Hamilton, Jeff Stuhr, Jeffrey Thomas, Jerome Uterreiner, Jim Kalvelage, Joan Baldwin, Joe Weston, John Elorriaga, John Carroll, John Meadows, John Russell, John Southgate, John Tess, John Thompson, Julie Vigeland, Ken Unkeles, Kurt Schultz, Laith Sayigh, Linda Czopek, Linda Dobson, Liz Mapelli, Lisa Watt, Marilyn Anderson, Mark Edlen, Mark Falcone, Mark Raggatt, Mark Siebert, Martha Bergman, Marty Houston, Marty Sevier, Mary Josephson, Mike Abbate, Mike Powell, Mitsu Yamazaki, Namita Wiggers, Nao, Neilson Abeel, Nolan Lienhart, Paddy Tillett, Pat Prendergast, Peter Walker, Phil Beyl, Phil Sylvester, Randy Gragg, Rich Ford, Richard Brown, Richard Singer, Rick Michaelson, Rick Gustaffson, Rod O'Hiser, Roger Shiels, Russell Keune,

Sam Adams, Sam Rodriguez, Sara Harpole, Spencer Beebe, Steve Cridland, Steve Pinger, Steve Schell, Susan Hodges, Tad Savinar, Terry Brandt, Tessa Papas, Tiffany Sweitzer, Tom Clark, Tom Benneke, Tom Jones, Tom Manley, Tony DeFalco, Vic Rhodes, Vicky Diede, Victoria Frey, and Zari Zantner.

INDEX